Torah Dynamics

PIRKEI AVOT
Looks at Life

SAMSON KRUPNICK and MORRIS MANDEL

FELDHEIM PUBLISHERS

Jerusalem • New York

Dedicated to

*Rose Anne Krupnick
and to families of
Kedem, Krupnick,
Allerhand, Lieberman*

*Shirley Mandel
and
Rabbi Allen
and Leah Mandel*

Contents

Introduction/1

1. This World and the World-to-Come/4
2. The Home/11
3. Time/16
4. Wisdom/20
5. Speech and Silence/25
6. Character and Personality/30
7. Contentment and Humility/35
8. Self-Esteem/39
9. Honor — Benefits and Pitfalls/43
10. Justice and Judgment/48
11. Community Service/53
12. Tzedakah and Gemilut Chasadim/59
13. Attitudes to Authority/69
14. Education/73
15. Teachers and Students of Torah/79
16. The Value of Work/86
17. Love/90
18. Envy/96
19. Lust/101
20. The Futility of Anger/105
21. Revenge — A Double-edged Sword/111
22. Hope and Perseverance/115
23. Retribution/118
24. Living a Life of Lovingkindness/121

Historical Background and Biographies/133
English and Hebrew text of *Pirkei Avot*/199
Glossary/272

We are grateful to Rabbi Eliyahu Chayim Krupnick for his advice and counsel in the editing of this book. His wide experience in the compilation and editing of *The Talmudic Encyclopedia* stood us in good stead.

The Authors

First published 1991
Copyright © 1991 by Samson Krupnick and Morris Mandel

All rights reserved. No part of this publication may be translated, reproduced, stored in a retrieval system or transmitted in any form or by any means, electronic, mechanical, photocopying, recording or otherwise, without prior permission in writing from the publishers.

Typsetting: Astronel, Jerusalem

Library of Congress Cataloging-in-Publication Data

Krupnick, Samson.
  Torah Dynamics / Samson Krupnick and Morris Mandel.
  288p.   15cm.
  ISBN 0-87306-541-7
  1. Mishnah, Avot—Criticism, interpretation, etc. 2. Ethics, Jewish.
  3. Conduct of life. I. Mandel, Morris
  II. Title.
  BM506.A23K77   1990
  296.1'23—dc20   90-3907
                                                         CIP

Phillip Feldheim Inc.   Feldheim Publishers Ltd.
200 Airport Excutive Park   POB 6525
Spring Valley, NY 10977   Jerusalem, Israel

Printed in Israel

10 9 8 7 6 5 4 3 2 1

Introduction

Enjoying the blessings of life is an art. To master this art, we must realize and acknowledge that everything we are and all that we have are gifts from the Creator, and that every day of our lives, these gifts are renewed. Knowing this, the thoughtful man will plan his life by following the advice found in God's Torah. How wise are the words of the Psalmist: "O teach us to count our days, that we may apply our hearts unto wisdom" (PSALMS 90:12). Now, the Psalmist in no way is telling us to count days, one by one. Rather, this is a prayer to make us constantly aware of how to live out our days — to make our days "count" — for this is indeed the supreme wisdom.

Pirkei Avot (Ethics of the Fathers) is comprised of the original five chapters of the Mishnah Tractate *Avot* and the added sixth chapter, called *Kinyan Torah*. Teaching us to "count our days" is, in fact, the message in this unexcelled guide to everyday living. Surely no book on human relations has ever been written that can improve upon this ancient but timeless Talmudic tractate.

There is no doubt that *Pirkei Avot* is the most widely known of all the sixty-three tractates of the Mishnah, for it is studied and recited publicly each Sabbath between Pesach and Rosh Hashanah. It is a foundation of Jewish life, and occupies a special place in the traditional Jewish home. Reading its well-loved counsel week after week, year after year, inspires improved behavior between man and his brother as well as between man and his Maker. In many homes the reading of *Pirkei Avot* is a family affair, with each member contributing his thoughts to a better understanding of the text.

We encounter many texts throughout our lives which teach tradition, texts which propound modern thinking, texts which advance new codes of human behavior. Many purport to give us formulas for happiness, but none can improve upon our Torah, given to us on Mount Sinai, and handed down from generation to generation. *Pirkei Avot* teaches us Torah ethics.

Traditionally, *Pirkei Avot* is studied *mishnah* by *mishnah*. In this book, however, we have taken what we feel is a novel and exciting approach. In addition to the accepted practice, we have linked the *mishnayot* by subject matter, thus enabling the reader to follow a single topic throughout *Pirkei Avot*, and thereby gain a comprehensive view. Each *mishnah* is treated fully, and each subject is elaborated by a wealth of Talmudic material, stories from our Rabbis, and a variety of ancient and modern parables which make the text more meaningful.

A lecturer on a specific topic will find this approach very helpful, and one who is a teacher of *Pirkei Avot* will find that this approach motivates and inspires his students to further study and research, thereby deepening their knowledge and appreciation of the work.

A special section is devoted to brief biographies of each Rabbi mentioned, with emphasis on the historical context, which is a contributing factor to understanding the fuller meaning of the Rabbi's teachings. Unfortunately, many who study this wonderful text do not understand enough about the historical setting or about the particular personality of each Rabbi. Although the biographies make no claim to be all-inclusive, they can add considerably to the reader's knowledge.

It is the authors' conviction that much of the restlessness and unhappiness that are characteristic of contemporary life is attributable to the fact that many have strayed from the path of Torah. Man could find contentment if only he realized that there exists a God-given code of ethics which can lead him to a meaningful and spiritual way of life. Herein are *Torah Dynamics*, through the eyes and hearts of a teacher and a family therapist.

If this volume proves helpful in inspiring Jews everywhere to more intense religious awareness and practice, then our fondest hopes will have been realized.

Samson Krupnick, Morris Mandel

1

This World and the World-to-Come

"This world is likened unto the eve of the Sabbath.
The World-to-Come is likened unto the Sabbath"
(KOHELET RABBAH 1:36).

"The World-to-Come is likened unto the day, while
this world is as the night" (PESACHIM 2b).

Each of the six chapters of *Pirkei Avot* opens with the well-known statement from the Mishnah: "All Israel have a share in the World-to-Come, as it is said (ISAIAH 60:21): 'Your people, all of them righteous, shall inherit the world forever; they are the flower of My plantings, the work of My hands, wherein I glory'" (SANHEDRIN 10). The Mishnah, following this declaration, immediately lists specific exceptions to the rule, in which those Jews who engage in certain violations of Torah and mitzvot are disqualified from their portion in the World-to-Come. These include: one who declares that according to the Torah there is no resurrection of the dead; his punishment is measure for measure, i.e., he himself does not experience resurrection and thus loses his place in the World-to-Come. The same is true of one who claims that the Torah is not Divine, but that Moses alone wrote it; the *epikoros* (heretic), and one who denies prophecy, and the Almighty's knowledge of the deeds of men; one who wallows exclusively in worldly pleasures, to the exclusion of spiritual values. The Mishnah further excludes from their portion in the World-to-Come certain kings who sinned and caused others to sin; the generation of the Flood; and the generation that wandered in the desert.

We can thus infer that the vast majority of Jews, and some righteous Gentiles as well, have an assigned portion in the World-to-Come. One may ask, what of those Jews who do not observe the Torah's mitzvot? If they, too, are included, is this not a contradiction of the fundamental principle of reward for good deeds and punishment for misdeeds, one of the thirteen articles of faith articulated by Maimonides? The answer provided by our Sages throughout Talmudic literature is: Truly all have a portion in the World-to-Come, "even one who has been sentenced to death by the court," provided that the wrongdoer does *teshuvah*, i.e., true repentance for his misdeeds, correcting the wrongs done to his fellowman, and making peace with his Maker. How great a portion one has in the World-to-Come, according to our Sages, depends to a large extent upon one's conduct in *this* world: one's observance of the mitzvot between man and man and between man and God.

In *Pirkei Avot* IV:2, we read: "The reward of a mitzvah is inherent in the mitzvah [as some interpret: the joy one experiences in performing a mitzvah] and the recompense of a sin is the sin itself." This, then, is the proper approach to living a life guided by Torah, a life which assures one his assigned portion in the World-to-Come. There are those who interpret the phrase "All Israel have a share in the World-to-Come" as meaning that, although the Jewish people as a whole has a share in the World-to-Come, each Jew must earn his portion individually — no one is assured a portion unless he merits it.

In chapter IV:1 we read: "Ben Zoma says...Who is rich? He who rejoices in his portion, for it is said (PSALMS 128:2): 'When you eat of the toil of your hands, happy shall you be, and it shall be well with you.' (*Happy shall you be* — in this world; *and it shall be well with you* — in the World-to-Come.)"

In the same chapter, Rabbi Ya'akov adds: "This world is like the vestibule before the World-to-Come; prepare yourself [adequately] in the vestibule, so that you may enter the banquet hall" (AVOT IV:16). Such preparation includes readiness to accept hardships. Rabbi Shimon bar Yochai warns (BERACHOT 5a):

"Three wonderful gifts has the Holy One, blessed be He, granted to Israel, and all three are acquired through suffering. They are: Torah, the Land of Israel and the World-to-Come."

There are many more statements found in Jewish literature, from ancient to modern times, which refer to the World-to-Come and to *Gan Eden*, interchangeably, and to Gehinnom as well, the abode of the wicked who receive Divine punishment. We also encounter the related concepts of the coming of the Messiah and the resurrection of the dead. Maimonides, in his commentary on *Sanhedrin* 10a, goes into a lengthy discussion of these basic Jewish concepts. He concludes that *Gan Eden*, like the original abode of Adam and Eve, must be a beautiful garden filled with luscious plants and fruit trees, pleasant to the eye and heavenly to the taste. Resurrection of the dead, a foundation of Jewish faith, is a certainty, promised by the Torah and repeated by the prophets. The soul and the body will be reunited (cleansed and healed, and dressed in white robes, according to Nachmanides) and will enjoy *Gan Eden*.

The coming of the Messiah, Maimonides tells us, will be an entirely natural occurrence. It will be marked by the return of the Jews to *Eretz Yisrael*, which will be a completely independent nation, and not subjugated by any other, led by a king greater than King Solomon, whose fame will spread throughout the world. There will then follow peace and security, nations shall not lift sword against each other, and Isaiah's prophecy of blissful amity among mankind will at last be realized. He subscribes to the Talmudic statement that there is no real difference between the nature of this world before and after the coming of the Messiah except the major removal of Israel's subjugation by foreign powers. After the resurrection of the dead, each person, including the resurrected, will enjoy long life, peace and tranquillity. All peoples will acknowledge the greatness of the Almighty and will live by His Torah.

Maimonides tells us that, in contrast to these detailed descriptions, the concept of the World-to-Come was not dealt with by the prophets as they dealt with the concepts of Messiah, resurrection, and *Gan Eden*. In Tractate *Berachot* 34b, this simple truth is recorded: "But the World-to-Come, no human eye has seen it, other than the Almighty alone." The reason that it has not been described, argues Maimonides, is that it is virtually impossible to imagine the bliss and joy in store for us.

The World-to-Come, following the coming of the Messiah and resurrection, will be a place which welcomes the worthy, and wherein "there is no eating, no drinking, no washing, no perfuming, and no sexual relations. The righteous recline, their heads adorned, and enjoy blissful happiness emanating directly from the holy spirit of the Almighty" (BERACHOT 17a). Attainment of this World-to-Come is then the ultimate desire of every human being, particularly Jews.

Our Jewish tradition records several instances of people who did not experience death, but were taken straight to Heaven by the Almighty — for example, the *tzaddik* Chanoch, and the prophet Elijah. An interesting account of one such occurrence is the report in Tractate *Ketubbot* 77b:

> About Rabbi Yehoshua ben Levi it is told that, when his time came, the Angel of Death was sent to him with instructions to grant him a wish. Rabbi Yehoshua requested of the Angel, "Please show me my assigned place." The Angel agreed. As they proceeded together, Rabbi Yehoshua requested of the Angel, "Please let me hold your knife. It makes me nervous." The Angel obliged. As they reached a certain point, the Angel lifted up Rabbi Yehoshua and showed him his assigned spot in the World-to-Come. Unceremoniously, Rabbi Yehoshua hurdled the fence and landed in his spot. In desperation, the Angel seized Rabbi Yehoshua's coattails in order to bring him back. Cried out Rabbi Yehoshua, "I hereby take an oath that I am not going back." Came the voice of the Almighty: "If Rabbi Yehoshua has ever made an oath before, and requested its annulment, he must return. If not, he may stay." Rabbi Yehoshua stayed. "But please return my knife," pleaded the Angel. Rabbi Yehoshua refused, until a *bat kol* [a Heavenly voice] ordered him to do so. Rabbi Yehoshua was welcomed to the World-to-Come by Elijah the Prophet.

Yet the exact nature of the World-to-Come and its Divine pleasures remains a mystery. The one thing that we do know, and that is self-evident, is that the World-to-Come is worth striving for — it is a challenge to every Jew. Hence the concept of *Chelek* — "share," or "portion" — serves as the most cogent inspiration for the study of *Pirkei Avot*, a treasure of morality and a guide for proper living.

In *Sanhedrin* 91a,b is recorded an extraordinary discussion between the Emperor Antoninus and the Sage Rabbi Yehudah *Ha-Nasi*.

"Look," the Emperor declared, "on the Day of Judgment, both body and soul should be able to win a sure, easy acquittal. The body can say in its defense: 'O God, it is not I who am guilty, but the soul. Ever since the soul left me, I have lain in my grave as still and unoffending as a stone. Obviously, it must have been the soul that caused me to sin.' The soul, on the other hand, can have an equally invincible defense. It can well say: 'Ever since I left the body, I have been fluttering in the upper realms, innocent and pure as the air. Certainly, then, it must have been the body in which I was encased that caused me to sin.'"

Replied Rabbi Yehudah: "Illustrious Emperor, I will explain the matter with a parable. To what may the matter be compared? To a king who once owned a beautiful grove of fig trees that bore luscious fruit. To guard the grove and its fruit, he employed two watchmen, one so badly crippled that he could not walk, and one who was blind. Tempted by the ripe figs, he who was lame said to the blind one, 'Take me upon your back and we shall have ourselves a feast.' The blind watchman consented and soon the grove was stripped of its ripe fruit.

"One day, the king came to inspect his orchard. To his dismay, he found that every last ripe fig was gone, whereupon he accused his watchmen of the deed. The blind one replied, 'How could I have stolen the figs? I cannot even see them.' The lame one replied, 'How could I have stolen the figs? I cannot even walk to the tree.' The king then ordered the blind watchman to lift the lame one onto his shoulders, and punished them both as one.

"And thus," the Rabbi concluded, "will God bring the body and soul together on Judgment Day and pass judgment on them as one."

A story is told about a man who was conducted on a tour of the other world. Upon reaching Gehinnom, he was surprised to find the people seated at a banquet, at beautiful tables piled high with appetizing food, appealing to the eye and to the palate. But then he saw that they looked starved and emaciated, and the reason became obvious: Long-handled spoons were tied to their hands, so long that no one could manage to get even a morsel of food into his mouth.

Afterwards, the man was taken to Heaven. There he saw exactly the same scene: The people were seated at a sumptuous banquet, and long-handled spoons were tied to their hands — yet they looked well-fed and happy. The man turned to his celestial guide and asked, "Why do the people look so happy and well-fed here?" The angel explained: "Here, my friend, the people have learned to feed one another."

One day, a villager noticed a woman carrying a pot of fire in one hand, and a pot of water in the other. "What are you going to do?" he asked her. She answered that with the fire she intended to burn Paradise, and with the water, to extinguish Gehinnom. When he asked, "Why?" her answer was quick in coming: "Because I do not want anybody to do good for the sake of going to Paradise as a reward, nor out of fear of Gehinnom — but simply for the love of God."

A wealthy American businessman, who was visiting Europe, decided to visit the Chafetz Chayim. When he arrived at the Rabbi's home, he was ushered into a room which contained a simple table and some benches. He imagined that this was some kind of outer hall, and was astonished when the famous Rabbi welcomed him in this room. He turned to the Rabbi and inquired, "But Rabbi, where is your furniture?"

The Rabbi, showing no surprise, replied, "And where is *your* furniture?"

"But I am only passing through this city, Rabbi. I don't need any possessions here."

"True," answered the Chafetz Chayim. "And I, too, am only passing through this world, and like yourself, I do not need any material possessions here."

❧ ❧ ❧

It happened that during his later years Reb Aryeh Levin, the *tzaddik* of Jerusalem, became critically ill. Just when the doctors had given up all hope for his recovery, he suddenly and inexplicably rallied, and completely recovered.

He later told his family and well-wishers that at the height of his illness he had a dream: The bed in which he was lying began to rise, floating up to Heaven. Suddenly snow began to fall upon his bed. The snowfall was heavy and weighed the bed down, and it slowly descended to earth once again. At that moment he realized that this was no ordinary snow — what had seemed to be snowflakes were, in fact, the myriad notes which he always carried concealed in the lining of his coat each time he went to visit the imprisoned Jewish freedom fighters.

No doubt these acts of pure *chessed*, repeated again and again during the years of the British occupation of Palestine, and at great peril to himself, had turned the tide of the Heavenly Tribunal in his favor. The crisis passed and Reb Aryeh became well again.

2

The Home

"How goodly are your tents, O Jacob,
your dwellings, O Israel" (NUMBERS 24:5).

When we think of the Jewish home and the preservation of its marvelous character throughout the centuries, we can think of it as a little Holland, wrested from the waters of materialism, paganism, and carnality; safeguarded against their deadly onslaught by dikes and dams constructed by Israel's inspired engineers in the days of old, under Divine guidance.

Judaism flourishes in homes where it is practiced in a proper atmosphere, well-integrated within the normal patterns of daily life. It is nurtured in homes where the Sabbath and the Holy Days are observed, where Torah is learned, where tradition is honored, where Jewish songs are sung. This is living Judaism.

Yosei ben Yoezer of Tzeredah counsels (AVOT I:4): "Let your house be a meeting place for scholars, and cover yourself with the dust of their feet, and drink in their words with thirst." The traditional Jewish home fills the religious, spiritual, intellectual, esthetic and emotional needs of the family. The home is thus the first school, and continues to be a school throughout life.

If one's home is to be a meeting place for scholars, one must strive to be of sterling character so that scholars will want to meet in his home. In addition, he must be both kind and hospitable, so that scholars and teachers will be happy to be there. The wise, the revered, the Torah scholars should be given seats of honor even while the host sits at their feet, drinking in their words of wisdom. The Talmud states: "Even the ordinary conversation of Sages [is instructive and] should be studied" (SUKKAH 21b).

It has always been known that education cannot be left completely to the school or the yeshiva. Knowledge is the light which illuminates the Jewish home. The light of wise men and the radiance of justice, truth, and prayer will strengthen the home. Unless religious practice is embedded in the home, no amount of religious practice in the synagogue can help. (One might say that at college the student can earn his A.B., but he must be taught the rest of the alphabet at home.)

Yosei ben Yochanan says: "Let your house be wide open" (AVOT I:5). At home there are no "office hours," no restricted times when visitors are not allowed to enter, or when the needy cannot come. The home teaches values — the value of hospitality, of friendship, of compassion. Our favorite description of a Jewish home has always been the dwelling of the Divine Presence (*Shechinah*), as was the Holy Temple. As the Psalmist tells us: "Except the Lord build the house, they labor in vain that build it" (PSALMS 117:1).

The location of a person's home is of great importance. Nittai of Arbel cautions: "Keep a distance from a wicked neighbor; and do not associate with an evil person..." (AVOT I:7). How often has it been said that a man is judged by the company he keeps! Environment plays a vital role in the development of family life.

When a person considers moving to a new neighborhood, or to a new city, he should not only consider the climate, the transportation facilities, or other amenities, but should also make inquiries about his neighbors. If a prospective buyer consults an expert to judge the value of the house he intends to purchase, how much more careful should he be in regard to the *people* who will be his neighbors. Undoubtedly, neighbors can be a powerful influence for good or for bad.

One can reflect: If you live near a perfumery, your home will be filled with delightful aromas; but if you live near a garbage dump, your home will be filled with foul odors.

A house does not mean a home. It doesn't matter whether one's house is built of brick, wood, or stone; it doesn't matter how it's furnished. Anyone can build a house, but we need God and His Torah to build a home. A home houses parents and children, and should express joy, love, and understanding. A house can be destroyed, but no power on earth can destroy a true home. Not even death itself can sever the binding of hearts joined together in the sacred union of family and home.

We can think of the home as the cradle into which the future is born, and of the family as the nursery in which the new world is being reared. The home should be a place where we enjoy the greatest freedom, and at the same time, in that freedom, we should be ever on guard to set the right kind of example for those who will follow us. The home is thus the irreplaceable cornerstone of Judaism.

And so, when our home becomes "a meeting place for scholars," they will bring with them lasting values. They will inspire the family to make its home not merely a shelter, but a lifelong inspiration. The Jewish home must function as the family's center of unity and strength, where values are taught and instilled, where children mature and add strength to the Jewish people and to society as well.

For a time the leaves on a tree were happy and contented. In the course of time, a merry flock of birds circled the tree, landing on its branches and then flying off again. The leaves, observing this, whispered to one another: "How fortunate the birds are. They can move freely, unfettered, and flit about under God's sky so lightly and gracefully. They can take wing and fly whenever and wherever they please. And we leaves? Oh, how unfortunate is it that we are always bound to the branch, imprisoned, chained! We cannot soar freely in the air. We are prisoners."

Without warning, a sudden whistling wind came up, angrily ripping a leaf from the tree and lifting it into the air. The leaf emitted a shout of triumph: "Ah, how kind the wind is. I am no longer tied to the detestable tree. I shall fly freely, without a care, wherever I shall please."

When the wind abated, the leaf tumbled and fell to the ground. Within a few hours, the leaf was shriveled up, dry, brittle and faded. Sensing that its last moments had arrived, the leaf lay faint and silent, and gazed with longing at the green, satiated leaves on the tree that had been its home. It lamented:

"How deceived and mistaken I was to think that the tree to which I was attached and bound was my enemy. Now I see that the tree nourished me, and gave me the strength to live. Too late, I realize that it was the very attachment to the tree, that I so resented, which gave me life. I am doomed to death because I rejected my home, the source of my life" (M. MANDEL, RECIPES FOR BETTER LIVING).

※ ※ ※

We read in *Bereshit Rabbah* 60:16:

"And Isaac brought her into his mother Sarah's tent" (GENESIS 24:67). It is said that as long as Sarah lived, a cloud hovered over her tent; but when she died, that cloud disappeared. When Rebecca came, it returned. As long as Sarah lived, her doors were wide open; at her death that hospitality ceased. But when Rebecca came, it returned. As long as Sarah lived, there was a blessing on her dough, and the lamp used to burn from the evening of the Sabbath until the evening of the following Sabbath. When she died, these ceased. But when Rebecca came, they returned. And so when he saw her following in his mother's footsteps, separating the dough when she made bread in purity, and handling her dough in purity, Isaac brought her into the tent.

※ ※ ※

Two men were crossing the desert. They had with them descriptions of the various landmarks which would guide them along their way. Suddenly a mighty sandstorm arose, which drove them into a cave for shelter. When the storm had abated, they realized that all the landmarks had been obliterated. The rocks were hidden, new dunes emerged, and the few sparse trees were nowhere to be seen. One of the men became panicky. "We shall never find our way now," he cried. "We are doomed to die in this desert!" But the other man was quiet. When evening came, he called to his companion and pointed to the clear desert sky. "You see?" he smiled. "Everything will turn out fine! The stars are still in the heavens."

When things go wrong, the fainthearted are thrown into a panic. The man of faith, however, knows that the stars, the heavens and their Creator are still there, as they always have been and always will be.

And so does the Jewish home serve as an eternal source of strength and light, illuminating the way, giving guidance, courage, and direction to all.

3

Time

"He who ignores time walks in darkness, and he
who explores it is illumined by a great light"
(IBN EZRA, SHIRAT YISRAEL).

A careful reading of *Pirkei Avot* reveals that, throughout this treasury of wisdom, emphasis is placed on the value of spending time wisely. It is said that in Heaven, as well as here on earth, time is noted. The Psalmist says: "Teach us to count our days, that we may apply our hearts unto wisdom" (PSALMS 90:12). "Applying our hearts unto wisdom" should teach us not merely to count our days, but to make our days count.

For everything a man receives, he pays with time. The wisdom of living consists of making the most of whatever time is available. But time itself does not act; it is an abstraction, the span of hours and days within which actions occur. It is only what man does with it that is of value. The supply of time is a daily miracle. Each morning when we awaken, God presents us with twenty-four hours. They are ours, the most precious of all possessions. If we ask where the time goes, the answer is that it goes into everything we do — and don't do. It was a wise man who remarked that the flowers of tomorrow are in the seeds of today.

From *Rabbenu* Bachyei we learn: "Say not 'Tomorrow I will do,' for the day of death is hidden from every living being" (CHOVOT HA-LEVAVOT, TESHUVAH, Chapter 7). The Chafetz Chayim stressed the importance of time when he remarked: "People say, 'Time is money,' but I say, 'Money is time,' for every luxury costs so many precious hours of your life."

A person's time, when well-used, can be compared to a cultivated field, whose few acres produce more of life's necessities than do extensive lands, even of the richest soil, which are overrun with weeds and brambles. If time is truly one of the most precious of all things, then wasting it must be one of the greatest prodigalities. Lost time is never found again; and what we so often call "time enough" generally proves little enough.

King Solomon explained: "To everything there is a season, and a time to every purpose under the heaven: a time to be born, and a time to die; a time to plant, and a time to pluck up that which is planted; a time to kill, and a time to heal; a time to break down, and a time to build up; a time to weep, and a time to laugh; a time to mourn, and a time to dance; a time to cast away stones, and a time to gather stones together; a time to embrace, and a time to refrain from embracing; a time to gain, and a time to lose; a time to keep, and a time to cast away; a time to reap, and a time to sow; a time to maintain silence, and a time to speak; a time to love, and a time to hate; a time of war, and a time of peace" (ECCLESIASTES 3:1-8).

The perceptive man realizes that time should not be spent in self-indulgence and his wise use of time teaches others. Living thoughtlessly brings about time-consuming people, and not people consuming time! The companionship of time is of short duration; it flies faster than the shades of evening. Plan for the future, learn from the past, but live in the present, in the "now." As Hillel asks us, "And if not now, then when?" (AVOT I:14).

Every point in time has a particular purpose for each person, and one must bear in mind the obligation of the particular moment and the realization that it cannot be postponed for a later moment. Today's moments have never before been present and will never be present again. Tomorrow's moment has a mission all its own. To do tomorrow what should have been done today is to deprive tomorrow of its due. This is why Hillel asks: "And if not now, then when?" What will become of this "now" if it is not utilized? It will die unused, and be lost forever.

Time is one of God's greatest gifts to us. The Roman philosopher Seneca said, "Nothing is ours except time." "And nothing is so dear and precious as time," added Rabelais. The Psalmist specifies *days* — not years — because each day is sacred, and each day counts. The future comes one day at a time.

Rabbi Tarfon observes: "The day is short; and the task is great...and the Employer is insistent" (AVOT II:15). Rashi explains: Life in this world is brief, and God is insistent, as it says: "You shall meditate in it [the Torah] day and night" (JOSHUA 1:8). The Rambam tells us: "This *mishnah* emphasizes the brevity of life, the magnitude of the wisdom of Torah, the effort needed to acquire that wisdom and the great reward for those who acquire it."

When Moses spent forty days on Mount Sinai, he refrained from sleep so that he would not lose a single gem of Torah wisdom. Man must realize that his obligation to God is unlimited. Material wealth should not be of first and continuous importance; rather, man must strive for perfection in Torah and in good deeds. When one considers what a parent expects of his children, one will realize what our Creator expects of us.

Rabbi Akiva notes: "All is given on pledge" (AVOT III:16). We are our brother's keepers, and as such are responsible for his actions and his use of time as well. A person's possessions are pledged to God, and may be taken away at any time. Since everything is given to us by the Almighty, we bear the obligation to discharge this debt in a way that will be accepted by Him.

No person can escape his obligation to God, and no unpaid debt is ever canceled. We might forget the debt, but God will exact payment in His own way and in His own time. This is what is implicated in the words: "A net is spread out over all the living" (AVOT III:16). No person escapes death or the Day of Judgment.

"The shop is open; the merchant extends credit," this *mishnah* continues. The world is compared to a shop, and we can continue the analogy: It contains a multitude of goods of various qualities. Some are expensive, and some are cheap; some are bitter, and some are sweet. The buyer has the freedom to choose whatever he desires. Man can choose either good or evil. The "extended credit" illustrates God's patience. One is not necessarily punished immediately.

Rabbi Yisrael Salanter made it very clear when he stated: "The world is like an expensive hotel; every pleasure must be dearly paid for." We pay a price for everything, and we must "count our days" with this in mind.

It has been wisely said that the future requires the past. Since our use of time will provide concrete illustration to those who come after us, we must set standards and values that are worthy of emulation. Although the past cannot be brought back, if it can teach lessons, then it will shape and mold the future.

The Sadigurer Rabbi taught: "We can learn from everything. The punctuality of the railroad train teaches us that every minute counts; a moment's delay in performing a good deed may mean the loss of everything. The telegraph teaches us that we must account for every word. The telephone teaches us that a word spoken here is heard elsewhere."

4

Wisdom

"Happy is the man who finds wisdom"
(PROVERBS 3:13).

To attempt to define the word *wisdom* would demand a careful reading of *Pirkei Avot*, together with deep and concentrated meditation on what has been read. Perhaps one explanation of wisdom is that it is the name which God gives to Torah living, for whatever is noble and good is to be found in Torah. Jewish wisdom is the accumulated body of knowledge of past generations. He is wise who knows the sources of knowledge — what has been written, and by whom, and where this is to be found.

Wisdom consists of the proper use of knowledge, for simply to know is not to be wise. Many men who know a great deal may yet be the greater fools for it; it is said that there is no fool so great as a knowing fool. True wisdom consists of knowing what is worth knowing, and doing what is worth doing.

Reading *Pirkei Avot*, one begins to realize that the wise man is just, pious, upright, and treads the path of truth. "The beginning of wisdom is the reverence of the Almighty" (PSALMS 4:7).

"Who is wise?" asks ben Zoma (AVOT IV:1). "He who learns from every man." In *Avot* I:4 we read: "Let your house be a meeting place for scholars, and cover yourself with the dust of their feet [i.e., follow them everywhere], and drink in their words with thirst." Hillel, in *Avot* II:7, counsels: "The more Torah study, the more life; the more study, the more wisdom." The implication is clear that materialism should not consume all of a person's time; overindulgence in physical pleasures shortens life, while increase in Torah study lengthens one's years. The wise man is he who knows the relative value of things, and King Solomon, the wisest of all men, taught: "Happy is the man who finds wisdom, and the man who attains understanding; for its merchandise is better than the merchandise of silver, and the gain thereof than fine gold. She is more precious than rubies; and all the things you can desire are not to be compared unto her. Length of days is in her right hand; and in her left hand, riches and honor. Her ways are ways of pleasantness, and all her paths are peace" (PROVERBS 3:13-17).

Rabbi Chanina ben Dosa says: "Anyone whose fear of sin precedes his wisdom, his wisdom shall endure; but he whose wisdom precedes his fear of sin, his wisdom will not endure." He added: "Anyone whose deeds exceed his wisdom, his wisdom shall endure; but he whose wisdom exceeds his deeds, his wisdom will not endure" (AVOT III:9). When a person learns Torah, and seeks its wisdom in order to understand his function in this world, and thereby to avoid sin, his wisdom will endure. When one learns Torah, and all one's learning is translated into practice, it becomes more deeply entrenched. Awareness of the importance of proper conduct can lead to learning Torah with this objective in mind, and this in turn will inspire a greater love of God and His Torah.

A sage was once asked, "To what would you compare a wise and pious man?" He replied, "He is like a craftsman with the tools of his craft in hand."

Ben Zoma says (AVOT IV:1): "Who is wise? He who learns from every man, as it is said (PSALMS 119:99): 'From all who have taught me I have gained wisdom.'" The verse in Psalms continues: "for your testimonies are my pursuits." A wise man is one who is continuously learning, and who realizes that there is always more to learn.

Ben Zoma implies: Which man may take pride in his wisdom? Only one who learns even from those less learned than he. Such a person can take pride in his own wisdom, since he perceives it as a means for spreading God's glory rather than as a vehicle for personal aggrandizement.

From *Tiferet Yisrael*, we learn: "One who wants to be considered wise and yet refuses to learn from everyone — and certainly not from an 'inferior' person — will remain ignorant forever." After all, a wise man will seek wisdom with the same sense of urgency as a man who has lost something of great value will ask everyone, regardless of his stature, to help him find it.

The wise man does not consider the main mission in his life to be making a living; one might say that he is more concerned with "making a life." He sees his life in this world as preparation for the World-to-Come, which is everlasting. It is interesting to note that the ancient philosopher and poet, Cato, said: "To succeed in the world, it is more important to possess the penetrating eye that discerns who is a fool than that which discerns who is a clever man."

Who is a fool, in the eyes of the Talmudic Sages? "There are three [kinds of[7] fools," we are told (CHAGIGAH 3b; YERUSHALMI TERUMOT 1:1):

> The one who loses, because of his indifference and disregard, that which was given to him.
> The one who walks alone at night.
> The one who rests in a cemetery.

The first one, because of his indifference to that which was given to him, becomes a fool in his personal life. One of the greatest deterrents in man's quest for happiness is his innate disregard for the things he already possesses. He is a *me'abed*, an abuser and detractor of the things that were given to him by God. He is that proverbial fellow who is looking everywhere for his lost treasure, being oblivious to the fact that it is in his own pocket.

The second one is a fool because he disregards society and endangers himself. Such a man is convinced that society is corrupt, and he makes no attempt to use his influence to change what is wrong; he just withdraws and endangers himself through his very isolation: "alone at night."

The third one, the man who "rests in a cemetery," is a fool because he constantly lives in the past, in the world of yesterday, and has little or nothing to do with the present world.

A most important word in all of the Book of Proverbs is the word *wisdom,* a word which comprises proper behavior in all human relationships. One of the many characteristics of wisdom that Proverbs mentions is prudence; the prudent man is one who will not be misled or enticed by impulse into dangerous paths. Prudence is his safeguard against temptation.

> A fool's anger is immediately known; but a prudent man conceals [his] shame (PROVERBS 12:16).

> A prudent man conceals knowledge; but the heart of fools proclaims foolishness (PROVERBS 12:23).

Another characteristic of wisdom is discretion. Discretion conveys the idea of careful planning toward a certain goal. The discreet man always looks ahead and makes detailed preparations for the future. Still another part of wisdom is known as discernment. Discernment is the power to distinguish between right and wrong, between what is good and what is bad. When God appeared to King Solomon in a dream and promised to grant him whatever he desired, Solomon asked for discernment: "Give therefore Your servant an understanding heart to judge Your people, that I may discern between good and bad" (KINGS I 3:9). This request pleased God and He granted Solomon "a wise and discerning heart" (KINGS I 3:12).

We read:

> The heart of the discerning one gets knowledge, and the ear of the wise seeks knowledge (PROVERBS 18:15).

Proverbs contrasts the attitudes of the wise man and the fool:

> Wisdom is before him that has discernment; but the eyes of a fool are at the ends of the earth (17:24).

> Scornful men set a city in a blaze; but wise men turn away wrath (29:8).
>
> The wise shall inherit honor; but as for the fools, they carry away shame (3:35).
>
> The wise in heart will accept commandments; but a babbling fool shall be punished (10:8).

In *Avot* V:7 we learn about the differences between a wise person and a boor:

> The wise man does not speak before one who is greater than he is in wisdom and experience; he does not interrupt the words of his companion; he is not hasty to answer; he asks what is relevant to the subject and answers to the point; he speaks on the first point first and on the last point last; regarding that which he has not learned, he says: "I have not learned this"; and he acknowledges the truth. And the opposite of these traits is the mark of the boor.

A young boy once decided to test the wisdom of the village wise man. He approached him with his fist closed and asked, "Wise man, tell me, you who know all: What do I have in my hand?"

"You have a bird in your hand," answered the wise man.

"How clever you are," answered the boy. "Now, tell me, is it living or is it dead?"

Now the wise man knew that if he said the bird was dead, the boy would open his hand and let it fly away. And if he answered that it was living, the boy would tighten his fist and crush it, to prove him wrong. Therefore, he replied sagely, "As you will it, my boy, as you will it."

The power within man's reach is very great; it is governed only by man's will.

5

Speech and Silence

"He who masters his speech will not be overcome"
(RABBI NACHMAN OF BRATSLAV).

"Even a fool, when he holds his tongue, is
counted wise" (PROVERBS 17:28).

The guarding of one's tongue is one of the exemplary virtues discussed in *Pirkei Avot*. Even scholars are warned to watch what they say. Avtalyon says: "Wise scholars, be careful with your words, for you may incur the penalty of *galut* [exile] and be exiled to a place of evil waters" (AVOT I:11). Silence is extolled in *Avot* I:17, where Shimon ben Gamliel says: "All my life I have grown up among the Sages, and I have found nothing better for the physical welfare of a person than silence... whoever speaks too much brings about sin." Shimon ben Shatach counsels: "And be careful with your words, lest through them they [witnesses] learn to falsify" (AVOT I:9).

Shammai says: "Say little but do much" (AVOT I:15); Rabbi Akiva says: "A fence for wisdom is silence" (AVOT III:13).

In *Avot* I:5, Yosei ben Yochanan of Jerusalem warns: "Do not engage in gossip with a woman. This they said even regarding a man's own wife; how much more so of his neighbor's wife." The idea being presented is that such conversation wastes the precious time set aside for Torah study. In no way does the injunction intend to belittle women. As a matter of fact, the sayings of the Sages are replete with maxims stressing the high esteem in which women should be held, the respect and honor due one's wife and particularly the great importance that a husband should attach to the views, opinions and counsel of his wife. In fact, this injunction is actually a compliment to women, for a man who truly respects his wife will have more to offer her than just gossip and idle chatter. He will want to discuss with her the serious concerns of life, the education of their children, plans for the future, etc. He will also want to discuss Torah with her.

Moreover, engaging in trifling talk with other women may lead to undesirable associations.

The story is told about two advocates who stood before Emperor Hadrian. One defended the virtues of speech and the other extolled silence. Asked by the Emperor to explain himself, the one who favored speech quickly replied: "My Lord, if it were not for speech, how would kings be proclaimed? How would ships be ordered to sail? How would brides be praised? How would business be carried on in the world?"

"Well have you spoken!" declared the Emperor, and then, turning to the second, asked, "Why have you praised silence?"

As the man was about to reply, the first advocate jumped up and interrupted him.

"My Lord!" he cried to the Emperor. "This man is unfair! I taught from what is mine concerning what is mine — that is, I taught by speech the value of speech. My companion, however, is using mine to teach his — he should defend himself by silence. Therefore I interrupted him."

"You are mistaken," replied the second advocate. "Solomon did not say that God would have you sit as a deaf mute. He said, 'In the multitude of words sin is not lacking; but he who restrains his lips is wise" (PROVERBS 10:19).

≈ ≈ ≈

Who could dispute the greatness of Aaron and Miriam — through Miriam's merit a well sprang up and gave drink; clouds of glory surrounded Israel through the merit of Aaron.

But because they spoke malicious gossip against Moses, they were punished at once.

It is told of *Rabban* Gamliel that he was preparing a feast and gave his servant tongues to cook. The servant prepared them, making some of them soft and some of them hard. First he served the guests the soft tongues, and then he brought them the hard ones. *Rabban* Gamliel called his servant aside and asked him, "For what reason have you done this, making some tender and some tough?" To which the servant replied, "To show how important and powerful is the tongue; if a man so wills, he can make it soft and tender; and if he so wills, hard and tough."

How realistic were the words of Rabbi Levi Yitzchak of Berdichev: "Two things have I learned from my master during my last visit to him: The less one speaks, the nearer he is to holiness; and the only good deed that is valuable is the one of which no one knows."

Many do not know how to be silent. Silence is the safest course for any man who is in doubt, and he is wise who knows when to hold his tongue. Silence, when nothing need be said, is the essence of discretion. We should never speak unless we have something to say. It is interesting to note that there are people who have something to say, and there are people who have to say something! The difference is clear.

Solomon observed: "The voice of the fool is known by a multitude of words" (ECCLESIASTES 5:2). Moderation is desirable in all matters, and speech is no exception. Solomon wisely commented: "To everything there is a season, and a time to every purpose under the heaven...a time to maintain silence, and a time to speak" (ECCLESIASTES 3:1,7).

A modern commentator noted in the vernacular: "Be sure brain is engaged before putting mouth in gear."

Orchot Tzaddikim, chapter 21, classifies speech into four categories:

1. Slander, profanity, curses; all of these are harmful and should be avoided completely.

2. Speech that praises a person in the presence of his enemy; the intention may be good, but the result can be harmful. This type of conversation should be avoided.

3. Giving idle judgments and opinions which are neither harmful nor beneficial; while this type of conversation is permitted, there is no real purpose to be served thereby.

4. What is left is discussion on Torah, and praising God; this has real and lasting value.

Our Rabbis again and again taught their followers the uses of speech. "Before I speak," writes Ibn Gabirol, "I am master of the word; after I speak, the word is master of me." He continues, "The less one speaks, the less one errs" (IBN GABIROL, CHOICE OF PEARLS 33).

"A fool says what he knows; a sage knows what he says" (RABBI SIMCHAH BUNIM).

Since speech is a gift from God, it must not be employed for that which is degrading. A scholar once advised, "It is more desirable to abstain from talking than to abstain from eating, since this practice will injure neither the body nor the soul."

How often have we been warned about the misuse of the gift of speech. The Rabbis, like *Rabban* Gamliel's servant, appreciated how unruly an organ the tongue can be. The proverb "Speech is silver, silence golden" has its counterparts in the Talmud: "A word for a *sela*, silence for two" (MEGILLAH 18a). "Silence is a healing for all ailments" (MEGILLAH 18a). "Silence is good for the wise; how much more so for the foolish" (PESACHIM 99a,b).

All wise men are in agreement regarding excessive talking. "They think too little who talk too much," wrote John Dryden. To which a philosopher added: "As it is the characteristic of great wits to say much in few words, so it is of small wits to talk much and say nothing."

"Why are fingers tapered like pegs?" asks Rabbi Elazar. "So that if one hears anything improper he can insert them in his ears" (KETUBBOT 5b).

The Rabbis taught that God provided the tongue with exceptional controls. "The Holy One, blessed be He, said to the tongue: 'All the limbs of man are erect, but you are horizontal. They are all outside the body, but you are inside. More than that, I have surrounded you with two walls, one of bone and the other of flesh'" (MIDRASH TEHILLIM 52:6).

A snake was once asked, "Why do you inject such deadly poison into your victims?"

The snake replied, "Why do you rebuke me? By means of my poison I am able to kill my prey. If you think that is despicable, then go and ask your questions of the gossip and the scandalmonger.

"I poison for my livelihood, while they poison for the sake of malice. And my venom affects only those whom I touch, but their venom spreads for miles" (TA'ANIT 8a).

6

Character and Personality

"Character, like a delectable dish, must be achieved with a proper recipe: of some traits, like modesty, man should take a large dose, and of others, like pride, fierceness, cruelty, he should take but little. Man should weigh carefully the measure of each ingredient, and he will attain the goal of the good"
                (ORCHOT TZADDIKIM, 15C, INTRODUCTION).

"He [*Rabban* Yochanan ben Zakkai] said to them [his disciples]: Go and see which is the right way [quality] to which a man should cling. Rabbi Eliezer says: A good eye. Rabbi Yehoshua says: A good friend. Rabbi Yosei says: A good neighbor. Rabbi Shimon says: One who has good foresight. Rabbi Elazar says: A good heart. He [*Rabban* Yochanan] said to them: I prefer the words of Elazar ben Arach to yours, for your words are all included in his" (AVOT II:9).

Rabbi Eliezer indicated that people should see the beauty in everything — beauty in learning, beauty in God's world, beauty in one's fellowman. Some interpret "a good eye" to mean the quality of generosity. Rabbi Yehoshua stressed friendship — help, understanding, and sensitivity toward our fellowmen. Rabbi Yosei chose good neighborliness — awareness of the consequences of our actions. This awareness keeps people on the right path, and prevents sin.

Rabbi Elazar advocated a good heart, an inclusive quality which comprises them all: A good heart will cause one to be appreciative, sensitive, pious, sin-fearing and understanding.

Rabban Yochanan saw the worth of each student's view, and realized that their views reflected their respective personalities.

Then he said to his disciples: "Go and see what is the evil way [quality] from which a man should distance himself. Rabbi Eliezer says: An evil eye. Rabbi Yehoshua says: A bad friend. Rabbi Yosei says: A bad neighbor. Rabbi Shimon says: One who borrows and does not repay... Rabbi Elazar says: An evil heart. He [*Rabban* Yochanan] said to them: I prefer the words of Elazar ben Arach to yours, for your words are included in his" (AVOT II:9). As with the "good heart," the "evil heart" included all the other (negative) qualities.

The overriding quality of "goodness of heart" is acknowledged many times in our sources. Maimonides regarded the heart as "the tabernacle of the intellect." In Psalms 51:12 we pray: "Create in me a clean heart, and renew a right spirit within me." Again in Psalms 86:11 we request: "Unite my heart to revere Your name."

In *Avot* V:10 we find another analysis of personalities. "There are four character types among men: He who says: 'What is mine is mine and what is yours is yours' is the average type; although some say, this is the character of Sodom. He who says: 'What is mine is yours and what is yours is mine' is an ignoramus. [Rashi defines *am ha'aretz* as 'uncultured'; others say this description is 'socialistic.] He who says: 'What is mine is yours and what is yours is yours' is a pious man. And he who says: 'What is mine is mine and what is yours is mine' is a wicked man."

The first case, the person who says, "What is mine is mine and what is yours is yours," is of average character. He is not particularly giving, but he doesn't expect anything from others either. In the second, it is clear that only an ignoramus can say, "What is mine is yours and what is yours is mine." For the social implications would mean that robbery is justified and every person would become vulnerable, with the ultimate result that society would not be able to exist. The third case describes the unselfish person who says, "What is mine is yours and what is yours is yours" — this is truly a pious person. Though he acknowledges individual ownership, he stresses the fact that what is his is available to those who need help. Finally, it is the wicked, selfish person who says, "What is mine is mine and what is yours is mine." He upholds the right of individual possession only as far as he is concerned — he is not willing to give, but expects to receive from others.

In *Avot* V:11 a third analysis of personality is made. "There are four kinds of dispositions: He who is easily provoked and easily pacified — his gain is canceled by his loss. He who is difficult to provoke and difficult to pacify — his loss is canceled by his gain. He who is difficult to provoke and easily pacified — is a pious man. He who is easily provoked and difficult to pacify — is a wicked man."

The various descriptions of human nature that we find in *Pirkei Avot* are very familiar to us, and we can all think of people we know who fit these categories. The enduring wisdom and insight of the Sages continue to be as relevant and illuminating to us in our time as they were in their own era.

Pirkei Avot also discusses four types of pupils; four types of givers to charity; four types of those who attend the house of study; and four types of those who sit before the Sages. Throughout the analysis of personality types, one can discern an emphasis on balance and moderation in behavior.

But each one of us is different; each is a unique individual. There are no duplicates in God's universe — all His creatures are original creations, and they differ from each other in some special way. And man alone, of all God's creatures, is conscious of his individuality. Accordingly, every person should feel that he has a unique offering for the world. In finding one's own way in life, and in guiding one's children in finding theirs, it is essential to acknowledge that each person was created with his own unique character. As we read in Proverbs 22:6, "Educate the child according to his way...."

Throughout *Pirkei Avot*, the ethical teachings stress the development of personality and character. There is hardly a *mishnah* that does not emphasize the value of a positive trait. For example, Antignos of Socho taught: "Be not like the servants who serve their master for the sake of receiving a reward, but be like servants who serve their master not for the sake of receiving a reward" (AVOT I:3). The influence of the home is described in *Avot* I:4: "Let your house be a meeting place for scholars, and cover yourself with the dust of their feet, and drink in their words with thirst."

One must be God-fearing, strive for humility, acquire a teacher, make good friends, consider carefully the neighborhood in which one lives, consider the poor, keep away from evil neighbors, love peace, increase knowledge, be aware of oneself, shun honor, be an active part of a community, and always remember to make Torah the center of one's life. Again and again values and choices are stressed.

"Only that which is acquired by hard labor and great struggle is of any value," taught the Vilna *Gaon*.

🌿 🌿 🌿

A king owned a precious gem, which he loved for its beauty and perfection. One day it fell and became badly scratched. Greatly distressed, the king summoned experts to remove the blemish, but they could not do so without cutting away a good part of the surface, thus reducing its weight and value.

Finally, another expert arrived, studied the jewel, and assured the king that he could fix it without reducing its value. The self-confidence of this expert was convincing, and the king told him to proceed. In a few days he returned, and the king was amazed to behold that in place of the ugly scratch was an exquisite etching of a rose. The deep scratch had become the rose's long and graceful stem.

The mistakes of life cannot be erased. We must live with them. But if we are wise, we can learn to use them as the basis for something new and beautiful that can enrich our lives.

🌿 🌿 🌿

One winter a teacher told his students that if they want to understand how character is developed, they should take notice of how icicles are formed. "You will see," he said, pointing to the icicles hanging from the roof outside the classroom window, "that each freezes a drop at a time, drop by drop, until it is a foot or more long. If the water is clear, the icicle will remain clear, and sparkle like diamonds in the sun; but if the water is slightly muddy, the icicle will look dull and its beauty will be spoiled."

Similarly are our characters formed — one little thought or action at a time. If each is pure and good, the soul will be clear and shine with joy; but if they are sullied, the soul will be sullied. One of our Sages expressed this in other words: "Pity the bread which was kneaded with improper dough."

7

Contentment and Humility

"Be always satisfied with life, but never with one's self" (G.C. NATHAN).

"With little or with much, be content" (BEN SIRA 29.23).

The Declaration of Independence of the United States calls "the pursuit of happiness" an inalienable right. Yet, sad to say, it seems to be ever pursued but not always found. Who among us can truthfully say: "I am completely happy. I have achieved peace of mind."

In *Avot* IV:1, we read: "Who is rich? He who rejoices in his portion, for it is said (PSALMS 128:2): 'When you eat of the toil of your hands, happy shall you be, and it shall be well with you.'" In other words, the rich person is not one who possesses great material wealth, but rather one who is satisfied with and grateful for what he has. Instead of envying what the other person has (and what may be unattainable for ourselves), and the imagined happiness other people supposedly enjoy, we are counseled to engage in honest labor and be satisfied with the livelihood we earn.

What depth of insight into human nature does this wise counsel contain! "Too much" does not mean "too good." The owner of a watch always knows what time it is, but when he has two watches he is never quite sure which is giving him the right time. Filling one's life with ever more material acquisitions does not ensure happiness, and we are reminded of this in *Avot* II:7: "The more property, the more concern...the more Torah study, the more life."

The greatest blessing a person can enjoy in this world is contentment. In *Musar Ha-Philosophim* we read: "If you want from the world just enough and no more, then a little will be enough; but if you want from the world more than enough, then the whole world will not be enough." Whatever the Almighty chooses to provide for a person is, in His judgment, best for his needs. A man uttered this prayer: "My God, give me neither poverty nor riches, but whatever it may be Your will to give; and give me, with it, a heart that knows humbly to acknowledge Your will." True contentment and fulfillment do not depend upon how much one owns; a tub was large enough for Archimedes, but the world was too small for Alexander.

It was a wise man who said, "I do not possess anything I do not want, and I do not want anything I do not possess." This is the secret of contentment: knowing how to enjoy what one has, and being able to curb one's desire for things beyond his reach. Years ago, it was customary to hang framed, embroidered mottos on the walls of one's home. A popular one read: "The City of Contentment is in the State of Mind."

Yet contentment must be appropriate — for absolute contentment would reconcile a man to whatever his condition is in this world, and make him accept his circumstances with finality. This is negative contentment, for no one should feel that his present circumstances represent the limit of his possibilities. While the beckoning visions of what one does not have should not blind him to the acknowledgment of what he does have, neither should a person accept himself without reservation. One should always bear in mind his potential for spiritual and material improvement.

Consider the person who rushes madly through his life trying to get rich, or worse, richer. Amassing wealth, he learns to live like the rich, indulging himself and his family in all sorts of material pleasures and delights. Unfortunately, his luxuries soon become necessities for him. And behind the life of luxury, every wealthy man is haunted, somewhere in the recesses of his awareness, by the specter of disaster, the possible plunge into the abyss of poverty. It is far, far better to live on a simple, modest scale, and to have inner peace, than to live with the gnawing anxiety of falling from the heights to the depths.

Our ancestors were distinguished by their humility. Abbaye said: "A man should always be humble in the awe of Heaven." And in *Berachot* 17a it is related of *Rabban* Yochanan ben Zakkai that no man ever greeted him first, even a heathen in the market.

Abraham, in his discourse with the Almighty on the fate of the wicked people of Sodom, declared simply: "I am but dust and ashes" (GENESIS 19:27). Moses and Aaron, in assuaging their angry fellowmen in the desert, stated humbly, "What are we...?" (EXODUS 16:8). King David offered meekly: "I am but a worm and not a man" (PSALMS 22:7).

Rebbe Mendel of Kotsk had a compromise proposal: "Each Jew should find a middle course — in one pocket should be: 'I am but dust and ashes,' and in the other pocket: 'For me was the world created' (SANHEDRIN 37a)."

A dear old Quaker lady, distinguished for her youthful beauty, was asked what cosmetics she used to preserve her appearance. She replied sweetly:
I use for the lips, TRUTH;
for the voice, PRAYER;
for the eyes, PITY;
for the hands, CHARITY;
for the figure, UPRIGHTNESS;
for the heart, LOVE.

The owner of a cottage decided to sell it, and consulted a real estate agent. After visiting the place, the agent wrote an elaborate description advertising it and submitted it to the owner for approval.

"Oh, my," said the owner after he read it, closing his eyes.

"Can you please read it aloud to me now?"

After a second reading, he was silent for a few moments. Then he said thoughtfully, "You know, I don't think I'll sell it after all. I've been looking for that kind of place all my life, but until I saw and heard that description, I didn't know I had it!"

If we could only see our blessings and privileges as others see them, would it not add to our contentment with our lot?

8

Self-Esteem

"As a man thinks in his heart so is he"
(PROVERBS 23:7).

A good self-image carries confidence, conviction and a cheerful outlook. A person cannot successfully meet life's challenges without self-esteem. In *Avot* I:14 Hillel says: "If I am not for myself, who will be for me? And if I care only for myself, what am I? And if not now, then when?" This profound statement tells us many things. While we should repudiate selfish egotism, we should at the same time have a healthy appreciation of our own worth. Self-depreciation is not a good thing — I must always be "for myself," to acknowledge that self that God created.

In addition, Rashi explains: "If I do not do for myself, who will do it for me? If I do not perform the mitzvot, who will perform them for me?" If I do not aspire to higher spiritual levels myself, who will do it for me? Motivation from internal sources is far more effective than motivation from external ones.

Everyone needs to feel important, to be "somebody," not just "anybody" in this world. But unfortunately, there are men and women who do not have any sense of self-worth, and who need the approbation of others to strengthen their own self-image; they depend on the validation of friends, relatives, and business associates if they are to think well of themselves.

Hillel advises that a man must find meaning in himself, that his self-esteem need not depend on the opinions of others. The very fact that God created each one of us and blew the breath of life into each of our souls should provide that inner strength that gives one the ability to encounter challenges with success. Life holds its surprises and disappointments but, equipped with inner strength, one is able to accept them. Think of Abraham, Isaac, Jacob, Joseph, Moses, and Aaron, to mention but a few of our great forefathers in the Bible who overcame great difficulties and thus inspired us by their example.

The realization that, since we are created in God's image, we are all intrinsically worthy should engender self-esteem. In *Avot* III:14 Rabbi Akiva says: "Beloved is man, for he was created in His image; still greater was the expression of this love in that it was made known to him that he was created in His image, as it is said (GENESIS 9:6): 'In the image of God did He create man.'" The knowledge of having been created in God's image, the privilege of living by the teachings of the Torah, the feeling of being one of God's children represent tremendous challenges, but at the same time should offer an individual strength of purpose.

Although in *Avot* III:1 we are reminded that man comes from a putrid drop, surely a belittling picture which encourages humility, Rabbi Akiva stresses the nobility of man, who was created in God's image. And in contrast to the statement in *Avot* III:1 that our destiny is a place of dust, decay, and maggots, Rabbi Akiva reminds us that we are "children of God" (AVOT III:14).

Reb Zusya of Hanipol remarked: "On Judgment Day, God will not ask me why I was not like Moses, nor like Isaiah, nor like Akiva. He will merely ask me why I was not like Zusya could have been." In other words, why did I not live up to my God-given capabilities? If He endows us with talents and skills, we must make proper use of them, and be all that we were made to be.

"Let man ever esteem himself," says Rabbi Elazar (TA'ANIT 11b), "...as though the Holy One dwells within him." In *Avot* II:5 Hillel advises: "Where there are no men, strive to be a man." Mankind was the prime purpose of Creation.

In *Avot* II:15, Rabbi Tarfon says: "The day is short; and the task is great; and the workmen are lazy; and the reward is great; and the Employer is insistent." Rabbi Tarfon is emphasizing that each person is allotted a limited time in this world, and so must make himself capable of seizing the fleeting opportunity. His self-esteem is thus a valuable and essential asset, and no one should minimize his own importance. He should consider:

> I am only one, but I am one;
> I cannot do everything, but I can do something;
> What I can do, I ought to do;
> And what I ought to do, by the grace of God, I will do.

And, as Hillel counseled, "If not now, then when?"

Said the Chafetz Chayim: "Every man enters this world with a certain endowment. It behooves him to make use of his endowment, for he will be held accountable regarding it."

"And if I care only for myself, what am I?" As important as self-esteem is, it must never fill one to the exclusion of others. One must be "for others" as well as "for myself." True concern for our fellowmen goes along with true concern for ourselves. It is the person who is not interested in his fellowmen who encounters the greatest difficulties in life. "There is no room for God in he who is full of himself," preached the Baal Shem Tov. "Many a man prays and is not heard, because he remains heedless of the plight and needs of others," warns the *Sefer Chasidim*. In a poem called "The Two Rabbis," John Greenleaf Whittier states:

> Heaven's gate is shut to him who comes alone,
> Save thou a soul, and it shall save thine own.

In Deuteronomy 5:5, Moses says: "I stood between the Lord and you." What is implied is that the "I" always stands between God and us. The proper balance of concern for self and concern for others ensures a rewarding life.

A man sought advice from the Baal Shem Tov in regard to his self-improvement. "I have tried for years to become a better person," the man complained, "but I am still very ordinary and simple."

The Baal Shem Tov listened and assured him, "My friend, to be aware that you are simple is an accomplishment in itself. Take pleasure in that" (MIDRASH RIVASH TOV).

Rabbi Shelomo of Karlin used to say: "The worst fault a person can have is to forget his intrinsic greatness as a human being" (DOR DE'AH, Vol. 1, p. 172).

9

Honor — Benefits and Pitfalls

> "He who promotes his own honor at the expense
> of his neighbor's has no portion in
> the World-to-Come" (BERESHIT RABBAH 1:5).

> "He who runs after honor remains behind one who
> flees from it" (YERUSHALMI AVODAH ZARAH 3:1).

One of the Divine gifts granted to man is his desire to extend honor, regard and respect to his fellowman. This gift must be highly cherished, and used extensively for those who merit it. On the other hand, the receiving of honor, albeit greatly appreciated, is fraught with perils and pitfalls. One is cautioned repeatedly in Rabbinic literature not to seek honor, nor to expect it by virtue of the fact that one is a great Torah scholar, or by the fact that he has performed mitzvot.

The great *Rabban* Yochanan ben Zakkai cautions: "If you have learned much Torah, do not take credit for yourself, for this is the purpose for which you were created" (AVOT II:8). In effect, one is then simply fulfilling an obligation, as it is written: "You shall meditate in it day and night" (JOSHUA 1:8). Hence no reward should be expected for Torah study or for performing mitzvot. On the other hand, *Rabban* Yochanan's teacher Hillel emphasized: "The more Torah study, the more life.... One who has acquired a good name — has acquired it for himself; one who has acquired the words of Torah — has acquired for himself the life of the World-to-Come" (AVOT II:7).

Inevitably, in acquiring this good name through one's Torah scholarship and consequent wisdom and good deeds, the honor will follow, as people generally acknowledge and appreciate a noble character. Should they fail to do so, a possibility in our age of hustle and bustle, the true *talmid chacham* will not resent or envy others who receive honors, the likes of which in fact are due him.

Bestowing honor is an emotional act that is akin to the emotion of love. The two are related in the commands to "love the Lord your God," and to pay due respects to *Melech Ha-Kavod* — the King of Honor. One honors God by honoring His Torah, and a natural extension of this honor is the honoring of those who are *oskim ba-Torah* — those who study the Torah, and those whose aid and encouragement make it possible for others to study Torah. The Tractate *Berachot* 63a tells of our Sages going from place to place, to speak and teach "in honor of the Torah." We honor the Torah by our conduct in the synagogue, as we rise when the Ark is opened and the Torah scroll is brought out for reading; it is the custom of some to remain standing during the Torah reading. Similarly, when a Torah scholar enters a room, we rise in his honor.

In the Fifth of the Ten Commandments, we are directed: "Honor your father and your mother, so that you may have length of days on this earth which the Lord, your God, has given you" (EXODUS 20:12). In the second recitation of the Ten Commandments, these words are added: "as God has commanded you...and so that it will be good for you" (DEUTERONOMY 5:16). In Leviticus 19:3 we read: "You shall have fear [awe] for your mother and father." The reward offered — length of days and "good" — is said to refer to the World-to-Come, "in which there is length of days and all the good" (KIDDUSHIN 39b). Rabbi Yehudah *Ha-Nasi* explains that the reason the father is listed first to be honored, and the mother first to be feared and held in awe, is that it is natural for a child to do just the opposite: to honor his mother because she feeds him, and cares for him constantly, and to fear and hold in awe his father, who is the teacher and disciplinarian. Therefore the Torah emphasized equality in our treatment of both parents (KIDDUSHIN 31a).

Our Sages infer from the word *and* (your father *and* your mother) that the commandment comprises respect for one's older brother as well (KETUBBOT 103a). Rabbi Shimon bar Yochai added: "Honoring one's father and mother is even greater than honoring the Almighty, for it is said: 'Honor the Almighty from your wealth' (PROVERBS 3:9). In other words, if you have the means, you are required to observe the directive. If you do not, then you are exempt. But in the matter of honoring your father and mother, you are required to provide for all their needs — food, drink, clothing, shelter, bringing them in and taking them out — even if you have to go begging" (YERUSHALMI PE'AH 1:1; KIDDUSHIN 32a). Respect for teachers is equated with respect for parents. For example, it is not permitted to sit in the chairs of either, to speak without permission in their presence, to contradict them (KIDDUSHIN 31b), or to call them by name (SANHEDRIN 100a).

One of the outstanding scholars of Kerem B'Yavneh, ben Zoma, taught: "Who is wise? He who learns from every man.... Who is strong? He who subdues his passions.... Who is rich? He who rejoices in his portion.... Who is honored? He who honors his fellowman" (AVOT IV:1).

This is a description of a person who has apparently attained all the attributes one should strive for, and is certainly worthy of honor, yet his chief concern is to see that others are honored. He derives great pleasure from that, and enjoys the honor bestowed upon others. He is a far cry indeed from the arrogant person who is filled with and ruled by envy, jealousy and the desire for honor, who is not only undeserving of honor but who cannot tolerate others who *are* deserving. It was this common destructive tendency which prompted Rabbi Eliezer Ha-Kappar to warn: "Envy, lust, and thirst for honor take a man out of the world" (AVOT IV:21). Maimonides comments that these serious flaws in the character of a person who has apparently lost control of his passions and desires can cause him such spiritual, moral, and physical harm that they may shorten his life. The evil inclination has taken control to the point where one strives endlessly to rise to honor, over the heads and upon the shoulders of others, not realizing what *Eruvin* 13b tells us specifically: "He who chases after honors and greatness, these cherished gains elude him; but he who runs away from these honors, they immediately run after him."

Rabbi Akavia ben Mahalalel, a student of Hillel, offers some very sobering words to anyone with the slightest tendency to arrogance: "Reflect upon three things and you will not come into the grip of sin.... Whence you came — from a malodorous drop; where you are going — to a place of dust, worms and vermin; and before Whom you are destined to render a strict accounting — before the Supreme King of kings, the Holy One, blessed be He" (AVOT III:1). This *mishnah* is recited solemnly at every funeral, and is most certainly the source of serious reflection.

Rabbi Yosei stated: "He who honors the Torah, will himself be honored by mankind; but he who dishonors the Torah, will himself be dishonored by mankind" (AVOT IV:6). The connection seems to be automatic for a true Torah student. Another student of Rabbi Akiva, Rabbi Elazar ben Shammua, who became the teacher of Rabbi Yehudah *Ha-Nasi*, added: "Let the honor of your student be as dear to you as your own; and the honor of your friend, as the reverence due to your teacher; and the reverence due to your teacher, as the reverence due to Heaven" (AVOT IV:12). Mutual respect should characterize the relationship between teacher and student.

In the sixth and final chapter of *Pirkei Avot, Kinyan Torah* (the acquisition of Torah), one is urged to be a perpetual student of Torah, and particularly to learn *lishmah*, sincerely, for its own sake and not for reward. The motivation should be the privilege of learning, teaching, and performing mitzvot. We are advised: "Do not seek greatness for yourself, and strive not after honor. Let your good deeds exceed your learning. And crave not for the table of kings, for your table is greater than their table, and your crown is greater than their crown; and your Employer is faithful to pay you the reward for your work" (AVOT VI:4).

※ ※ ※

There was a king who wanted to live humbly, despite his honored status. He therefore attired himself in old garments, took up residence in a small hut, and forbade anyone to demonstrate reverence before him. But when he honestly examined his inner thoughts, the king found himself filled with more pride over his apparent humility than he had ever had before. A philosopher thereupon remarked to him: "Dress like the king that you are; live like a king; allow the people to show due respect to you as their king; but be humble in your heart."

10

Justice and Judgment

> "A judge must have these seven qualifications: wisdom, humility, fear of God, disdain of gain, love of truth, love of his fellowmen, and a good reputation" (MAIMONIDES, SANHEDRIN, 2:7).

Our patriarch Abraham referred to the Almighty as "the Judge of all the land," when he pleaded for a fair judgment for the people of Sodom (GENESIS 18:25). As we are urged constantly to emulate the attributes of our Maker, it is our grave responsibility to assure society that justice shall be properly and equitably discharged. One of the first major functions of Moses in the desert was to act as judge for the multitude who went out of Egypt. The task being enormous, Moses followed the wise advice of his father-in-law, Jethro, and relegated much of the responsibility to local judges, proof positive of the tremendous importance attached to the administering of justice among the Jewish people (SANHEDRIN 18a; EXODUS 18:25). Judges are even referred to as *Elokim* — the name of the Almighty — because they do the work of the Almighty (EXODUS 22:8). In Tractate *Shabbat* 10a, this thought is amplified. "Every judge who judges a case truthfully, even for one hour — it is recorded on his behalf as if he has become a partner to the Holy One, blessed be He, in the works of Creation." Hence the command was urgent: "Judges and officers shall you appoint in all your gates" (DEUTERONOMY 16:18), to enable everyone to enjoy justice.

Throughout *Pirkei Avot* we find emphasis on the vital importance of justice and upon the critical role of the judges in administering justice. From the very start, the *Anshei Knesset*

Ha-Gedolah, who fixed for the Jewish community the order of prayer and religious conduct that is followed to this day, cautioned the judges: "Be cautious in judgment" (AVOT I:1). Judges should not permit themselves to treat any matter routinely, but must always judge each individual case on its merits. For the experienced judge, there is ever-present the temptation to succumb to the natural tendency to think "I have heard these matters many times," and therefore rule hastily. Much harm can result from such thoughtless action.

Both the *Nasi* of the Sanhedrin, Shimon ben Shatach, and his associate, Yehudah ben Tabbai, suffered personal anguish as a result of the miscarriage of justice during the very trying times of the reign of King Yannai in the second century B.C.E. This was a period during which the Sadducees had succeeded in acquiring domination of the Sanhedrin by influencing King Yannai to eliminate the Pharisees, stalwarts of tradition. The King's brother-in-law, Shimon ben Shatach, fought a losing battle to maintain true Torah Judaism; finally he was forced to go into hiding. Yehudah ben Tabbai also escaped capture, and found refuge with the large Jewish community in Alexandria, Egypt. After some critical years, and with the influence of Queen Shlomtzion, Shimon ben Shatach returned to power, removed the Sadducees from the Sanhedrin and restored the Torah to its rightful position (KIDDUSHIN 66a).

He immediately brought back Yehudah ben Tabbai, and in their haste to correct the many wrongs committed, each made costly errors. Shimon ben Shatach hurriedly had executed — in one day — eighty accused witches in Ashkelon, in order to eliminate the spreading practice of witchcraft in Israel. As a result, his enemies brought trumped-up charges against his son, and brought false witnesses to testify, causing his conviction and execution.

Yehudah ben Tabbai ruled in error that a false witness (*ed zomem* — not one who contradicts the testimony of another witness, but one who casts doubts upon the other's presence at the time of the crime) be put to death. This was an error in interpretation of the law. Shimon ben Shatach thereafter forbade Yehudah to issue judgments.

As a result of these bitter experiences, Shimon ben Shatach urges: "Be persistent and thorough in examining the witnesses; and be careful with your words, lest through them they learn to falsify" (AVOT I:9). And Yehudah ben Tabbai cautions, "In the function of judge do not act the part of the counsels; and while the litigants stand before you let them be as guilty in your eyes; but when they depart from you, let them be innocent in your eyes, once they have submitted to the judgment" (AVOT I:8).

In other troubled times, those which followed Bar Kochba's revolt against the powerful Roman legions and during which the Jews suffered under the decrees of the Emperor Hadrian, *Rabban* Shimon ben Gamliel was restored to the *Nesiut*. In his valiant attempt to revive Torah living, he was aided by great scholars, the students of the martyred Rabbi Akiva. *Rabban* Shimon stressed the three basic foundations of society: "By virtue of three things does the world endure: Upon justice, and upon truth, and upon peace, as it is said (ZECHARIAH 8:16): '...administer the judgment of truth and peace within your gates'" (AVOT I:18). This formula was effective and there followed the very fruitful years of *Rabban* Shimon's son, the outstanding personality known as *Rabi* — Rabbi Yehudah *Ha-Nasi*.

A conscientious judge is naturally awed by his weighty responsibility, for his judgments affect the very lives of the litigants. In Tractate *Yevamot* 109b, it is recommended that a judge should envision himself as if there were a sword between his loins and "Gehinnom open beneath him." Hence it is understandable that many scholars hesitated to take on this precarious task.

Rabbi Ishmael ben Yosei, head of the yeshiva in Sepporis in the Galilee, was wary of being a judge. He preferred to assign this function to others, explaining, "He who avoids a judicial position, rids himself of hatred [from the loser in a trial], robbery [in cases of error], and perjury, but he who arrogantly renders legal decisions — is foolish, wicked, and brutish." He

Justice and Judgment 51

advised further: "Do not judge alone [in spite of the fact that a true scholar is permitted to judge singly], for none may judge alone, except One. And [when co-opting two more judges] do not say: 'Accept my view,' for it is they and not you who have the authority" (AVOT IV:7-8).

Justice must be rendered correctly and swiftly. "The sword [of war]," we are told, "comes into the world for the delay of justice, and for the perversion of justice, and upon those who misinterpret the Torah" (AVOT V:8). In Tractate *Shabbat* 32b this thought is even more forcefully expressed: "If you see a generation that suffers great misfortunes, go quickly and examine carefully the integrity of the judges in Israel, for all the punishments that descend upon this world do not come except for the misdeeds of the judges in Israel." The administration of true justice, by judges of impeccable integrity, is the foundation of a healthy and decent society.

Pirkei Avot also comments cogently on the subject of personal judgment. Human weaknesses are acknowledged, and the general advice is to think and act positively. Yehoshua ben Perachiah counsels, "Judge every person favorably" (AVOT I:6). We should give everyone the benefit of the doubt. Or, as the Sefat Emet recommends, "Judge the whole of the person. Maybe if you see one fault, he may have other offsetting qualities" (SEFAT EMET on PIRKEI AVOT). Enduring advice comes from Hillel: "Do not judge your fellowman until you have been in his position" (AVOT II:4). We are called upon to consider what would be our own reactions under similar conditions and circumstances, and to wonder if we would have done any better. There is also the implication: "Would you like to be in his unfortunate position?" The answer is: "Obviously not" — in which case we should not judge him at all.

In truth it is the Almighty Who sits in judgment upon all our actions. Tractate *Shabbat* 127b promises: "One who judges his fellowman favorably, he too will be judged favorably." Akavia ben Mahalalel reminds us: "Before Whom you are destined to render a strict accounting — before the Supreme King of kings, the Holy One, blessed be He" (AVOT III:1). Rabbi Akiva describes life in this world as a shop, with full credit extended, and payment collected, knowingly or unknowingly, the ultimate accounting being "a judgment of truth" (AVOT III:16). He points out that as Jews we have a special relationship with the Almighty, for we are His children, as it is written, "You are the children of the Lord your God" (DEUTERONOMY 14:1). We are the recipients of the Almighty's greatest gift, with which the world was created, as it is written: "I have given you a good portion. Forsake not My Torah" (PROVERBS 4:2). Hence we are judged accordingly. Rabbi Akiva concludes with a profound thought (which the Rambam described as "containing words of great significance"): "Everything is foreseen [by the Almighty]; yet freedom of choice is given; and the world is judged with goodness; yet the judgment of all is according to the predominance of man's kindly deeds" (AVOT III:15). The Almighty combines justice with mercy and lovingkindness to all.

❧ ❧ ❧

Rabbi Ya'akov Berlin, father of the Netziv, was a wealthy merchant as well as a Torah scholar. It is told that once he purchased some expensive glassware, and when he brought it home, the maid handled it carelessly and broke one of the glasses. Reb Ya'akov's wife was naturally upset and reprimanded the maid; when her husband heard this, he told her that it was not permitted to hurt the maid's feelings, but, that if she expected the maid to pay for the damage, she should take her to a *Din Torah* for a Rabbinical ruling.

His wife consented and, as she put on her coat to go to the *Beit Din* with the maid, she noticed that her husband was also putting on his coat. She remarked to her husband that it was not necessary for him to accompany her, since she was quite capable of presenting her case. Whereupon Reb Ya'akov replied, "It is not for you that I am going to the *Beit Din*, for I am confident about your ability. I am going, instead, to speak in behalf of the poor maid, who will have no one to do so."

11

Community Service

"One appointed to a position of importance
has his sins completely forgiven..."
(YERUSHALMI BIKKURIM 3:3).

Our Rabbinical literature abounds with references to the importance of the individual. Typical is the all-inclusive remark of the Sages in Tractate *Sanhedrin* 37a: "One who supports one soul in Israel, is as if he supports the entire world." The individual, created by the Almighty, is a treasured entity and is to be given every consideration; and it follows that he in turn must give every consideration to his fellowman.

Rabbi Akiva taught this basic principle when he declared, "'You shall love your fellowman as yourself' (LEVITICUS 19:18) — this is a great principle in the Torah" (YERUSHALMI NEDARIM 9:4). Rabbi Akiva enlarged upon this concept in *Pirkei Avot* III:14, declaring: "Beloved is man, for he was created in His image; still greater was the expression of this love in that it was made known to him that he was created in His image, as it is said (GENESIS 9:6): 'In the image of God did He create man.'" Rabbi Akiva carried this thought further when he added: "Beloved are Israel, for they are called the children of God; still greater was the expression of this love in that it was made known to them that they are called the children of God, as it is said (DEUTERONOMY 14:1): 'You are the children of the Lord your God.'"

It follows logically that, out of proper consideration for one another, a viable community life is the aim of each person within society. Jews have in fact been the prime model for organized community life, operating for the mutual benefit of each and all of the members of the community. On the basis of the thesis that "All of Israel are responsible one for the other" (SHAVUOT 39a), through the ages, *kehillot* were formed to deal with education, aid to the poor, care for the ill and needy, burial arrangements, and all other beneficial services needed by a community. Most of these functions were traditionally carried out by dedicated volunteers, ordinary men and women of the community. Today, when huge and complex organizations deal with the many and varied needs of vibrant Jewish communities, trained staffs and highly qualified personnel direct their manifold activities. However, the foundation of all these organizations remains a loyal corps of dedicated volunteers who serve as board members, advisers and "foot soldiers" in fund raising, in *gemilut chasadim* and in all areas of public service.

It is for the welfare of these volunteers and for the encouragement of more such volunteers that we recite on Sabbaths, and on Festivals that occur on the Sabbath, the following prayer: "And all those who are engaged in performing communal functions faithfully, may the Holy One, blessed be He, give them their recompense, and remove from them every affliction, sustain them in health and forgive them any wrongdoing. May He send blessings and success to all their handiwork, together with all Israel, and let us say Amen."

So highly valued was community service that the Sages equated it with the study of Torah, declaring: "One who is engaged in community work, it is as if he were engaged in Torah study" (YERUSHALMI BERACHOT 5:1). *Rabban* Gamliel, son of Rabbi Yehudah *Ha-Nasi*, advised: "And all those who work for the community should do so only for the sake of Heaven [honestly and sincerely], for the merit of their fathers will sustain them and their righteousness will endure forever. 'As for you [says God], I credit to you a great reward, as if you had accomplished it all'" (AVOT II:2).

Maimonides lauds those who do community service with vigor and sincerity, noting that the effect alone, regardless of actual accomplishments, merits great reward and satisfaction, both by the community and by the Almighty.

In *Avot* II:4, Hillel cautions: "Do not set yourself apart from the community." Samson Raphael Hirsch, in his commentary on *Pirkei Avot*, discusses the place of the Jew within the community and his responsibilities thereto. He explains, "It is not to the individual, but to the community that God entrusted His Torah as an inheritance for all the generations to come. For this reason every individual is duty-bound to join forces with his community in thought, in word, and in deed, in loyalty to share in its tasks and obligations, so long as that community proves to be a faithful guardian and supporter of the Torah. Indeed it is essential in the discharge of his own life's task that the individual be part of a larger community. For whatever he may be able to do on his own is inadequate and short-lived."

Jewish life is inseparable from communal arrangements. The Torah is read only in the presence of a *minyan*, ten men; the *Kedushah* and *Kaddish* are recited only when there is a *minyan*. Historically, the Jewish people have experienced many dangers both to their physical and spiritual existence, all of which required joint communal action. Their ability to join together in emergencies has been a major source of survival throughout the ages. This particular blessing from the Almighty has come into vital use during Israel's War of Independence and all of the struggles thereafter.

Our Sages have left us instructions on personal conduct toward the community. Rabbi Yosei *Ha-Kohen* taught: "Let the property of your friend [the community] be as dear to you as your own...and let all your deeds [for the community] be done in the name of Heaven" (AVOT II:12). Thus one's attitude to the handling of public funds must be as prudent and as diligent as if he were dealing with his own money, which he is anxious to preserve and protect, as well as to increase. Rabbi Chanina ben Dosa, a student of *Rabban* Yochanan ben Zakkai (about whom are related many miracles ascribed to his great piety and righteousness), said: "Anyone whose deeds exceed his wisdom, his wisdom shall endure.... He who is pleasing [by his attitude and actions] to his fellowmen is pleasing also to God; but he who is not pleasing to his fellowmen is also displeasing to God" (AVOT III:9,10).

One's relations with his fellowmen within the community must be characterized by humility, and respect for the opinions of others. Ben Zoma says: "Who is wise? He who learns from every man, as it is said (PSALMS 119:99): 'From all who have taught me I have gained wisdom'" (AVOT IV:1). Wisdom of this sort should be well applied in public relations. Further excellent advice comes from ben Azzai: "Do not despise any man, and do not deem anything unworthy of consideration" (AVOT IV:3). And Rabbi Levitas adds: "Be exceedingly humble in spirit" (AVOT IV:4).

Through involvement in community affairs, it is inevitable that there arise differences of opinion among people. The manner in which these differences are resolved is a measure of the leadership's maturity and sincerity in its work. If one's motives are not personal prestige and honor, but rather devotion to the communal good, differences of opinion can be settled. In *Avot* V:17 the Sages describe just such a situation and provide a means of assessing the problem. They state: "Any controversy which is for the sake of Heaven [a noble purpose], will result in abiding value; but that which is not for the sake of Heaven, shall not in the end be of permanence. Which controversy was for the sake of Heaven? The controversy between Hillel and Shammai. And which was not for the sake of Heaven? The controversy of Korach and all his company."

A great and lasting responsibility is entrusted to the leadership of the community, along with a challenge for positive accomplishment. The Sages tell us: "He who leads the people to righteousness, no sin shall occur through him; but he who leads the people to sin, shall not be granted the opportunity to repent" (AVOT V:18).

Living together peaceably is the necessary basis for any society. Participation in community affairs, whether as a leader or an ordinary member, demands this skill. When genuine interest of the community is at stake, there is no room for envy, jealousy, striving for personal glory, or needless controversy. Hence the Sages conclude: "At all times shall your sincere efforts be to get along well with your fellowmen in the community" (KETUBBOT 17a); and "At all times let the awe of the community be upon you" (SOTAH 40a). You are serving the needs of all, and thereby you benefit along with all the other members of the community.

Long ago in ancient times, a big wedding was being celebrated in a village. All the townsfolk attended, dressed in their best clothes. They sat down at the wedding feast and, with hearty appetites, began to eat the rich food. Since knives and forks had not yet been invented, they ate with their fingers.

After eating his fill of the delicious food, one of the guests wanted to wipe his greasy hands. "I shall put my hands under the table and wipe them with the garment of the man sitting next to me," he decided. "No one will see me, and as long as my own hands are clean, I don't care about getting his clothes dirty."

The only trouble was that his neighbor had the same idea, and quietly did the same thing. In fact, everyone seated at the table had the same idea, but each thought that he was the only one soiling his neighbor's garment. As they rose to leave the table at the conclusion of the feast, they all stared with amazement at their own dirty clothes.

A story is told of a man in Maine who, after regularly attending the Sabbath services of his congregation, suddenly stopped coming one winter. The Rabbi inquired about him and was informed that the man was in good health. One chilly evening he decided to pay him a visit; he found the synagogue member seated comfortably at the fireplace, reading a book. Sitting himself next to his host in the glow of the warm fire, the Rabbi silently took the fire tongs and removed a live, glowing coal from the flames, setting it down quietly in a corner of the fireplace. While the rest of the fire blazed and crackled, the isolated piece of coal grew paler by the minute, until it was cold and dead. Saying not a word, the Rabbi arose, bade his congregant good night, and went home.

On the following Sabbath the man returned to synagogue.

Choni *Ha-Me'agel* once met an old man who was planting a carob sapling. "Why are you planting this tree?" Choni asked him. "Don't you know that it takes seventy years for a carob to mature and bear fruit? Are you so sure you will live another seventy years?"

"Ah, but I am not planting it for myself," answered the old man. "When I came into this world I found ready carob fruit. And so just as my forefathers planted for me, so I shall plant for my grandchildren and for theirs after them."

Choni then sat down to eat, and fell into a deep sleep. He slept for seventy years. When he awoke, he saw a young man sitting under a majestic carob tree, contentedly eating the sweet, rich fruit.

"Do you know who planted this tree?" asked Choni.

"Yes, I do," answered the man. "My grandfather planted it seventy years ago."

One who is concerned with the needs of others preserves the past, creates a present, and prepares the way for the future.

12

Tzedakah and Gemilut Chasadim

"Tzedakah and gemilut chasadim are great angels of merit for the children of Israel and their Father in Heaven" (TOSEFTA PE'AH 1:1).

The Hebrew terms *tzedakah* and *gemilut chasadim* defy accurate translation into English. The accepted translations — "charity" for *tzedakah* and "lovingkindness" for *gemilut chasadim* — aim to convey the spirit of these lofty concepts, the very foundations of Judaism. Charity as such implies a beneficence on the part of the giver, and suggests a certain condescension to the recipient, a bestowing of mercy — a gesture worthy of recognition and public acclaim. But the Hebrew word *tzedakah* has no such implications. The root of the word is *tzedek* — justice or righteousness. One who does *tzedek* is a *tzaddik* — a righteous person. He who gives *tzedakah* is thus only doing what is the right thing to do. He must do so with kindness and good will, and without condescension, so as not to shame or embarrass the recipient. The obligation to give *tzedakah* is just that — an obligation, not an option. In some Jewish communities it is even enforceable by law. The basis of this approach, unique to the Jewish people, is the acknowledgment that all one "owns" actually belongs to the Almighty, and that one holds it on loan, to be distributed to others who are in need, at the behest of the Almighty.

In Deuteronomy 15:7,8 we read: "You shall not harden your heart, nor shut your hand from your needy brother, but you shall open your hand wide and lend him sufficient for his need."

Rabbi Hai Gaon wrote: "By benevolence, man rises to a height where he meets God. Therefore do a good deed before you begin your prayers."

In *Bava Batra* 9b we read: "The Holy One, blessed be He, sends him [who hastens to give *tzedakah*] fitting recipients of *tzedakah* so that he may be rewarded." Rabbi Yehoshua ben Levi adds: "He who gives *tzedakah* habitually will have sons who are wise, wealthy, and eloquent" (BAVA BATRA 9b, 10a).

In Deuteronomy 15:9,10, we are warned: "Should you look with evil upon your brother, the poor person, and refuse to give to him, he will then cry out to God, and you will then have incurred a sin. Give generously and continue to give, and let not your heart feel bad in your act of giving to him, for in this proper act will the Almighty bless you in all your deeds, and in all your undertakings."

To enlarge upon this basic concept — that an act of *tzedakah* is, in effect, a sharing of God's gift with one's fellowman, who has a right to it — we have the cogent statement in *Avot* III:7 of Rabbi Elazar of Bartota: "Give to Him what is His, for you and all that you have are His. And thus King David said (CHRONICLES I 29:14): 'For all things come of You, and of Your own have we given You.'"

Rabbi Elazar, a close friend of the sainted Rabbi Akiva, indeed practiced what he preached about *tzedakah*. In Tractate *Ta'anit* 24a, an incident is related which sheds light upon the zealousness with which Rabbi Elazar regarded the giving of *tzedakah*: Two *tzedakah* collectors, upon seeing Rabbi Elazar from a distance, tried in vain to elude him, for he was known to give to *tzedakah* collectors all that he had in his possession, and they did not want him to remain destitute. Rabbi Elazar pursued them, however, and upon meeting them said, "I direct you [under oath] to tell me for what worthy cause you are presently collecting." Haltingly, they replied, "With the matter of arranging for the marriage of two poor orphans." Rabbi Elazar, who had been on his way to the market to purchase a trousseau for his own daughter, promptly took all the money that he had and gave it to the collectors, saying, "By my word, they definitely have precedence over my daughter."

Meticulous instructions about *tzedakah* are related in Tractate *Ketubbot* 67b and 68a, as well as in Tractate *Bava Batra* 8b and 9a. Giving less than 10 percent of one's income is considered inadequate; 10 percent is proper; 20 percent is admirable. We are told: "One should not spread out more than 20 percent of his income, lest his livelihood be endangered." No less than two collectors in a community shall be engaged in *tzedakah* collection, and no less than three shall dispense *tzedakah*. Collectors shall wear cloaks without pockets, and shall place the money in a special *tzedakah* purse, and disburse only from that purse, so as not to engender any suspicion about their honesty and integrity.

The Torah commands us: "[Give the poor person] all that he now lacks" (DEUTERONOMY 15:8). The Sages interpreted this phrase almost literally. About Hillel it is told that he provided a formerly wealthy man, who had become poor but who was accustomed to a horse and a runner before him to announce his arrival, with a horse and runner. One day Hillel could not find him a runner, so he himself ran in front of the horse for three miles in order to fulfill the obligation.

The great scholar Rava received a poor man, and inquired of him what his regular fare was for meals. "A stuffed hen and old wine," was the prompt reply. Rava, taken aback, asked, "Do you not fear being a burden upon the community?" "Why?" replied the man. "Am I eating what is theirs? What I eat is God's." Rava's sister brought in a stuffed hen and old wine for the poor man, and Rava promptly apologized to him.

Nevertheless, a person should not accustom himself to overindulgence, for we are told of Rabbi Nechemiah who, upon asking a similar question of another poor man, received the same request for stuffed chicken and old wine. Rabbi Nechemiah was a man of limited means, however, and invited the poor man to join him in his meal of lentils. The poor man ate the lentils, and died shortly thereafter, to Rabbi Nechemiah's great sorrow.

Maimonides, in a lengthy discussion of *tzedakah*, describes seven ways of giving. The least desirable is giving with an ulterior motive or with a lack of enthusiasm, and the very best is that neither the donor nor the recipient know the other's identity. *Pirkei Avot* has a great deal to say about attitudes and approach in giving *tzedakah*, and their effect upon both the donor and the recipient. Hillel advises: "The more [one gives to] *tzedakah*, the more [he contributes to] peace" (AVOT II:7). And it is written: "And it shall be that the achievement of *tzedakah* shall be peace" (ISAIAH 32:17). By the giving of *tzedakah*, one creates a feeling of well-being in the heart of the needy person, so that he is at peace with himself and his Maker.

Rabbi Akiva noted that opportunities are presented to one who gives *tzedakah* that increase his income and thus his ability to give more and more *tzedakah* (AVOT III:13): "Tithes are a protective fence to wealth." We read in Tractate *Ta'anit* 9a: "Give tithes [one-tenth] so that you will receive tenfold in return."

Pirkei Avot V:13 lists four types of donors to *tzedakah*, and analyzes their motives: "He who desires to give but that others should not give — begrudges the privilege of others. He who desires that others should give, but will not give himself — begrudges himself. He who gives and also wants others to give — is pious. He who will not give and does not want others to give — is wicked." One who urges another not to give, even though he may have the good intention of helping him to conserve his assets, is making a grievous error, for it is said that what one gives to *tzedakah* is the only permanent possession that he retains as a mitzvah to accompany him in the hereafter. That one should give, and inspire others to give, is the ideal approach to *tzedakah*.

This principle is illustrated vividly in *Bava Batra* 11a regarding the meritorious action of King Munbaz "who distributed large quantities of his treasures, and those of his predecessors, in order to feed the needy in a year of famine. His family criticized him severely and declared, 'Your predecessors amassed wealth and added more wealth to their predecessors' — and you are squandering all this wealth!'

"He replied, 'My predecessors amassed wealth below, while I am amassing "wealth" Above; they stored their wealth in an insecure place, while I am placing my wealth where no human hand can touch; they amassed wealth that does not produce fruits, while I amassed wealth that does produce fruits; they amassed wealth for their successors, while I amassed wealth for myself; they amassed treasures of money, while I amassed treasures of souls; they amassed wealth for this world, while I amassed wealth for the World-to-Come.'"

In fact, our Sages emphasize (Tractate *Kallah* 2a): "The act of influencing others to give is even greater than the act of giving oneself." The implication is that if one is unable to give fully, he is not absolved from the responsibility of influencing others to give. The sharing of the burden equitably by all members of the community is the foundation of Jewish communal life, and this is to be accomplished in a spirit of cooperation and joy at fulfilling the great mitzvah of giving *tzedakah*. (It is interesting to note the significant change in approach taken by the United Jewish Appeal in its current fund-raising campaign. Its posters used to cry out: "Give until it hurts." Now they state, in a more constructive and satisfying call: "Give until it feels good."

Tzedakah not only provides the needy with physical sustenance. Equally important is provision for the spiritual needs of the individual and the community. Hence, Rabbi Elazar ben Azariah warns: "Where there is no bread, there is no Torah" (AVOT III:17). It is incumbent upon each person to support not only individual scholars who learn Torah but, even more so, the institutions that teach Torah. The classic example of such an arrangement wherein one undertakes the support of scholars and shares in the mitzvah is the arrangement between the tribe of Zevulun, who were merchants, and Issachar, who were Torah students: Issachar learned Torah and Zevulun provided the required sustenance. A similar midrashic arrangement exists between the Almighty and each Jew today, as it did in ancient times. The Almighty states: "You care for my four — the Levite, the stranger, the orphan, and the widow, and I shall care for your four — your son, your daughter, your servant, and your maid" (RASHI ON DEUTERONOMY 16:11, BASED ON MIDRASH TANCHUMA, PARASHAT R'EI).

Tzedakah and *gemilut chasadim* are closely related. The same basic principle applies in both instances: A person's wealth is not his own, but belongs to the Almighty, and is given in trust to be used wisely and to be shared with the less fortunate. That one gives *tzedakah* does not release him from the obligation to practice *gemilut chasadim*. Both are among the most important of our mitzvot.

Gemilut chasadim, however, involves a much wider scope of activities, all designed to help a person in need such that he will not have to request *tzedakah*. *Gemilut chasadim* includes every benevolent act that helps another, whether the recipient is rich or poor, while *tzedakah* is to be given to the poor. We are all familiar with the many *gemach* funds — an acronym for *gemilut chasadim* — available to those in need of temporary assistance, whether for business, marrying off children, medical care, or any other pressing matter.

Maimonides specifically advises us to help any person in need of assistance, wherever possible, not merely by giving alms, but more so by helping to rehabilitate him so that he will not require *tzedakah*. That help may take the form of a loan which will help him establish a business, the provision of gainful occupation, etc. In this way the recipient preserves or regains his self-respect.

Our forefather Abraham is associated with the mitzvah of *gemilut chasadim*. His hospitality — *hachnasat orchim* — is a good example of this kind act. He would prepare sumptuous meals for travelers and transients, and personally serve them.

Upon completion of the meal, the guests would wish to thank their host, whereupon Abraham would raise his arms Heavenward and declare, "Please thank the Almighty, for it is He Who created the world and provides us with food" (SOTAH 10b).

Jews have cherished and observed this mitzvah through all the generations, as it is recorded in Tractate *Kallah* 10a: "Whoever has these three attributes: mercy, modesty, and *gemilut chasadim*, is surely of the seed of our father Abraham." Tractate *Berachot* 8a assigns an even greater achievement to one who performs this mitzvah: "So says the Holy One, blessed be He: 'One who is occupied with Torah and with *gemilut chasadim*, and who worships with the congregation, I consider it as if he has redeemed Me and My children from among the nations of the world.'" Proverbs 10:2 relates that "*tzedakah* saves one from death." Rabbi Elazar, in Tractate *Sukkah* 49b, praises *gemilut chasadim*, explaining: "*Tzedakah* is greater than all the sacrifices, yet *gemilut chasadim* is greater than *tzedakah*, as it is written (HOSEA 10:12): 'Sow for yourself in righteousness [*tzedakah*], reap in mercy [*gemilut chasadim*].' When one sows, it is questionable whether or not he will merit to eat of the crop, but when one already reaps he is certain to eat."

The Sages supported this thesis, declaring: "In three things is *gemilut chasadim* greater than *tzedakah*: the giver of *tzedakah* gives his money, but the giver of *gemilut chasadim* gives of himself as well as of his money; *tzedakah* is given only to the poor, but *gemilut chasadim* can benefit the rich as well as the poor; *tzedakah* is given to the living, but *gemilut chasadim* may be for both the living and the dead" (SUKKAH 49b).

In *Pirkei Avot* these thoughts are reflected with even greater emphasis. We read: "Shimon *Ha-Tzaddik* was one of the last survivors of the Great Assembly. He used to say: On three things the world stands: on the Torah, on the service of the Almighty [*avodah*], and on acts of lovingkindness [*gemilut chasadim*]" (AVOT I:2). These three pillars support and maintain this world, and all of us are required to do our part in perpetuating this arrangement. How? By constant involvement in Torah study or by the support of Torah institutions and their scholars; by the service and worship of God, or — as some interpret the word *avodah* — the actual work of plowing, planting, and harvesting, thus "assisting" the Almighty in the task of creating; and by becoming involved in the full gamut of mutual aid and assistance, in the spirit of "All of Israel are responsible one for the other" (SHAVUOT 39a).

Yosei ben Yochanan's advice enlarged upon the third of these pillars, *gemilut chasadim*: "Let your house be wide open, and let the poor be members of your household" (AVOT I:5). Treat the stranger as your brother and extend to him aid and assistance as needed. Shammai, associate of Hillel, cautioned: "Say little but do much; and receive every person with a kindly countenance" (AVOT I:15), as did our father Abraham, the classic model of *gemilut chasadim*. Rabbi Ishmael, associate of Rabbi Akiva, added: "And receive all men with cheerfulness" (AVOT III:12). This causes a guest to feel wanted and not a burden to his host.

Pirkei Avot contains numerous references to the great necessity of performing good deeds as a logical concomitant of Torah study, for one without the other is incomplete. Shimon, the son of the elderly *Nasi*, Gamliel, learned from his experiences in the house of the *Nasi* that "the teaching and study of Torah are not the most important things, but rather the practice of Torah" (AVOT I:17).

Rabbi Elazar ben Azariah, at age 18 the youngest of all *Nesi'im* in Jewish history, described this precept in a picturesque manner: "One whose wisdom exceeds his deeds...[is like] a tree whose branches are many, but whose roots are few, and the wind comes and uproots it and overturns it upon its top ....But he whose deeds exceed his wisdom...[is like] a tree whose branches are few, but whose roots are many; even if all the winds of the world come and blow upon it, they cannot move it from its place, as it is said (JEREMIAH 17:8): 'For he shall be as a tree planted by the waters, that spreads out its roots to the stream of water, and shall not see that the heat comes, and its leaves are ever fresh and green; and shall not be troubled in the year of drought; neither shall it cease from bearing fruit'" (AVOT III:17).

The Sages conclude in the final chapter: "Great is the Torah, for it gives life to those who practice it in this world and in the World-to-Come" (AVOT VI:7). Clearly, *tzedakah* and *gemilut chasadim*, in all their vast implications and broad ramifications, are the guideposts of living a Torah life, acceptable to the Almighty and to man alike.

🌿 🌿 🌿

One cold winter, the famous Rabbi Meislish was gathering money to buy coal for the poor. When he was received in the home of the wealthy merchant Pozansky, in a warm and beautifully furnished room, the Rabbi thanked the merchant for his welcome and, begging his pardon, asked him to be kind enough to speak with him in the street, noting that it was important.

The merchant immediately obliged and, thinking that it would only take a few minutes, didn't bother to put on his overcoat. Once outside, the Rabbi appeared to be in no hurry. His conversation was slow and drawn out, as he moved from one subject to another. As time passed, the merchant started to feel the sting of the bitterly cold weather. Finally, when he could bear it no longer, he cried, "Rabbi, you must excuse me, but I am almost frozen. May we return to the house?"

"Now," answered the Rabbi, "I will tell you the real nature of my visit to you. This is a cold winter, and the price of coal is too high for the poor to pay. They have no heat in their homes and they are freezing. I want a donation from you for this purpose."

The merchant immediately proffered a generous sum, and as he handed the money over, he asked, "Now tell me, Rabbi, why did you have to bring me out into this freezing cold? Couldn't we have done this in my living room?"

"No," answered the Rabbi. "There is a proverb that states: 'The satiated person does not believe the hungry one.' I came to ask for money to buy fuel for the poor, who are freezing. Do you think that, sitting in your warm and cozy home, you would have appreciated what it is to suffer from the cold?"

In *Bava Batra* 10a we read of an incident in which the Roman Governor Turnus Rufus inquired of Rabbi Akiva, "If your God loves the poor, why does He not support them?" Rabbi Akiva replied, "In the merit of the help that we extend to them we are saved from Gehinnom." Turnus Rufus argued, "In that case, you should be punished for interfering with God's decrees." To which Rabbi Akiva replied with a parable: "A king was angered by his son and ordered him imprisoned and denied food and water. Then someone came and provided the son with food and water. When the king, repentant over his harsh decree, heard of this kindness to his son, would he not reward the person who did it?"

13

Attitudes to Authority

"Three things shorten a man's life...[one being]
the acceptance of the role of authority"
(BERACHOT 55a).

The Rabbinic literature is filled with words of caution to those who hold positions of authority, as well as to those who have to deal with the ruling authorities. Those who would take upon themselves such roles are warned against the effects on their way of life, and on the length of their life as well. In Tractate *Berachot*, quoted above, it is taught that Joseph, having been appointed Viceroy of Egypt, lost at least ten years of his life. He died at the age of 110, while all of his brothers were still alive. His position of authority and the consequent strain involved undoubtedly shortened his life. The inference is that, if one desires to lead an unfettered life, he should at all costs avoid positions of power. Wielding power will force him to compromise his beliefs, detract from his freedom of thinking and expression, and ultimately make him a slave to his position. These attitudes toward the holding of authority in no way reflect upon our responsibility to share in communal service both as lay leaders and as active participants. It is rather the seeking of power that is discouraged.

Shemayah, who was *Nasi* at the end of the Hasmonean period and at the beginning of the Herodian (the first century C.E.), was a student of Shimon ben Shatach, whose sad experiences with King Yannai had a great effect upon his view of authority. Shemayah concluded that it is best to steer a course which does not clash with authority. Consequently, he advised:

"Love work; and hate holding offices of authority; and do not seek intimacy with the governing officials" (AVOT I:10). This formula assures independence of action, for concentration on constructive efforts will benefit both the individual and his community, and avoid dependence upon authority. Shemayah and his close associate Avtalyon, the Head of the *Beit Din*, followed this astute policy carefully and successfully under the precarious conditions which prevailed during Herod's rule.

Rabban Gamliel, son of Rabbi Yehudah *Ha-Nasi*, experienced the harsh Roman decrees banning the observance of mitzvot, Torah study, Sabbath observance, circumcision, and the ordaining of Rabbis, which were repealed after his father established a good relationship with Emperor Antoninus. Nevertheless, *Rabban* Gamliel cautioned: "Be cautious with the ruling authorities, for they do not befriend a man except for their own interests; they appear as friends when it is to their advantage, but they do not support a man when he is in distress" (AVOT II:3).

During his time, the Jewish community in Babylon had begun to assume its centrality in Jewry, and prominent Jewish leaders were close to the Babylonian authorities. The warning of *Rabban* Gamliel was timely not only for the Jews of Babylon, but indeed for all the Jewish communities and their leadership in the many countries of exile, through the ages. Don Isaac Abarbanel, who was Finance Minister in fifteenth-century Spain and Portugal, also drew from his own varied experiences when he wrote on this subject in his commentary on *Pirkei Avot*.

Rabbi Chanina, who was assistant to the High Priest in the waning days of the Second Temple, and witnessed the baseless hatred among Jews which led to its destruction, urged peace among Jews and between the Jews and the Romans. "Great is peace," he said, "for it is measured as equal to all the works of Creation" (SIFRI NASO 41:11). He also said: "Pray for the welfare of the government, since were it not for the fear of it, men would swallow each other alive" (AVOT III:2). Jews have been witness to this fact on many occasions. During revolutionary times, when authority ceases and chaos reigns, the Jews have always been the first to suffer. Atrocities and pogroms were particularly prevalent during the Cossack Rebellion in the seventeenth century and during and after the Soviet Revolution in 1917.

In Chapter Six of *Pirkei Avot*, Rabbi Meir, who suffered greatly during the difficult times which followed the anti-Roman uprising, looks to a different kind of authority which will one day preside over Israel and the entire world. This authority will be vested in an individual who occupies himself with Torah sincerely and devotedly. "Through him men benefit from counsel and sound wisdom, understanding and strength...[Torah] gives him kingship and dominion and sound wisdom and discerning judgment" (AVOT VI:1). This will be at the time prophesied by Zechariah (14:9): "And the Lord shall reign over all the earth. On that day the Lord shall be One and His Name One." Although Rabbi Meir's message deals not only with the days to come and the Messiah, we can also infer from it that everyone who engages in Torah sincerely and devotedly can achieve the level of development described.

The ancient historian Josephus, in both his books — *Antiquities of the Jews* and *Jewish Wars* — teaches us why the Jews were advised to "not seek intimacy with the governing officials":

> Herod, when he was governor of the Galilee, executed a number of Jews whom he claimed were bandits, when in fact they were Jewish patriots who objected to the growing Roman influence in the country. Herod was consequently summoned by the Sanhedrin to stand trial. In a deliberate affront, he appeared dressed in princely robes, accompanied by a contingent of his warriors. It was evident he was exhibiting his contempt for the highest court in the land.
>
> Shemayah ordered Herod to send the soldiers away and to dress more appropriately, but Herod refused. Shemayah then turned to the other members of the Sanhedrin and asked their opinion. When most remained silent, fearing retribution from

Herod, Shemayah, disappointed and angry, warned them: "You have lowered your heads. One day Herod will be king and will also lower your heads."

As Shemayah had predicted, Herod became king and executed almost all the members of the Sanhedrin, although Shemayah and Avtalyon were saved.

Shemayah and Avtalyon did not fear Herod but they avoided any contact or intimacy with him. They were determined to live as Jews and to help others maintain a religious life, and thus wanted as little as possible to do with him.

14

Education

"Educate the child according to his way.
Even when he ages, he will not depart from it"
(PROVERBS 22:6).

Study — "learning" — has always been emphasized by our Sages and Rabbis. Education builds men, strengthens character, gives light and meaning to life. It broadens the vision, and brings man closer to God. In Deuteronomy 6:7 we are taught: "You shall teach them diligently unto your children." Rashi, in a commentary to Exodus 13:14 — "And it shall be when your son asks...What's this?" — counsels, "We must endeavor to teach even the unintelligent."

In *Iggeret Ha-Ramban* we read: "Busy yourself as much as possible with the study of Divine things, not to know them merely, but to do them; and when you close the book, look around you, look within you, to see if your hand can translate into deed something you have learned."

If one is to learn properly and adequately, he must have a teacher. Yehoshua ben Perachiah says: "Provide yourself with a teacher" (AVOT I:6); *Rabban* Gamliel gives identical advice in *Avot* I:16.

But it is not sufficient to find any teacher; one must find a good one. Our Sages have described the qualities that a good teacher should possess. Hillel stated: "An impatient man cannot teach" (AVOT II:5). And we read in *Orchot Tzaddikim*, chapter 2: "A teacher should explain again and again, in accordance with the pupils' intelligence, the difficult parts so that they understand them fully."

The classic example of a teacher's patience is related in *Eruvin* 54b: Rabbi Preida had a student with whom he would repeat each lesson 400 times, until the student finally understood the material. One day Rabbi Preida was called away to perform a mitzvah. Before leaving, he repeated the lesson 400 times as usual — but this time the student failed to grasp the material. Rabbi Preida, unperturbed, inquired of the student the reason for his failure to understand. The student replied, "I was unable to concentrate from the moment that I knew you must leave, and I feared that you would leave at any moment." Rabbi Preida immediately stated, "Please concentrate now, and I will teach the lesson to you 400 times once more." Rabbi Preida is reported to have been rewarded with length of days and a goodly share in the World-to-Come for himself and his entire generation.

Teachers deserve to be held in the greatest respect and esteem. Our Sages counsel: "To oppose a teacher is to oppose the *Shechinah*" (SANHEDRIN 110a); "[Let] the reverence due to your teacher [be] as the reverence due to Heaven" (ELAZAR BEN SHAMMUA, AVOT IV:12); "He who pleases his teachers is destined for the World-to-Come" (CHANINA BEN CHAMA, SHABBAT 153a); "To serve one's teacher is greater than to study Torah" (SHIMON BAR YOCHAI, BERACHOT 7b).

Ibn Gabirol states: "As the day adds to the vision of the seeing and the blindness of the bat, so does instruction help to enlighten the wise" (MIVCHAR HA-PENINIM). The purpose of education is not just to learn what to do, but to enjoy the doing as well. King Solomon defines the object of studying: "To know wisdom and instruction; to perceive the words of understanding; to receive the instruction of wisdom, justice and judgment, and equity; to give prudence to the simple, to the young man knowledge and discretion" (PROVERBS 1:27). If one can attain, understand and put into practice these goals of education as defined by Solomon, then he will merit a greater understanding of life and will judge all people charitably.

"Education does not mean teaching people what they do not know," said John Ruskin. "It means teaching them to behave as they do not now behave." One might say that education is the process of learning from others and through experience the meaning of the following verbs, and acquiring the personal power of each:

I AM — the power of self-knowledge.
I THINK — the power to investigate.
I KNOW — the power to master facts.
I FEEL — the power to appreciate, to value, to love.
I WONDER — the power of reverence, curiosity, worship.
I SEE — the power of insight, imagination, vision.
I BELIEVE — the power of daring faith.
I CAN — the power to act and the skill to accomplish.
I OUGHT — the power of conscience, the moral imperative.
I WILL — the power of will, loyalty to duty, consecration.
I SERVE — the power to be useful, to be devoted to a cause.

Hillel warns: "He who does not add to his knowledge decreases it" (AVOT I:13). The thought that a person who does not increase his knowledge will forget even what he has learned previously is very compelling. No person should believe that he knows all that there is to know about something, and hence feel that there is no necessity for him to acquire a teacher. Certainly there is no one more justified in making such a statement than Hillel. According to the account in *Yoma* 35b, Hillel was so poor in his youth that he earned no more than one tropaikon per day, a pittance, for his labors. Of this, he had to give half to the doorkeeper of the house of study as admission fee, while the other half had to do for his and his family's needs. It came to pass one day that he could find no work, and hence could not pay the doorkeeper. Unable to enter the house of study, he climbed up to the roof and lay atop the skylight. From that position he listened all night long to the learned discourses of Shemayah and Avtalyon, his great teachers. The next morning it seemed to be unusually dark in the house of study, and when Shemayah investigated the cause, he came upon Hillel lying on the skylight, buried under a foot of snow that had fallen during the night. Hillel was immediately rescued, revived and permitted thereafter to continue his studies undisturbed. Therefore it is said that, if a man pleads poverty and economic worries as a reason for not studying, let him be reminded of the example set by Hillel.

There are those who might believe that they can rely on their own logic when they study, and therefore are in no need of a teacher. Both Yehoshua ben Perachiah and *Rabban* Gamliel wisely counsel such people not to rely on their own reasoning, but to "provide yourself with a teacher" (AVOT I:6,16). Even great scholars are in need of master teachers. Rabbi Eliezer tells us, "Warm yourself beside the fire of the Sages" (AVOT II:10). If one studies alone, he may encounter many questions that he cannot answer. *Rabban* Gamliel thus counsels that when you have a teacher, you "liberate yourself of doubt" (AVOT I:16). Thus one does not grow over-confident in deciding matters of Halachic importance. Also Rashi counsels that one should always endeavor to resolve all doubts and reservations regarding the Torah, by consulting a master.

If one respects the teacher he has acquired, and lives up to the values he espouses, one will "acquire...a companion" for himself, an aide for guidance in living (AVOT I:6). In this way, theory is translated into action and reality, and so becomes integrated into daily living.

The beginning of true wisdom is the desire for instruction that will bring one closer to God. Knowledge alone cannot bring wisdom.

There is an interesting legend that tells of God's love of Wisdom. Because of His love, He adopted her as His daughter, and lovingly raised her. Before He made heaven and earth, she was His delight...and He took counsel with her....Then, because God loved man, He sent Wisdom to walk upon the earth, that her delightful employ be with man, who would choose her in order to survive unto great salvation (SATANOV, MISHLEI ASAF, 1789).

A Sage was once asked, "Why are you wiser than your friends?" Without much hesitation, he replied, "Because I spend more on oil [to keep my lamps burning] than they on wine" (IBN GABIROL, MIVCHAR HA-PENINIM).

A provincial Jew once came into town, entered a Jewish bookstore and said, "I would like to purchase a *Siddur* for my son." The bookseller, understanding that this simple Jew's son must not be much of a scholar, took an ordinary prayer book and offered it to him.

"No, not one like that," the villager protested. "I want a thick prayer book, one which is full of many commentaries and laws."

"Is your son such a scholar," the bookseller asked in wonder, "that you need such a *Siddur* for him?"

"Not at all," smiled the customer. "My little boy sometimes rips the pages out of the prayer book. Now, if I buy him a thin *Siddur* in which the prayers start on the very first page, then when he starts to remove the pages, nothing will be left. But if I get him a thick one, full of commentaries in the front and in the back, even though he tears out a lot of the pages, the prayers will remain!"

Once there was a man who always had difficulty finding his clothing and other items when he got up in the morning. One evening, he took paper and pen in hand and, as he undressed, he noted down exactly where he placed every item of clothing. The next morning he eagerly grasped the slip of paper in hand and read: "Hat is on the chair. Pants and jacket are in the closet. Shoes are under the bed." Joyfully, he got dressed, and then looked at the last item on his list: "I am in bed." He glanced with alarm at the empty bed, and began to search for himself fruitlessly, after a while crying out in frustration: "I have found everything that belongs to me, but what good is it when I myself am lost!"

How true of our time! Our inventions and achievements are immense, our discoveries colossal. But sometimes we ourselves are lost.

Only when we are imbued with the spirit of God and the love of man, when our lives are guided and directed by the teachings of Sinai, can we say: "I may feel alone at times, but I am not lost, for how can one be lost on the mountain of God?"

15

Teachers and Students of Torah

"Let the...reverence due to your teacher [be as dear to you] as the reverence due to Heaven" (AVOT IV:12).

"He who pleases his teachers is destined for the World-to-Come" (SHABBAT 153a).

"Torah commanded to us by Moses is the inheritance of the Congregation of Jacob" (DEUTERONOMY 33:3). "She is a tree of life to those who lay hold upon her, and happy is everyone who retains her" (PROVERBS 3:18). Clearly, the Torah — this great treasure granted to us by the Almighty as an inheritance — is worthy of the most prudent care. Therefore, it is incumbent upon every generation to produce the best teachers it can, to teach students on every level, in accordance with their capabilities and understanding of Torah. The chain of tradition began with Moses, who is always called "Moshe *Rabbenu*" — Moses our Teacher. It continued to the *Anshei Knesset Ha-Gedolah* in the fifth century B.C.E., and was passed from them to our Sages in *Eretz Yisrael*, in Babylon, and through all the generations down to our own. The *Anshei Knesset Ha-Gedolah* advised, "Raise up many students; and make a fence for the Torah" (AVOT I:1), and its surviving disciple, Shimon *Ha-Tzaddik*, added, "On three things the world stands: on the Torah, on the Service of the Almighty, and on acts of lovingkindness" (AVOT I:2). Learned Rabbis of every generation issued injunctions to spread the learning of Torah among the Jewish people at all costs, even at the cost of the lives of both teachers and students.

During the troubled times of the Emperor Hadrian's decrees, in the second century C.E., ten of our greatest scholars gave up their lives *"al kiddush Hashem,"* sanctifying God's Name rather than permit the neglect of Torah teaching and learning. Rabbi Chanina ben Teradyon was burned alive, wrapped in a Torah scroll. Rabbi Akiva, one of Israel's greatest scholars and teachers of all time (who was as worthy, it is said, to have been given the Torah as was Moses), explained his martyrdom to Papus ben Yehudah by commenting upon the command in the Torah: "'And you shall love the Lord your God with all your heart and with all your soul' (DEUTERONOMY 6:5) — even if He chooses to take your soul."

In Tractate *Berachot* 61b, the detailed conversation between the two is recorded. When Papus found Rabbi Akiva teaching large groups in public (he is said to have had 24,000 students), he inquired, "Akiva, are you not afraid of the Romans?" Rabbi Akiva replied patiently, "I shall cite you a parable. [This was a favorite teaching technique of Rabbi Akiva, and one followed diligently by his brilliant student, Rabbi Meir.] A fox was strolling along a river bank, and noticed that the fish were swimming hurriedly downstream. The fox asked them: 'From what danger are you fleeing?' Replied the fish: 'From the fishing nets that the people are casting.' Offered the fox: 'Why don't you come ashore and we can live together in peace, as did your forefathers and mine?' Scoffed the fish in derision: 'And you are said to be the wisest of animals? Not only are you not wise, but you are an outright fool! If, in our own natural habitat, we are afraid, how much more so would we fear for our lives on dry land — where we cannot possibly survive!'" Concluding the parable, Rabbi Akiva added, "So it is with us. Now we sit and study Torah, in which it is written: 'For she is your life and the length of your days' (DEUTERONOMY 30:20). Thus if we abandon the Torah, our source of life, how much more so do we decree our death."

Shortly thereafter Rabbi Akiva was arrested and put to a violent death, whereupon his devoted and dedicated students —

Rabbi Meir, Rabbi Yehudah, Rabbi Yosei, Rabbi Shimon, and Rabbi Elazar ben Shammua — arose and "filled all of *Eretz Yisrael* with Torah" (YEVAMOT 62b; BERESHIT RABBAH 61:3).

The first requirement of any prospective student is: "Provide yourself with a teacher; [and then] acquire for yourself a companion [a *chaver*]" (AVOT I:6), one who will be your *chavruta* in learning as well as your companion in life.

"Be of the disciples of Aaron, loving peace and pursuing peace, loving your fellowmen and bringing them nearer to the Torah" (AVOT I:12), Hillel advises the teacher. And he counsels both the teacher and the student: "A timid man will not learn [for he is ashamed to ask questions], and an impatient man cannot teach" (AVOT II:5), he counsels both the teacher and the student.

Avtalyon, the teacher of Hillel and Shammai, stressed the gravity of the responsibility of teaching Torah, cautioning teachers: "Wise scholars, be careful with your words, for you may incur the penalty of *galut*" (AVOT I:11). Since *galut* (exile) is the judicial punishment for manslaughter, this suggests that careless teaching could bring about the moral decline and "death" of a student. A case in point was the result of a misinterpretation of the statement by Antignos of Socho, a student of Shimon *Ha-Tzaddik*, who taught: "Be not like the servants who serve their master for the sake of receiving a reward, but be like servants who serve their master not for the sake of receiving a reward" (AVOT I:3). Two of his students, Tzadok and Baytos, misunderstood this statement, thinking that it implied that there is no reward for good and no punishment for evil — and that, therefore, there is no hereafter. They founded the sects of the *Tzadokim* (Sadducees) and *Baytosim*, which were a source of great strife and dissension for many years (AVOT D'RABBI NATAN 5:2).

The study of Torah is to be a lifetime experience: "At five years of age [one is ready] for the study of Torah; at ten for the study of Mishnah; at thirteen, for the fulfillment of mitzvot; at fifteen, for the study of Talmud" (AVOT V:21), and thereafter continuously for as long as the Almighty grants one years. A student should strive to attain a level of learning at which he becomes "quick to learn and slow to forget" (AVOT V:12).

Rabban Yochanan ben Zakkai, the great Torah teacher, saved Judaism after the destruction of the Second Temple by establishing the yeshiva and Torah center Kerem B'Yavneh. His students later founded yeshivot in Lod under the direction of Rabbi Eliezer and Rabbi Tarfon; in Bnei Brak under Rabbi Akiva; and in Usha, Sepporis, Tiberias, and Caesaria.

He recognized different learning approaches, describing what he called "Sinai" — one who retains his learning like a "cemented cistern which does not lose a drop," as in the case of his outstanding student, Rabbi Eliezer ben Hurkanos — and what he called *"Oker Harim"* (one who moves mountains), an innovator and creative thinker like Rabbi Elazar ben Arach, who "is like a spring which ever increases its flow" (AVOT II:8). A controversy over these basic educational principles was resolved later, taking into account an era in which the bulk of the Oral Law had not yet been recorded and retention was vital. In Tractate *Berachot* 64a, the answer is given: "Sinai or *Oker Harim*? Sinai is preferred." However, even after the completion of the Talmud in 500 C.E., the issue has remained to this day a subject of heated discussion.

In his teachings, Rabbi Elazar ben Azariah emphasized the obligation incumbent upon a student of Torah to take his proper place in society and thereby set an example, for he represents Torah to the community. "Where there is no Torah, there is no proper conduct [*derech eretz*]; where there is no proper conduct, there is no Torah.... Where there is no bread, there is no Torah; where there is no Torah, there is no bread" (AVOT III:17). Rabbi Ishmael bar Rabbi Yochanan also considered Torah learning to be inseparable from one's behavior in the larger community: "He who learns in order to teach will be granted the opportunity to learn and to teach; but he who learns in order to practice will be granted the opportunity to learn and to teach, to observe and to practice" (AVOT IV:5).

The sixth and final chapter in *Pirkei Avot*, a *baraita* rather than the original *mishnah*, is aptly called *Kinyan Torah* — the acquisition of Torah. Therein Rabbi Meir, a brilliant and popular teacher — whose curriculum consisted of one-third *Halachah*, one-third *Aggadah* and one-third parables (he is said to have used 300 parables about foxes!) — offered the greatest reward of all to sincere students: "He who occupies himself with Torah with a sincere purpose merits many things; moreover, he is deserving that in his merit the whole world exists. He is called: friend, beloved; he loves God, he loves mankind, he pleases God, he pleases mankind" (AVOT VI:1). However, the student is cautioned that he must study Torah under any and all conditions, including physical discomfort if such is his lot: "This is the way of the Torah: To eat bread and salt; to drink water by measure; to sleep upon the ground; and to live a life of hardship while you study the Torah diligently. If you do so, '...happy shall you be, and it shall be well with you' (PSALMS 128:2): *happy shall you be* — in this world, *and it shall be well with you* — in the World-to-Come" (AVOT VI:4).

The above description of the meager fare and humble conditions under which Torah is to be studied is directed to the student, who should be willing to suffer material hardships for the sake of Torah. However, insisted the Lublin Rabbi, Rabbi Meir Shapiro, for those whose task it is to solicit funds for supporting yeshivot and their needy students, the injunction must be understood as a rhetorical question: "Such is the way of Torah, etc.?" Certainly not! Therefore, contributors must do their share to ensure that these hardships are not too severe, and should take to heart the verse describing Torah as "a tree of life to those who lay hold upon her, and happy is everyone who retains [supports] her" (PROVERBS 3:18).

Despite all this, a teacher's lot left much to be desired, even those teachers who were highly regarded and greatly respected by their students. Many of our Sages were poor, barely eking out a living from their handiwork. Hillel was a woodsman; Rabbi Yehoshua was a blacksmith; Rabbi Yochanan was a shoemaker; Rabbi Meir was a scribe. None took compensation for his teaching, a practice which continued until recent times. Then teachers were not paid for teaching per se, but rather received a nominal amount of compensation for time lost from their studies or from occupations from which they earned their livelihood. To this day, teachers, and particularly those in yeshivot, earn much less than other, comparably trained workers. While the Almighty will undoubtedly grant teachers of Torah their just reward, it is nevertheless incumbent upon the Jewish community to express appropriate respect for their sacred work.

A legend tells of a shepherd boy who was grazing his flock on the mountainside and noticed a strange flower that he had never seen before. Intrigued, he picked it and suddenly found a cave opening at his feet. As he ventured in, he encountered a heap of sparkling diamonds. Hurriedly discarding the flower, he filled his hands with the shining gems. As he started to leave, a voice said: "Don't forget the best." But what could possibly be better than these diamonds? thought the boy, and hurried out. The cave immediately closed up behind him, and the gleaming jewels crumbled to dust in his hands. For he had forgotten the best — the magic flower, without which nothing from the cave had lasting value.

It is wise to remember that we take nothing material with us when we leave this world, that the aim of life is to live by the Torah, to love God, to walk in His ways, and to love one's fellowman. It follows that learning this, and teaching this, are of the highest value.

A boy was taken by his father on a camping trip in the mountains. Wanting to leave the beaten trails, they hired a guide and spent a week in the depths of the woods. The boy was greatly impressed by the guide's ability to discern all sorts of things which were invisible to the ordinary eye. One day, after the guide had been pointing out some of nature's hidden secrets, the lad asked in an awed voice, "Mister, can you see also God?" The old man smiled and replied, "My boy, it's getting so that I can hardly see anything else when I'm out in the woods!"

※ ※ ※

A young scholar who taught in a yeshiva found it difficult to support his family on his meager income. He approached the Chazon Ish and asked him whether he thought it advisable for him to learn a trade, adding that he was considering becoming a diamond polisher.

"And until now," replied the Chazon Ish, "have you not been polishing diamonds?"

Thus should teachers always be encouraged to remember the value in their work and to keep it a labor of love.

※ ※ ※

A young blacksmith decided to open his own workshop. He bought a brand-new forge, anvil, hammers, and all the other tools needed for his work. But when he tried to use the bellows to fan the flames, nothing happened — not a single spark came to life. When he inquired of his old master what could be the reason for his failure, the latter smiled and told him: "You have everything you need, young man, except for one thing: a few live coals. Without these, not even the best bellows could fan the flames."

Every teacher and student of Judaism must bring into his teaching and his learning "live coals" — those burning sparks that will, with a little effort, be fanned into a great and holy fire.

16

The Value of Work

"The sanctity of labor must be declared, for man has been placed on earth to work, to employ and to develop his person"
(RABBI SAMSON RAPHAEL HIRSCH).

Man must work for his living. Even in *Gan Eden*, he was enjoined "to till it [the garden] and to watch over it" (GENESIS 2:15). Work can be interesting, exhilarating, and a source of energy, health, and satisfaction in addition to livelihood; yet our work is not always agreeable, and we must accept the problems and frustrations that may be inevitable. We must also try to rid ourselves of the false notion that manual work is degrading. Shemayah says: "Love work" (AVOT I:10). Many of our Sages were skilled craftsmen and artisans: Rabbi Yochanan was a shoemaker; Rabbi Yehoshua was a blacksmith; Hillel was a woodcutter. It was through the merit of Jacob's working with his hands that God saved him from the evil designs of Laban (GENESIS 31:5-13).

King Solomon asks: "What profit has man of all his labor in which he labors under the sun?" (ECCLESIASTES 1:3). In no way does this mean that all endeavors for the sake of livelihood are in vain. On the contrary, this statement teaches that while it is God's will that we work, each at his own vocation, excessive labor will not necessarily yield a greater profit. Man should also realize that the blessings he receives in this world are not solely a result of his own strenuous efforts, and that God provides for all His children.

Shimon *Ha-Tzaddik*, in *Avot* I:2, tells us that the world stands on three things: on the Torah, on *avodah*, and on deeds of lovingkindness. The word *avodah* in this *mishnah* is generally understood to mean the Divine Service, prayer, or the observance of the mitzvot. However, another interpretation holds that *avodah* here means, simply, work: through plowing, sowing, and reaping, etc., man becomes, as it were, God's partner in Creation; through the merit of labor, the world is maintained.

The lack of gainful occupation can lead to boredom, fatigue, and illness. The Talmud tells us: "Idleness leads to unchastity" (KETUBBOT 59a). And Rashi adds: "even to insanity."

Rabbi Akiva describes man's task on earth: "Everything is foreseen; yet freedom of choice is given; and the world is judged with goodness; yet the judgment of all is according to the predominance of man's kindly deeds" (AVOT III:15). The emphasis is on deeds, and the concept of "work" is expanded to include the performance of mitzvot for one's own benefit and for that of the community.

Rabbi Tarfon and the elders were assembled in the garret of Nitheza's house in Lod when the question was asked, "Which is more important: learning or doing?" Said Rabbi Tarfon: "doing." Said Rabbi Akiva: "learning." All agreed: "Great is learning for it leads to doing."

In *Avot* III:17 Rabbi Elazar ben Azariah says: "One whose wisdom exceeds his deeds, to what is he compared? To a tree whose branches are many but whose roots are few, and the wind comes and uproots it and overturns it upon its top, as it is said (JEREMIAH 17:6): 'For he shall be like a lone tree in the desert, and shall not see when good comes; but shall inhabit the parched soil in the wilderness, a salt-saturated land which is uninhabitable.' But he whose deeds exceed his wisdom, to what is he compared? To a tree whose branches are few, but whose roots are many; even if all the winds of the world come and blow upon it, they cannot move it from its place."

We read in Deuteronomy 14:29: "that the Lord your God may bless you in all the work of your hand which you do." And in Psalms 128:2: "When you eat of the toil of your hands, happy shall you be, and it shall be well with you."

A spectator watched three men working at a construction site. "What are you doing?" he asked the first one. "I'm working for $40 a day," was the reply. He then asked the second man the same question. "I'm cutting stone," was his reply. When he asked the third man, the answer was, "I am building a school."

Here indeed is the exhilaration of labor. An American poet, James Russell Lowell, wrote:

> No man is born into the world, whose work
> Is not born with him; there is always work
> And tools to work withal, for those who will;
> And blessed are the horny hands of toil!

Yes, happy is the man who finds joy in his work, and fortunate is he who can direct all his energies toward a given task. Life is a complex endeavor, consisting of many separate actions which become significant in their contribution to the larger whole. One should strive to work by the light of life's greater goals, and lift every bit of work to a plane of higher significance.

A man should never say, "I will eat and drink and will enjoy myself, and Heaven will have compassion upon me." For this reason it is written, "I will bless you in all that you do." It is man's duty to *do*, for "Happy is he who fears the Lord, who walks in His ways" (PSALMS 128:1). "His ways" clearly implies gainful occupation and labor in the field of Torah and mitzvot.

A secret of Tchaikovsky's success may be found in his comment: "Work, work, work, and on top of the work comes the inspiration."

On the wall of his office, Dr. Charles Mayo kept the following motto: "There is no fun like work." Of these words, Mayo wrote: "I have always liked that motto, for I believe in it. To be without work is almost to be without life. For it is work that creates interest in life."

It is not doing the thing which we like to do, but *liking* to do the thing which we have to do, that makes life blessed.

A magnet in a chemist's laboratory was suspended against a wall, and loaded heavily with weights hung upon an armature. When asked the reason for this, the scientist explained: "The magnet was losing its power by lying around here without being used; I am restoring its force by giving it something to do — more and more every day."

17

Love

"One who is loved Above is most pleasing below" (BERACHOT 17a).

"Love His creations and honor them. And the Torah — honor it" (DERECH ERETZ ZUTA 1.1).

In Deuteronomy 6:5 we read: "And you shall love the Lord your God with all your heart and with all your soul and with all your might." How can one be *commanded* to feel love? After all, it is either present or absent, and can hardly be mandated. The answer is that there is an innate affection of the human soul for God. Being of Divine origin, the soul is naturally drawn to its source. Therefore, if one does not experience love of God, it is because he has allowed barriers to interfere. When he removes them, his natural love for God will prevail.

And yet, man asks, "How can I love God when I have never seen Him?" In Genesis 5:1 we are told: "In the day that God created man, in the likeness of God He made him." Rabbi Akiva taught: "Beloved is man, for he was created in His image" (AVOT III:14). And God manifested additional love for man in that He revealed to him that he was created in His image. It follows that in order to love God, one must love His creations.

"Rabbi Shimon ben Elazar explained the connection between the words, 'You shall love your fellowman as yourself,' and the immediate succeeding phrase, 'I am the Lord' (LEVITICUS 19:18), thus: I, the Lord, created man. If you love man I will be sure to reward you, but if you do not, I am also the Judge who exacts punishment" (AVOT D'RABBI NATAN 16:15).

Rabbi Akiva taught in *Yerushalmi Nedarim* 9:4: "'You shall love your fellowman as yourself' — this is a great principle in the Torah." Hillel interpreted it: "That which is hateful to you, do not do unto your neighbor" (SHABBAT 31a). In *Sefer Ha-Mevakesh*, we read, "What you love for yourself, love also for your fellowman." Love is the desire, the will, and the ability to understand and give to another. When we love someone we trust him, regard him kindly, overlook his shortcomings and in general judge him favorably. We think of him as a person of dignity and merit. We seek the well-being of all those whom we love — husband or wife, children, parents, friends — ourselves as well.

A poet described love with these words:

> True love is the gift which God has given
> To man alone, beneath the Heaven.
> It is the secret sympathy,
> The silken link, the silken tie
> Which heart to heart, and mind to mind
> In body and soul can bind.

Perhaps one of the greatest contributions of Chasidism to Jewish life was its emphasis of the doctrine that love of God must always be accompanied by love for His creatures. The following story is told of Reb Moshe Leib of Sassov:

> Reb Moshe Leib loved his fellow Jews so much that he searched daily for lost souls. In one of his excursions he found himself in a tavern and overheard the following exchange between two Russian peasants:
>
> Declared the first: "I love you, my friend!"
> "No, you don't," rebutted his comrade.
> "But I do!" protested the first. "Why, I love you more than anything or anyone!"
> His comrade remained adamant. "Then do you know what gives me pain?"
> The first responded: "How can I know what gives you pain!"

"Ah," sighed the other. "If you really loved me, then you would know what pains me and what I suffer."

The Rebbe of Sassov left the tavern, shaken by the insight into the meaning of love provided by these two coarse peasants.

A teacher asked a student: "How do we know that love of man precedes love of God?" The student could not find an answer, whereupon the teacher explained: "In the prayer book the opening instruction is: 'Before you pray, say the words: Love your fellowman as yourself'" (MIDRASH: TORAT KOHANIM ON LEVITICUS). Thus the teacher pointed out that to love God one must love His works. Rabbi Levi Yitzchak of Berdichev wrote: "Whether a man really loves God can be determined by the love he bears for his fellowmen." If one claims to love God, but has no love for His creatures, he speaks falsely. Cultivating love of one's fellowman calls for the constant awareness that all of us are the children of one Creator. The more one loves his fellowman, the more closely he approaches God.

Martin Buber interpreted the commandment to love one's neighbor as oneself to mean: "Look upon your neighbor as a person like yourself. Do not regard him as a thing ... He is not to be manipulated and used for one's own selfish ends. As you are a person, so, too, he is a person."

Man cannot be selective in his love of mankind. An example of such selectivity is given in the remarks of Rabbi Yehoshua, student of *Rabban* Yochanan ben Zakkai. He taught that hatred of mankind may remove a man from the world (AVOT II:11). What is the meaning of this unusual teaching? Rabbi Yehoshua explains: "No man should think of saying, 'I love the scholars but hate the disciples,' or 'I love the disciples but hate the ignoramus.' On the contrary, love all these, for God has created all. Hatred of mankind puts a man out of the world" (AVOT D'RABBI NATAN 16:1). Being "put out of the world" does not necessarily mean that one's life is shortened. Rather, it implies that one's worthiness on earth is diminished when he fails to exercise his innate natural tendency to love others. Hillel advised: "Be of the disciples of Aaron, loving peace and pursuing peace, loving your fellowmen and bringing them nearer to the Torah" (AVOT I:12).

In Proverbs 10:12 Solomon explains: "Hatred stirs up strife, but love draws a cover over all transgressions."

Shimon *Ha-Tzaddik* taught: "On three things the world stands: on the Torah, on the Service of the Almighty, and on acts of lovingkindness" (AVOT I:2). In Psalms 89:3 we learn: "The world is built on lovingkindness." Love is the basic element in all enduring relationships — essential for every marriage bond, necessary in all friendship.

Pirkei Avot cautions: "All love which depends on some sensual object will soon pass away when the object passes away; but if it does not depend on a sensual object, it will never pass away. Which love was dependent upon a sensual object? The love of Amnon and Tamar. And which did not depend on any such object? The love of David and Jonathan" (AVOT V:16). In this way, the *mishnah* differentiates between two kinds of love: that which is prompted by external factors, and that which flows from spiritual affinity, independent of external causes.

When love depends upon material advantages or physical gratification, it will cease when its source ceases, for there will be nothing to sustain it. Love which is not generated by external factors, but which flows from an inner mutual appreciation, will never cease.

The love of Amnon for Tamar was motivated by lust, but when that lust was gone, "Then Amnon hated her with an exceedingly great hatred" (SAMUEL II 13:15). But in the love of David and Jonathan, which was spiritual in character, like the love of a father for his son, "The soul of Jonathan was bound unto the soul of David, and Jonathan loved him as his own soul" (SAMUEL II 18:15). And when David heard of the death of Jonathan, he cried out: "Our love was greater than the love of women" (SAMUEL II 2:26).

God's love for us is even greater than the love of a father for his son. Meir ben Isaac Nehoral (author of the prayer *Akdamut*, recited on Shavuot) described God's love in these words:

> Could we with ink the ocean fill,
> Were every blade of grass a quill,
> Were the world of parchment made,
> And every man a scribe by trade,
> To write the love of God above
> Would drain the ocean dry;
> Nor would the scroll
> Contain the whole
> Though stretched from sky to sky.

He who loves brings God and the world together. On the commandment to love God "with all your heart, with all your soul, and with all your might," we read in *Berachot* 54a: "Love Hashem *with all your heart* — with both your good and evil inclinations; *with all your soul* — even when He takes your soul; and *with all your might* — with all your possessions."

"And Jacob served seven years for Rachel; and they seemed unto him but a few days, for the love he had for her" (GENESIS 29:20). Where there is love, time does not count, and seven years of labor is as naught. If husband and wife truly love one another, no hardship will be too difficult to bear, no weather will be too stormy, no sacrifice will be too great. "One who loves his wife as himself and honors her more than himself, concerning him does Scripture say (JOB 5:24), 'And you shall know that there is peace in your tent'" (YEVAMOT 62b).

❧ ❧ ❧

God sent an angel down from Heaven to locate the most beautiful thing on earth, and to bring it back to Heaven. When the angel came across budding flowers that appeared with the first breath of spring, he said, "These certainly must be the most beautiful things on earth." Immediately, he gathered a beautiful bouquet and proceeded on his way.

On the way he met a little girl of pure, unspoiled beauty. She had silky, golden hair and a warm, friendly smile. When he saw the child he felt he had erred in selecting the flowers. "Surely," he said to himself, "this must be the most beautiful thing on earth. There can be nothing more beautiful than the smile of a young and innocent child."

Further along, as he passed through a small village, he came across a humble cottage where a mother sat in the doorway with her baby on her lap. He watched as she soothed and comforted her infant, and said to himself, "This must indeed be the most beautiful thing on earth. I will also take that mother's love back with me to Heaven."

When the angel reached the gates of Heaven, the flowers in his hand had wilted and faded; the smile on the little girl's face had changed to anger; but the mother's love was as full and untarnished as before.

It has been said that a mother's love is God's vehicle for leading His children toward goodness and righteousness. The love of parents and children for each other, of man and wife, and of one friend for another are all but a reflection of the Divine love of God for man.

18

Envy — a Killer

"Who sows envy reaps regret"
(IMMANUEL, MACHBAROT, chapter 9 [ca. 1300]).

Much has been written about envy, and about its destructive powers. *Bava Kama* 92b aptly illustrates it: "The envious one has sixty toothaches when another smacks his lips."

The viper and the cobra have deadly poison in them, but it only hurts others, and not themselves; envy is so deadly that it not only kills others, but those who harbor it as well. The envious man frets when he sees that others do well. He cannot eat or sleep unless the person he envies encounters some misfortune. Job states, "Wrath kills the foolish man, and envy slays the witless one" (5:2). In Exodus 20:14 the Ten Commandments conclude: "You shall not covet your neighbor's house, you shall not covet your neighbor's wife, nor his manservant, nor his maidservant, nor his ox, nor his ass, nor anything that is your neighbor's."

A sculptor once created a statue that symbolized envy. He formed it so that it reminded all who saw it of the blighting and distorting power of envy when it is permitted to enter the human heart. The sculptor's figure of envy had crooked legs, representing its twisting, devious ways; the arms of the statue were abnormally long, and the hands huge and coarse, for envy is ever reaching out to clutch at the good fortune of others. The sculpting of the head was symbolic as well — the ears were long and donkey-like; they drooped down, for envy is always listening to the voices of those below, in hate and suspicion, and never to the voices of Heaven; the eyes bulged hideously and were glazed and short-sighted. Its protruding tongue was forked, for all envy's speech is deceitful and cruel.

Envy is like poison, never failing to have its way, to wrap its victim in the mantle of death. Rabbi Eliezer Ha-Kappar says: "Envy, lust, and thirst for honor take a man out of the world" (AVOT IV:21).

At the very inception of human history, we find the power of envy driving Cain to murder his brother Abel. We find it in the revengeful spirit of Saul, who plotted for years to murder David. We find it in the hearts of Joseph's brothers, who, trapped in the clutches of envy, sold him into slavery. Isaac became embroiled with the Philistines because of their envy for his possessions.

Korach envied Moses' authority and incited the Israelites to rebel against their Divinely appointed leader. Consider Datan and Aviram and all of Korach's band, who, figuratively speaking, dug their graves with their own hands. The story of Korach is the story of the triumph of envy, and how it ruined a brilliant man and his followers. Korach himself was of the tribe of Levi, socially prominent and a profound scholar. He aspired to leadership, but was extremely envious of Moses and his influence. And so Korach went about the camp, stirring up the people against Moses. Moses pleaded with Korach not to rebel, but to no avail.

Evidently, envy of the great is something that has been with mankind since antiquity. King David's assertion that envy assails the noblest — that the wind howls around the highest peaks — seems to have been as applicable then as now.

As a moth gnaws a garment and ultimately destroys it, so can envy consume a man. A good lesson can be learned from this poetic rendition of *Sotah* 9a:

> Who'er his greedy eyes doth set
> On what to him belongeth not,
> What he desires he shall not get,
> And he shall lose what he hath got.

Solomon Ibn Gabirol observed: "Who seeks more than he has, hinders himself from enjoying what he has." Hillel cautioned: "The more property, the more concern...but the more Torah study, the more life" (AVOT II:7). In *Pesikta Rabbati* 21 we are told: "To covet is to violate all the Ten Commandments."

One might say that there is truly enough in this world for everybody's need — but not for everybody's greed.

The wealthy are indeed the objects of envy, but what do our Rabbis say about the nature of wealth? Ben Zoma stated: "Who is rich? He who rejoices in his portion" (AVOT IV:1). He who desires more than he has is never rich, for his greed is never satiated. The man who rejoices in his lot is called rich, for he desires nothing beyond what he has; the wealthy man who is *truly* wealthy delights in the opportunities for service that his wealth provides. Ben Sira advises: "With little or with much, be content."

There is no greater poverty than envy; the surest way to avoid it is to realize that everything belongs to God and is given to all in trust by Him, and that there is always justice in His distribution, even though we human beings may not always be aware of it.

The Radzviller Rebbe commented: "The commandment *You shall not covet* is placed at the end of the Decalogue because he who has observed this commandment is certain to have observed all those which precede it."

The mental anguish suffered by the envious is so great that Moses preferred death to envy. "Better a hundred deaths," he said, "than one occasion for envy."

And yet, envy can have its good uses in some areas of endeavor. Scholarship and Torah study are encouraged through the spirit of competition. "The envy of scholars increases wisdom," says the Talmud (BAVA BATRA 21a).

Rabbi Nachman states: "Is envy [the evil inclination] a very good thing? However, if there were no envy, a man would not build a house, would not marry, would not give birth, and would not engage in commerce" (MIDRASH RABBAH BERESHIT 9:7).

And so has remarked King Solomon: "I considered all travail and every right work, that for this, a man is envied of his neighbor" (ECCLESIASTES 4:4).

However, these references imply a strict measure of control over an emotion that can prove very damaging to an individual consumed with envy and to a society which can deteriorate to violence and anarchy.

We should be guided by the wisdom of the sage who commented: "God grant me the serenity to accept what I cannot change, courage to change what I can, and wisdom to know the difference."

A little watch, dissatisfied with being kept in a pocket all the time, envied Big Ben, the great tower clock. "I wish I could be up there like him," it sighed. "There, I could serve the multitude."

And suddenly, the little watch's wish came true. It was drawn up to the tower, but alas: from below, it was invisible. Its elevation had become its annihilation.

There was once a woman who was so riddled with envy that she even envied her own children. This poison took hold of her completely; it became the master of her every waking hour, and brought unrest to her dreams.

One day, at a friend's home, she was introduced to a young woman with large, beautiful eyes. The envy that was always with her overpowered her once again. "How I detest wearing eyeglasses," she confided to her new acquaintance. "I wish I had eyes like yours."

"How I wish I could wear eyeglasses," replied the young woman quietly. "You see, my eyes are completely sightless."

A canary and a goldfish were neighbors, for the master of the house had placed his birdcage and his goldfish bowl together on the windowsill. One hot day, he overheard the goldfish complaining. "Oh," cried the fish, "how I wish I were up there in the fresh air and sunshine like my friend. Then I too would be able to sing sweetly."

Meanwhile, the canary was eyeing the fishbowl. "How cool it looks!" he cried. "How I wish I were there, swimming about in that refreshing pool."

"Well," said the master, "let it be as you wish." He placed the fish in the birdcage, and the canary in the fishbowl, whereupon each saw the folly of his envy.

❧ ❧ ❧

A man was strolling in the park on a beautiful, warm summer day. As he was walking, he met a friend who remarked, "It's a glorious day, isn't it?"

"It certainly is," came the sullen reply.

"Then why do you look so glum?" asked the friend.

"Because my enemies are enjoying it as well!"

19

Lust

"Ben Zoma says... Who is strong?
He who subdues his passions" (AVOT IV:1).

In Unit 18 we quoted Rabbi Eliezer Ha-Kappar: "Envy, lust, and thirst for honor take a man out of the world" (AVOT IV:21). That unit was devoted to the first killer, envy. In this unit we will discuss lust and its devastating effect on people.

Lust is not conducive to long life, and our sources contain many warnings against succumbing to it. In *Niddah* 13b we read, "He who indulges in lustful thoughts will not be admitted into the compartment of the Holy One." "Wine causes lust" (MIDRASH RABBAH BEMIDBAR 10:6). Fighting lust is the grand battle of life. It is an enemy to every person, and its conquest is one of the highest endeavors of a person's existence. Man has been warned again and again that God's grace never descends upon one who is a slave to lust.

Impure thoughts awaken impure feelings, and these lead in turn to impure expression. What consumes men today? Envy, lust, and the quest for fame and wealth. This constant craving weakens the will and keeps man distant from Torah.

A formula for avoiding these pitfalls is found in the counseling of Proverbs 30:7-9:

> Two things have I asked of You;
> Deny me them not before I die:
> Remove far from me falsehood and lies:
> Give me neither poverty nor riches;
> Feed me with my allotted bread:
> Lest I become sated, and deny You, and say,

> "Who is the Lord?"
> Or lest I be poor, and steal,
> And profane the Name of my God.

The prophet Jeremiah (9:22) offers us his wisdom for a life free of lust and envy:

> Thus saith the Lord:
> Let not the wise man glory in his wisdom,
> Neither let the mighty man glory in his might,
> Let not the rich man glory in his riches.

The wisdom of living consists of making the most of what one is given, and not lusting for what one has not. Life is what one makes it; so it has always been and so it always will be. It can be bitter or sweet, good or bad, valuable or valueless. If one can remove envy and lust from his heart, he has eliminated two killers that destroy lives.

The person who lusts for what he does not have destroys his own peace of mind and disposition. Many of our sources point out that a cheerful disposition is an estimable treasure. It preserves health, promotes convalescence, and helps us cope with adversity. In *Chochmah U'Musar* (volume 2, pp. 331-32) we read that the truly happy person does not allow his happiness to be dependent on external factors, for over these he has no control. A person who allows his happiness to depend upon fame, success, wealth, or the satisfaction of his lust will find it almost impossible to acquire true happiness. It is wise to remember that the sources of happiness are not outside ourselves, but rather within us, as ben Zoma counsels: "Who is strong? He who subdues his passions... Who is rich? He who rejoices in his portion" (AVOT IV:1).

The Slonimer Rebbe listed ten rules for happiness. We include three that are appropriate to this unit:

> Happy is he who constantly examines his actions and regrets every unworthy act.
> Happy is he who withstands temptations.
> Happy is he who reminds himself at all times to fear the Lord and His retribution.

What the Rebbe was teaching with these rules is that the essence of happiness is the attainment of holiness and the knowledge of God. The better the man, the more he will attain. Every temptation that is resisted, every impulse that is not heeded, every sinful act that is repressed, every bitter word that is withheld, adds to a person's character and personality. All of us should learn the art of self-control, which is beneficial to the individual and especially pleasing to God. In Psalms 1:1 we read: "Blessed is the man who has not walked in the counsels of the wicked." Rabbi Yehoshua ben Levi (AVODAH ZARAH 19a) states: "Blessed is the man — one who acts like a man and conquers his evil impulse." The truly great person disciplines himself so that his better nature is always in command.

Rabbi Assi stated in *Sukkah* 52a: "The evil impulse is, at the beginning, like the thread of a spider, but at the end it is like cart rope, as it is stated: 'Woe to those who draw iniquity with cords of vanity and sin as it were with a cart rope' (ISAIAH 5:18)."

The highest form of rulership is to rule over oneself, and not to be a slave to impulse. It naturally follows that if one overcomes his impulses and controls his conduct and actions, his life will be more productive. The principle that it is a good thing to sow wild oats in one's youth is fallacious, for it is the control of lust, not the submission to it, which can prevent ruin.

It is wise to recall that:

> God appears:
> In the best thought,
> In the truest speech,
> In the sincerest action.
> And His bounty
> Is manifested
> In the bounty
> Of great hearts.

One should *be aware* of temptation and *beware* of it as well. The best victory a man can achieve is to take control of his thoughts and actions. When a man's fight begins within himself, then the battle is worth waging. When he wishes to live up to God's wishes, he can fight temptation. Or, as the Yiddish proverb states: "Be master of your will and slave to your conscience."

❧ ❧ ❧

Many years ago, the Russian government offered to its peasants a gift. All the land a man could traverse in a single day, from sunrise to sunset, would become his. Lured by the offer, a peasant determined to set out at the crack of dawn. Hour after hour he jogged on, increasingly exhausted by the exertion. After several hours, he looked up and saw the sun was high overhead — a sign that the day was half over and he should turn back. But the thought that all this land and more could belong to him compelled him to keep on. Another hour passed; now surely he would have to turn back if he were to reach the starting point before sunset. His heart pounded fiercely as he turned about in his tracks; his breath grew shorter and shorter; a great weariness permeated every fiber of his body. But he drew another heavy breath and forced himself to run faster and faster. He could now see a small group of men standing at the starting point awaiting his return. Gasping, with his last ounce of strength he reached the group, collapsed on the ground, and died. The people buried him, and on his tombstone they inscribed the words: *All the Land a Man Needs.*

20

The Futility of Anger

"Anger and temper are Death's executioners"
(MIDRASH TEHILLIM 6:7).

"Anyone can become angry — that is easy," noted Aristotle. "But to be angry with the right person, and to the right degree, and at the right time, and for the right purpose, and in the right way — that is not within everyone's power and is not easy. But it is advisable."

In *Avot* V:11 we learn: "There are four kinds of dispositions: He who is easily provoked and easily pacified — his gain is canceled by his loss. He who is difficult to provoke and difficult to pacify — his loss is canceled by his gain. He who is difficult to provoke and easily pacified — is a pious man. He who is easily provoked and difficult to pacify — is a wicked man."

Proverbs 25:28 states: "He who has no control over his own spirit is like a city that is broken down, and without walls." Allowing one's emotions to rule him can be compared to driving a car without a steering wheel. It leads to catastrophe. In Ecclesiastes 7:9 we read: "Be not hasty in spirit to be angry; for anger rests in the bosom of fools." In *Sotah* 3b we learn from Rabbi Chisda: "Anger in a house is like a worm in a sesame plant."

Anger is blindness. In Proverbs 16:32 we are counseled: "He who rules his spirit is better than he who conquers a city." From Rav we learn: "Anyone who becomes angry, if he is wise, his wisdom departs from him" (PESACHIM 66b). "He who grows angry gives no consideration even to God Himself. He forgets his learning and increases folly" (NEDARIM 22b).

Anger and hatred are the outward manifestations of social and intellectual immaturity. When anger rises, it is wise to think of the consequences, for, if not restrained, anger can frequently be more harmful than that which provoked it. A wise proverb counsels: "If you are patient in one moment of anger, you will escape a hundred days of sorrow."

It has been said: "All men of anger are fools. Most angry people ultimately allow themselves to be pacified"; "Grow not angry and you shall not sin; grow not drunk and you shall not offend"; "All men of anger are men of pride"; "The angry man's speech is like scalding water which overflows from a boiling kettle."

Rabbi Shimon ben Elazar said: "He who rends his garments, breaks a vessel, or scatters his money in a moment of anger shall be dominated by the evil inclination to the point of worshiping idols."

Again and again, we are reminded: "He who hates a man is as if he hated God."

The students of Rabbi Nechunia once asked him, "What is the secret of your longevity?" "I have never accepted gifts," he replied, "and I have always forgotten the wrongs done to me" (MEGILLAH 28a).

"You shall not hate your brother in your heart" (LEVITICUS 19:17). Our Rabbis taught that since this precept might be explained to mean only that you must not injure him, or insult him, or vex him, the words "in your heart" are added — thereby forbidding us even to feel hatred in our heart.

In Tractate *Shabbat* 31a, we read the story of a man who made a wager with a friend that he would be able to provoke the ever-patient Hillel to lose his temper. If he succeeded, he was to receive 400 *zuzim*; but if he failed, he was to give his friend this sum.

> The Sabbath eve was approaching, and Hillel was engaged in his ablutions, when a man, passing his door, stopped and called out: "Who here is Hillel?"

Wrapping a towel about his wet hair, Hillel came out to ask the man what he wanted.

"I want to ask you a question," the man replied.

"Ask, my son," said Hillel.

"I want to know why the Babylonians have such round heads," the man stated.

"My son, you have asked a great question," said Hillel. "The reason is that their midwives were not apt."

An hour later he returned, shouting, "Who here is Hillel, who here is Hillel?"

Hillel appeared and listened to his next question.

"Why are the eyes of the Pacmyreans bleared?"

"My son, you have asked a great question," replied Hillel. "It is because they live in sandy places."

The man departed, tarried a while, returned and called out, "Who here is Hillel, who here is Hillel?"

Hillel appeared and listened carefully to his next question: "Why are the feet of the Africans wide?"

"My son, you have asked a great question," said Hillel. "It is because they live in watery marshes."

"Oh, I have many more questions, but you will lose patience with me and become angry," taunted the questioner.

"Ask whatever you wish," smiled Hillel.

The man then cried out in vexation, "May there not be many like you in Israel! Because of you I have lost 400 *zuzim*!"

"Better it is that you should lose 400 *zuzim* and another 400 after that," Hillel replied, "than that Hillel should lose his temper."

Proverbs 1:8 cautions: "Hear, my son, the instruction of your father, and forsake not the teaching of your mother." Accustom yourself to speak in gentleness to all men, at all times. Thus will you be saved from anger, the fertile cause of sin. We learn in the Talmud from Rabbi Yonatan: "Over the man of wrath rules every manner of Gehinnom, as it is written: (ECCLESIASTES 11:10) 'Remove anger from your heart, and put away eveil from your flesh'" (NEDARIM 22a).

"Being delivered from anger, there will arise in your heart the quality of humility, better than all things good. For the reward of humility is fear of the Lord" (IGGERET HA-RAMBAM).

Proverbs 22:24-25 counsels: "Make no friendship with an angry man; and with a furious man you shall not go; lest you learn his ways, and get a snare to your soul."

In his efforts to keep anger from mastering him, one must guard himself against hasty temper in his treatment of his children and other members of his household. An angry man cannot be a teacher. "The angry man fills his mouth with live coals and with needles, sharp and hard," a wise man declared.

Numerous passages from our sacred Scriptures and the Talmud could be cited to show how failure to control one's anger leads to ignorance, sickness, discontent and sinfulness. The best of all possible traits for the person who seeks peace in this world and in the World-to-Come is control of his temper. Let him be wise and never become angry, never insist on revenge and always forgive the person who wrongs him.

Elijah advised Rabbi Natan: "Eat one third [of one's fill], drink one third, and leave one third, should you anger [lest you suffer ill health]" (GITTIN 70a).

"Break your anger by showing mercy to the one with whom you are angry," advised Rabbi Nachman of Bratslav, and continued as follows:

"Anger and cruelty arise from lack of understanding. Study the Torah to improve understanding.
He who is overcome by anger loses his image of God.
Anger prevents God's abundance from descending to one.
He who subdues his anger achieves a good name.
Anger causes a man to be far from truth.
An angry man cannot pray properly.
An angry man cannot attain the goal to which he aspires.
Anger leads to contempt and to sin.
Anger after meals is dangerous to life.
Anger is injurious to health and to eyesight.
Anger is caused by falsehood and jealousy.

Anger shortens the days of one's life.
Anger is followed by melancholy.
The sins of the angry man will surely outweigh his merits."

One must learn to dismiss a quarrel the moment it is over. One should not encourage bitterness, resentment, and the desire for retribution in his heart.

Proverbs 19:11 advises: "The discretion of a man makes him slow to anger; and it is his glory to pass over a transgression."

When one must show anger to someone for that person's benefit, one should exercise care, and know exactly how much anger is necessary to achieve the purpose. The Rambam (DE'OT 2.3) advises that a person should always remain internally tranquil and show external anger only where it can have productive use.

There was a wise Rabbi who made it a rule never to express his displeasure with anyone on the same day that he was offended. The next day he would say, "I was displeased with you yesterday."

Rabbi Shimon ben Elazar said, "Do not attempt to pacify your fellowman in the time of his anger" (AVOT IV:18). Should one attempt it, the effort would be in vain. It is extremely difficult for a man, in the heat of anger, to accept an apology or to offer one. The Talmud relates that God told Moses to wait until His anger passed away before pleading on behalf of the nation (BERACHOT 7a).

It is good to remember that anger can be compared to an acid, which can do as much or more harm to the vessel in which it is stored than to anything on which it is poured.

The Rozdoler Rebbe said: "When I feel angry at a person, I delay the expression of my anger. I ask myself: 'What will I lose if I postpone my anger?'"

The Dubner Maggid told this story of a man who had suffered a heart attack and called in a cardiologist. The doctor examined him but forebore to prescribe medication, offering instead the following advice: "Avoid anger; live in a friendly and harmonious way with everyone; do not be overambitious; and avoid worrying about business affairs."

Two of the patient's friends came to visit him, and heard of the specialist's "prescription." One remarked in astonishment, "Is good moral counsel not the domain of a preacher?"

The second friend replied, "It is the domain of both a doctor and a preacher. Through the very same counsel, the physician cares for the bodily welfare of his patient — leading a quiet, sound life will save him from mortal illness — and the preacher cares for the spiritual welfare of his congregants — for if he counsels a quiet, sound way of life, this is for the salvation of the soul."

Though their concerns are different, their counsel is the same, and from this we learn that medicine for one's soul is often also medicine for one's body.

21

Revenge — a Double-Edged Sword

> "You shall not avenge nor bear any grudge against the children of your people, but you shall love your fellowman as yourself: I am the Lord" (LEVITICUS 19:18).

He who believes the old saying, "Revenge is sweet," should look into the faces of those who have lived on it for years. Revenge does people more harm than the initial injury which caused the revenge. One might say that the time and energy invested in "getting even" would be better spent in "getting ahead"! Revenge is like a boomerang; although for a time it flies in the direction in which it is hurled, it can take a sudden curve and return, delivering to its sender the heaviest blow of all. The best manner of avenging oneself is by making the effort *not* to resemble the person who has caused the hurt.

In *Avot* IV:19, Shmuel Ha-Katan quotes: "Rejoice not when your enemy falls, and let not your heart exult when he stumbles; lest the Lord see it, and be displeased, and He turn away His wrath from him" (PROVERBS 24:17-18).

It is interesting to note that it is men who take revenge; God punishes.

In the Jerusalem Talmud (NEDARIM 9:4) we read, "He who takes vengeance or bears a grudge acts like one who, having cut one hand while handling a knife, avenges himself by cutting the other hand." Similarly, the Chafetz Chayim stresses that all Jews are part of the same spiritual entity (one large *neshamah*). It is therefore pointless to seek revenge against oneself (SHMIRAT HA-LASHON, SHA'AR HA-TEVUNAH). To illustrate this point, he described a group of Jews on a sea voyage. One of them began to drill a hole in the floor of his cabin. When the others tried to stop him, he cried out, "It's my cabin — I paid my fare," not realizing that his action would involve all of his companions. In other words, we are all "in the same boat"!

The commandment "You shall not avenge" (LEVITICUS 19:18) forbids repaying evil with evil. In fact, the Talmud counsels: "If a man finds both a friend and an enemy in distress, he would first assist his enemy in order to subdue his evil inclination."

Our Torah praises the virtue of forgiveness both by precept and example, as evidenced in Joseph's conduct to his brethren, as well as David's to Saul. It is significant to note that when the Egyptians were drowning in the Red Sea, and the angels wanted to sing songs of exultation, the Holy One, blessed be He, disapproved, declaring, "The creations of My hands are drowning in the sea, and you are engaged in song?" (MEGILLAH 10b).

A Talmudic legend tells how a Rabbi once met Elijah in the crowded marketplace. "Master," he asked, "can you tell me who, among this throng, are assured of eternal life?" The prophet, in reply, pointed out two men of undistinguished appearance.

The Rabbi rushed over to them. "Tell me," he asked, "what are your special merits?"

"We have none," they answered, "unless it be that when people are in trouble we comfort them, and when they quarrel we make them friends again" (TA'ANIT 22a).

In *Avot d'Rabbi Natan* 41:11, Rabbi Yehudah ben Teima states: "If you have done even a tiny injustice to your friend, let it be in your eyes like a major thing. If you have done to your friend a great deed, let it be in your eyes as a mere nothing. If your friend has done for you a very small favor, let it be in your eyes as if he had done a great thing. And if your friend has done you a grave injustice, let it be in your eyes as a small thing."

If a person cannot forgive others, how can he ask forgiveness of God? It is difficult for a person to overcome the desire for revenge, for people are sensitive to humiliation and suffer greatly from it. To one who is wronged, taking revenge appears to be even sweeter than honey. Nevertheless, we must resolve to avoid this pitfall. The words of the Baal Shem Tov can help us understand this: "One knows that he has many faults; nevertheless, one still loves oneself. That is how one should feel toward the person who has caused him hurt. Despite what he had done, try to love him nevertheless" (LIKKUTEI AVRAHAM, 221).

"Who is a true hero? He who converts an enemy into a friend" (AVOT D'RABBI NATAN 23:1). Vengeance can wreak disaster, but joy can result when the desire for revenge is curbed and replaced by understanding and friendship. There is excellent advice found in *Sanhedrin* 7a: When someone insults you, we are told, remain silent. In this way you will save yourself the trouble involved in a quarrel. No doubt this is difficult, yet in the long run there is much more to be gained by refraining from responding to insults.

What is the difference between vengeance and bearing a grudge? Vengeance is when a person says to his neighbor, "Lend me your sickle," and he refuses, and the next day the neighbor asks him, "Lend me your axe," and he replies, "I will not lend you anything, just as you refused to lend me." A grudge is when a person says to his neighbor, "Lend me your axe," and he refuses, and the next day the neighbor comes and says, "Lend me your garment," and the person replies, "Here it is: I'm not like you, who declined to lend me what I wanted." He who forgoes retaliation, his sins are remitted; when his pardon is asked, he grants it (YOMA 23a).

The Koretzer Rebbe said: "When a man injures or abuses you, it does not lie within your rights to seek revenge. It is as if a man stood in the presence of a king, and another smote him on the cheek. The only course open to him is to keep silent. The king witnessed the blow, and if he believes the man deserved it at the hands of his neighbor, the injured person cannot go against the king's wish. If, however, the king believes that the blow was undeserved, then he will surely punish the offender. In the same way, one should remember that he is always in the presence of the King of kings; He will inflict punishment upon one's adversary if one is undeservedly abused by him."

One can find inspiration in the meaningful message of Jeremiah 9:23:

> But let him that glories, glory in this,
> that he understands and knows Me, that
> I am the Lord Who exercises lovingkindness,
> judgment, and righteousness, in the earth:
> for in these things I delight, says the Lord.

The *Sefer Ha-Chinnuch* observes (mitzvah 241) that we must recognize the Hand of the Almighty in all that happens to us, and must strive to correct our ways, if some measure of evil befalls us.

※ ※ ※

A child was attacked and killed by a neighbor's dog. The bereaved father knew that vengeance was forbidden, so he found a better way to relieve the agony of his heart. When a famine had plagued the people and the neighbor's fields lay bare because he had no corn to plant for the next year's harvest, the troubled father went out one night and sowed the neighbor's field, explaining: "I went out and sowed seed in my enemy's field, so that God should see that I did not plot revenge."

※ ※ ※

A young farmer was insulted by his neighbor. In order to take revenge he traveled to a neighboring village and obtained a hardy, wild grass that, once planted, is almost impossible to destroy. One night he sowed his neighbor's field with this dreaded weed, and within a short time the grass came up and did great damage to the farm. Its thick, fast-growing roots spread and destroyed many of the crops.

A few years later this young man fell in love with his neighbor's daughter and married her. When her father died, his daughter inherited the farm. For thirty years now, this man who succumbed to revenge has been fighting that grass, quite literally reaping what he had sown.

22

Hope and Perseverance

"Surely the measure of Divine goodness is greater
than that of evil dispensation" (SANHEDRIN 100b).

Ben Azzai declares: "Do not despise any man, and do not deem anything unworthy of consideration; for there is no man who does not have his hour and no thing that does not have its place" (AVOT IV:3).

Here ben Azzai is cautioning us not to disregard any man or his ideas. One should not dismiss a man as unworthy because he has not made his mark in the world; he may possess remarkable qualities which he has not yet had the opportunity to exercise. Nor should one condemn an idea because it does not appeal at the moment, or does not fit into one's present framework or environment. In other words, ben Azzai is telling us that there is a purpose to everything, even though it may not be obvious. Respect the potential in every man and every matter, large or small, and do not form hasty judgments and opinions.

Optimism has always been the lifeblood of Judaism. Hope and perseverance in the face of sorrow can banish despair. "Even when a sharp sword is at his neck, man should not despair of being rescued" (BERACHOT 10a). Shadow and light accompany us in this world; when it seems that there is more shadow than light, one should consider: Every object casts a shadow, and it is that very shadow that sets the light into relief. How could we appreciate the warmth of the sun if it were summer all year round? Similarly, we could not appreciate life's joys were it not for frustration and sorrow. In the words of the prophet: "Though I am fallen, I shall rise again. Though I dwell in darkness, God is my light" (MICAH 7:8).

"The world is judged with goodness" (AVOT III:15). Ultimately the good must prevail. How true is this bit of wisdom: "In the day of prosperity be joyful, but in the day of adversity, consider: ...God made one as well as the other" (ECCLESIASTES 7:14). "The Lord will give strength unto His people" (PSALMS 29:11). A person should never abandon hope and lose faith in God's help. King Solomon wisely observed: "Hope deferred makes the heart sick" (PROVERBS 13:12). And we read: "Hope in the Lord, be of good courage and He shall strengthen your heart, and hope in the Lord" (PSALMS 27:14); one "hope" follows the other, much strengthened.

The classic prayer of renewed hope is in Psalms 23:4:

> Yea, though I walk through the valley of
> the shadow of death,
> I will fear no evil: for You are with me;
> Your rod and Your staff they comfort me.

Faith in God gives one the strength to accept and face disappointment, failure, and even crisis. The person facing a crisis might think of this passage: "It is good for me that I have been afflicted, that I might learn Your statutes" (PSALMS 119:71). Two Chasidic sayings are very appropriate: "The man who cannot survive bad times will not see good times"; "If you carry your own lantern, you will endure the dark." Perseverance, hope, and faith in God are the Jew's lantern.

We have often been told that opportunity knocks at least once in everyone's lifetime. Happy is the person who, waiting and watching, hears the knock and opens the door. For every person has his share in life, "his hour," as *Pirkei Avot* tells us. Expecting one's "hour," one should recognize it when it comes.

Those who reject an idea because it is unappealing, because it upsets preconceived notions, or because it appears to be impractical, are addressed by our *mishnah*. There is not a cause, it says, if it is a true one, which will not finally find its place. And if one is convinced of the truth of his cause, he should work for it, energetically. "It is not up to you to complete the work; yet you are not free to evade it" (AVOT II:16). It is those who carry on with steadfast perseverance whom ben Azzai encourages: "For there is no man who does not have his hour and no thing that does not have its place."

"Each day is an opportunity to start all over again," counseled a Rabbi, "to cleanse our minds and hearts anew, and to clarify our vision. Let every dawn of a new morning be to you as the beginning of life, and every setting sun be to you as its close."

A few years ago a man died — an exceptional person who had set a record in his lifetime for formal education. When he was very young, he had received a bequest which offered him an allowance of two thousand dollars a year for as many years as he might wish to remain in school. He accepted the opportunity that had been given him, and, until he died at the age of seventy-eight, he was still attending classes. During this time he earned eleven degrees in a variety of subjects.

A saintly man said: "If there is any good that I can do or any kindness that I can show, tell me now and let me do it quickly, for I shall not pass this way again, and so must take advantage of the moment."

When Napoleon was making plans to invade England he was told that an American visitor was waiting to see him. "I can give him only two minutes," Napoleon replied. Unfortunately, the allotted two minutes were not long enough for Robert Fulton to convey the significance of the steam-propelled ship he had invented. Had Napoleon but taken the opportunity to listen, his own "hour," as well as the history of the world, might have been different.

23

Retribution

"He who digs a pit will fall into it, and he who rolls
a stone, it will come back upon him"
(PROVERBS 26:27).

"He [Hillel] also saw a skull floating on the surface of the water. He said to it: Because you have drowned others, you were drowned, and in the end those who have drowned you will themselves be drowned" (AVOT II:6).

In a few brief words, Hillel has painted a vivid picture, which teaches a principle that humanity has failed to absorb. The evil that a man does returns, comes back to him, sooner or later. No sin goes unpunished. The wheels of justice grind slowly but, in the long run, evenly. There is a Divine justice which in the end metes out the proper retribution to the evildoers. In Proverbs 5:22 we read: "His own iniquities shall take the wicked, and he shall be holden with the cords of his sins."

Initially, the sinner experiences a sort of pleasure and enjoyment in his sin, and believes that he is immune to retribution. This is evident to us daily, as we see people who are steeped in vice and yet seem to be enjoying themselves to the full, apparently none the worse for their wrongdoing. These people don't realize that judgment for sin can be delayed days, months, and even years, but it is assured. This is the thought so vividly stated by Hillel in addressing the human skull floating upon the water: no one escapes the consequences of his sin. Nittai of Arbel counsels: "Do not give up your belief in retribution" (AVOT I:7).

Moreover, it is the evil itself that visits the evildoer: "The wicked man shall die by his iniquity" (EZEKIEL 3:18). Because he is punished by the sin itself, the man who gives in to temptation prepares his own gallows. Perhaps he begins hesitantly, but eventually he allows himself to be drawn by passion until finally he finds himself a slave to his own vices. Then he is unable to extricate himself, and sinks deeper into the mire he created. "The evil impulse is, at the beginning, like the thread of a spider, but at the end it is like cart rope" (SUKKAH 52a). The words of King Solomon ring with truth: "There is a way which seems right to a man, but at its end are the ways of death" (PROVERBS 14:12).

Hillel's cogent message — that by the evil men do they are themselves destroyed — was explained by the Rabbis thus: "The measure with which man measures will be measured out to him"; that is, as man deals with others, so will others deal with him. This concept of measure for measure also portrays the relationship of the Almighty with man in all His ways.

Yet, mere vengeance and retaliation can be base and injurious, and lead to the continuation of the evil. Taking revenge for a wrong can beget another wrong: "Those who have drowned you will themselves be drowned."

The Almighty holds every man answerable for his actions. "Man stands forewarned" (BAVA KAMA 3b). He can choose — and if he chooses wrongly, he does so on his own responsibility. "Everything is foreseen; yet freedom of choice is given" (AVOT III:15). The eye of God watches the actions of man, even though he is a free agent; he may choose good or evil, but should bear in mind that he will have to render an account.

All the good that man does accrues to his credit; and as every act of goodness is counted, so is every evil one. Nothing is lost, though one may not see the results immediately. "And your Employer is faithful to reward you" (AVOT II:16). One must have faith in God and in His justice; retribution is not the province of man.

"The reward of those who live exactly according to the Law is not silver or gold, nor a garland of olive branches... nor any public sign of commendation; but every good man is content with the witness that his own conscience bears him" (JOSEPHUS, AGAINST APION).

"The reward of the righteous in the World-to-Come is spiritual bliss; the punishment of the wicked [in the World-to-Come] is exclusion from it: light everlasting for the one, death to the other" (MAIMONIDES, YAD: TESHUVAH 8.1).

24

Living a Life of Lovingkindness

"Chasidim are quick to do mitzvot"
(RASHI, MENACHOT 40b).

"The highest form of wisdom is kindness"
(BERACHOT 17a).

Through the entire fifth chapter of *Pirkei Avot* there prevails a central theme: that of conducting ourselves, in our relationship with the Almighty as well as with our fellowmen, in the manner of lovingkindness — *chasidut*. Thus we emulate the Almighty in His relations with us, His creations. In Psalms 145:7 we read: "The Lord is righteous [*tzaddik*] in all His ways, and acts with lovingkindness [*chasid*] in all His deeds." In Jeremiah 3:12 the prophet is instructed: "Go and proclaim these words toward the north, and say, 'Return, O Israel, says the Lord, and I will not cause my anger to fall upon you, for I am a *chasid*, says the Lord, and I will not keep anger forever.'"

We learn that Noah was a *tzaddik*. But although he was a *tzaddik*, he was apparently no *chasid*, for he had no influence upon the people of his generation, nor did he plead for them before the Almighty as did our father Abraham, whose acts of lovingkindness, particularly in regard to *hachnasat orchim* — the welcoming of guests — are the hallmark of his descendants, Israel, to this day. The mutual love of the Almighty for Abraham and of Abraham for the Almighty was exemplified by ten trials, or tests, which Abraham passed, and which strengthened him. Through his merit the Almighty performed miracles for us in Egypt and on the Sea of Reeds, and tolerated with great patience the ten series of complaints from the children of Israel during their forty years of wandering in the desert.

With great compassion and lovingkindness the Almighty wrought ten miracles for our fathers in the services at the Temple Sanctuary, not the least of which were that "the people stood tightly pressed together [even to the point where their feet were lifted off the ground], yet they found ample space [six square feet, to ensure privacy during the confession of sins] to prostrate themselves; never did a snake or scorpion do injury to anyone in Jerusalem; and no man ever said to his fellow: 'There is insufficient space for me to lodge overnight in Jerusalem'" (AVOT V:5). Implied tribute is paid to both the Jerusalemites and the many visitors, whose *chasidut* made this miracle an actuality in the holy city of Jerusalem. The Almighty has created a perfect world. When His creations follow His example and emulate His acts of lovingkindness, they in effect become partners in the creation of God's world. This partnership was apparently achieved in Jerusalem during the times of the First and Second Temples when there was full observance of the Holy Days.

In Tractate *Kallah* 2a it is stated that "*Chasidut* brings one to modesty and humility." In addition, it is noted that "*Chasidut* brings one to a condition where he attains the holy spirit — *chasidut* is greater than all virtues." By definition, a *chasid* is one who does *chessed*, that is, he performs deeds of lovingkindness, "*lifnim mishurat ha-din*" — more than is required of him. His spiritual attainment is measured both by example, in his general conduct, and by his actions for the good of his fellowmen. Accordingly, his behavior exemplifies the *chacham*, one who is careful not to interrupt another person in his speech, or to speak in the presence of those wiser than he, and yet is not hesitant to add to the general knowledge of others, and is well-organized in his thought and logical in his presentation (AVOT V:7). His attitude to society, as reflected in his dealings with his fellowmen and his use of the means and talents that he has been granted, is clearly the one summed up as: "What is mine is yours and what is yours is yours." He is prepared to help any and all who are in need, with no regard for recompense. He gives of his time and of his efforts for the general welfare of society, unlike those who would say: "What is mine is mine, and what is yours is yours," and "Don't bother me with the troubles of others, for they are not my concern." He is certainly the antithesis to the wicked person who would say, "What is mine is mine and what is yours is mine" (AVOT V:10) — one who covets what belongs to others and would certainly not come to their aid.

A *chasid* exercises self-control in all his actions. Anger is not part of his natural makeup, for he recognizes the inherent dangers to one's mental and physical state that anger can bring, as recorded in all our literature. "Anyone who becomes angry, if he is wise, his wisdom departs from him," he is warned in *Pesachim* 66b. In Tractate *Nedarim* 22b a worse fate is described for one who is in a state of anger: "Anyone who angers forgets his learning and replaces it with foolishness."

Clearly the *chasid*, more than others, must avoid anger at all costs. However, the *chasid* is a human being, not an angel, and on occasion may lose his temper for good cause. We have such examples even on the part of the most modest of men, Moses. In one such incident, by losing his temper over the grave sin of worshiping the golden calf, he taught the Jews a lesson that cost them dearly, for 3,000 idol-worshipers lost their lives (EXODUS 32:19-29). In another incident, Moses, in a fit of anger, failed to use the opportunity to sanctify the Almighty before the people, and therefore forfeited his role of leadership (NUMBERS 20:7-14). Pinchas also succumbed to anger, and in his zeal slew the *Nasi* of the tribe of Shimon, as well as the Midianite princess he had brought with him, and thereby halted the plague in which 24,000 Jews died (NUMBERS 25:7-9). And so, while on rare occasions one may become angry, only the one who is quick to pacify or be pacified is designated as a *chasid*. On the contrary, he who is *quick* to become angry and *slow* to be pacified is described as "wicked" (AVOT V:11). A *chasid*, emulating the

Almighty, is quick to forgive anyone who has possibly wronged him, or has caused him to become angry.

"A person's character is evident through three things: his cup [how he acts after drinking wine or liquor], his pocket [how liberal he is with *tzedakah* and *gemilut chasadim*] and his anger [how he controls it]" (ERUVIN 65b). The *chasid* is judged by his fellowmen in much the same manner. He is a moderate individual, who does not go to extremes in any of his actions, and certainly not in the matter of excessive drinking. Nevertheless, in the observance of the Sabbath and Holy Days, a little wine or liquor can add to the *simchah*, and in that spirit he joins others gladly. The same is true of any other joyous occasion, such as a wedding, a *brit milah*, a *bar mitzvah*, etc. Many of our Sages considered it a great mitzvah *lesame'ach et ha-kallah* (to add to the joy of the bride) by dancing and participating actively in the merriment. The same attitude was encouraged in other public *semachot*, such as the *Simchat Beit Ha-Sho'evah* (the celebration of the drawing of the water), which was observed with great joy by the Sages in Temple days, and is now commemorated once again in Israel. The *chasid* should be a leader in setting an example for others in serving the Almighty *b'simchah* — with unbounded joy.

The *chasid*, rich or poor, also sets an example in another basic sphere of Torah Judaism: "All of Israel are responsible one for the other" (SHAVUOT 39a). His influence is measured by the extent to which he is involved in communal efforts and *tzedakah* — by his contribution to others in material sustenance as well as in spiritual and educational endeavors. He gives *tzedakah* with a full heart, and influences others to do their utmost to help their fellowmen. Such a person is designated as a *chasid* (AVOT V:13).

Conversely, one who does not give or does not give with a full heart, and prefers that others not give, is designated as wicked. The *chasid* does even more than is expected of him. He seeks out every opportunity to perform deeds of lovingkindness. Our Sages emphasized the great value of *gemilut chasa-*

dim and set it above the giving of *tzedakah*. In *Sukkah* 49b they declare: "In three things is *gemilut chasadim* greater than *tzedakah*: the giver of *tzedakah* gives his money, but the giver of *gemilut chasadim* gives of himself as well as of his money; *tzedakah* is given only to the poor, but *gemilut chasadim* can benefit the rich as well as the poor; *tzedakah* is given to the living, but *gemilut chasadim* may be for both the living and the dead." (This is called *Chessed shel Emet* — respectful attention to the departed in the ritual and burial.) Our Sages made a rather startling statement, no doubt to give greater emphasis to *gemilut chasadim* as a matter of regular and continuous practice: "Anyone who denies [the vast importance of *gemilut chasadim*], it is as if he were denying the basic principle of Judaism" (KOHELET RABBAH 7:4) The Rambam gives examples of concrete help for a person in need: It is better to give some constructive help which puts him on the path to recovery than to give him alms. "Make him a partner in your business," he suggests.

In *Avot* V:14, the *mishnah* depicts a scenario wherein a scholar comes to a *beit midrash* — a house of study — and retains his learning well, putting it into practice in his daily life. He is called a *chasid*. Another, who comes to the *beit midrash* but does not apply the learning in his daily life, nevertheless has *sechar halichah* — the reward for coming (applied also today to one who walks a distance to a synagogue for services). Still another, who does not come to the *beit midrash* to learn but does observe what is required, is a doer and receives his reward for "doing." One who does not come to learn and is not a doer is designated as wicked. Our commentaries ask the cogent question: Why, in the case of the *chasid*, does the *mishnah* not state: "He gets his reward for coming to the *beit midrash* and also for being a doer?" The answer given typifies the character of the *chasid*: He cares not about any reward. He learns and he does because that is his nature — to do, without any thought of recompense. At the time this *mishnah* was written (about 200 C.E.), the only way a scholar could really learn was to come to the *beit midrash* and learn orally from the Sages. The Oral Law still consisted, in great part, of learning directly from the teacher and from one's fellow scholars. However, the general principle of learning and doing, as the proper combination and application of Judaism, is the way of the *chasid* and worthy of attainment by all Jews.

The *chasid*'s attitude to basic emotions such as love and hate should be consistent with his general outlook on life. He sees himself as a creation of the Almighty who loves all His creations and expects His creations to love each other. To nurture hate, then, is totally out of the question. We are warned: "You shall not hate your brother in your heart.... You shall not avenge nor bear any grudge against the children of your people" (LEVITICUS 19:17-18). As far as love is concerned, the basic principle governing this emotion remains: "You shall love your fellowman as yourself: I am the Lord" (LEVITICUS 19:18).

A dramatic tale makes this great principle most vivid. Two very dear friends once happened to come to a town where a murder had just been committed. One of them was arrested and immediately led away to be hanged, whereupon his friend began to shout: "He is innocent! I am the guilty one!" Each then proceeded to argue as to his own guilt and the innocence of the other. This most unusual situation came to the attention of the king, and upon further investigation it was found that both were innocent, and the guilty man was subsequently apprehended. The king was fascinated by this demonstration of friendship and inquired of the one who had volunteered to die in place of his arrested friend, "Were you really prepared to give up your life for your friend?" "Yes," replied the man. "Our friendship is so binding that I could not have gone on living without him." The king, overwhelmed, requested humbly: "I beg you, please accept me as your third friend as well." Thus the Almighty tells us: "If you love your fellowman as yourself, then I too am your friend" (REBBE YISRAEL OF RHIZIN).

The love of the Almighty which we profess in the recitation of our prayers three times daily, as well as the love of our fellowmen and of the stranger, are all expressions of our love and appreciation of the Almighty for our very existence. This love is not dependent upon any particular object or specific cause. This is the subject of *Avot* V:16, wherein is mentioned the lustful Amnon who raped his half-sister Tamar, and whose love afterwards turned to hate. It is rather more like the love of David and Jonathan, whose enduring love for each other is related in Samuel I 18:1: "And the soul of Jonathan was bound unto the soul of David, and Jonathan loved him as his own soul." The *chasid* merits that kind of love, for he gives the same to others, and his love for the Almighty is enduring.

What is the *chasid*'s position on the matter of *machloket* (controversy)? There is no simple answer. There are many considerations, for no two people think exactly alike. Our Sages recognized this phenomenon and made allowances for differences of opinion, differences of interpretation (even of the same quotation from the Torah), and differences of judgment and decrees of decisions. It is stated in *Sanhedrin* 38a: "In three things is one person totally different from another: in voice, in appearance and in opinion." In this respect, man is the only creation of the Almighty with the inherent right of independence of thought and decision. Throughout our Torah and Rabbinic literature he is urged to do the right thing in his relationship with both his Creator and his fellowmen. But should his evil inclination prevail, then he proceeds as he chooses. Undoubtedly this unique grant from the Almighty is reflected in the daily life of the individual as well as in that of the community.

As a general rule, one should avoid controversies, for the risks involved of generating anger, with its concomitant evils of insults, tale-bearing, etc., are great and are to be avoided at all costs. However, while our Sages have remarked wisely: "Envy, lust, and thirst for honor take a man out of the world" (AVOT IV:21), they nevertheless emphasized: "Jealousy [including controversy] among scholars will increase knowledge" (BAVA BATRA 21a). *Pirkei Avot* cites an example of a desirable

128 TORAH DYNAMICS

controversy which in fact contributed to the issues at hand: that of Hillel and Shammai (AVOT V:17). Their points of conflict were only on three matters, but their followers, the schools of *Beit Hillel* and *Beit Shammai*, continued controversies for over a hundred years, controversies which included not only matters of *Halachah*, but also philosophical issues, such as whether it is worthwhile for a person to have been born. (They took a vote, and decided that it would be better not to have been born, but since one has no choice, he should examine his deeds carefully [ERUVIN 13b].)

There are also examples of controversies among our great Sages which, although dedicated to *Halachah*, nevertheless had undesirable effects upon the community. One classic example is the controversy between Rabbi Eliezer and the other Sages, led by Rabbi Yehoshua, which dealt with the question of "the oven of Achnai" and its propensity to become unclean (impure). Rabbi Eliezer ruled "clean," and the Sages ruled "unclean." Whereupon Rabbi Eliezer, certain that he was right, ordered: "If I am right, let that nearby carob tree move." The carob tree moved promptly — 150 feet. The Sages responded: "One cannot derive proof from a carob tree." Undaunted, Rabbi Eliezer continued: "If I am right, let this stream of water change its course." Immediately the stream changed its course. The response of the Sages was the same: "One may not bring proof from a stream." Rabbi Eliezer dared once again to convince the Sages: "If I am right, let the walls of the *beit midrash* prove it." The walls then began to bend. In anger, Rabbi Yehoshua shouted at the walls: "If great scholars are debating with each other on matters of *Halachah*, what right have you to intervene?" The walls were confused — out of respect for Rabbi Eliezer they remained partially bent, but out of respect for Rabbi Yehoshua they bent no further. Rabbi Eliezer made a final attempt: "If I am right," he declared, "let the proof come from Heaven." A voice was heard from above saying: "Why do you question Rabbi Eliezer's ruling? The *Halachah* is always according to Rabbi Eliezer's opinion." Rabbi Yehoshua arose and quoted: "The Torah is 'no longer in Heaven' (DEUTERONOMY 30:12). Therein it is written 'majority rules' (EXODUS 23:2)" (BAVA METZIA 59b).

An interesting postscript to this incident was the question asked of Elijah the Prophet by Rabbi Natan: "How did the Almighty react to all this?" Elijah reported: "The Almighty laughed and remarked: My sons won the controversy" (BAVA METZIA 59a-b). Rabbi Eliezer refused to accept the majority opinion and was isolated by his colleagues.

A similar controversy involving Rabbi Yehoshua and the *Nasi, Rabban* Gamliel of Yavneh, resulted in the temporary replacement of the *Nasi* by the young Rabbi Elazar ben Azariah. Obviously one who engages in controversy treads on dangerous ground. Examples of controversies that are not *l'shem Shamayim* ("for the sake of Heaven," that is, sincere and entirely impersonal) are myriad. They have plagued entire communities and their Rabbis everywhere and in all generations. The classic example cited by *Avot* V:17, of Korach and his band who were engaged in the controversy against Moses and Aaron, doesn't even mention Moses and Aaron. The latter had no argument as appointees of the Almighty, whereas the complainants had each his own personal interest. The futility of such a controversy is indicated by the judgment from Heaven. Whereas on earth one's acts are not liable for punishment until one reaches the age of 13, and in Heaven, it is said, until the age of 20, the punishment for Korach's controversy was meted out even to babies, for all were swallowed up by the earth — men, women, and children. This was most certainly not a controversy *l'shem Shamayim*. The Rebbe of Kotsk once remarked: "Even a controversy that is obviously *l'shem Shamayim* must be conducted by means that are themselves as well *l'shem Shamayim*." All things considered, a *chasid* would do well to avoid any controversy that contains inherent risks.

A *chasid* is by nature community-minded, for he shares the problems of each member of the community. That he receives a reward for his service to the community in that he is assisted from above to avoid sin (he is no angel and hence may be tempted on occasion) is of course gratifying, but that is not his reason for devoting all his talents and all his means to helping others. Just as Moses our teacher worked selflessly for his people, so we are all expected to do. Conversely, Israel's King Jeroboam sinned and caused others to sin (for political reasons, in order to maintain his independent kingdom of the Ten Tribes) in idol worship. His punishment was cumulative, and covered the sins of those he influenced. Hence it is said that he has no part in the World-to-Come and has no opportunity to repent (AVOT V:18).

Avot V:19 designates our father Abraham as the *chasid* par excellence, whose followers we are and whose example we should emulate. Among his many outstanding attributes, three are emphasized: a good eye (not jealous of anyone, but rather happy for the next person's good fortune); a humble spirit (devoid of arrogance, and befriending all, as in his *hachnasat orchim*); and a modest soul (not demanding a wide range of earthly pleasures which lead to immorality). In all these areas, Abraham excelled. The precise opposite is characteristic of Bil'am the wicked and his followers, who are punished both in this world and in the World-to-Come. The followers of Abraham, performing good deeds with enthusiasm, joy and loving-kindness, are the recipients of good fortune in this world, and even more so, in the World-to-Come. This then is the right and proper way of the *chasid*, and in the words of Rabbi Meir: "He who occupies himself with Torah with a sincere purpose...qualifies to be a...*chasid*" (AVOT VI:1).

Rabbi Levi Yitzchak of Berdichev stood with a smile upon his face as he watched the wagoner, in *tallit* and *tefillin*, applying grease to the wagon wheels. A Jew nearby remarked to the Rabbi critically: "Look at that one, smearing his dirty wheels while wearing *tallit* and *tefillin*." Rabbi Levi Yitzchak, however, raised his head Heavenward and remarked: "*Ribbono shel Olam*, look at this devout Jew! Even when he smears his wheels, he wears his *tallit* and *tefillin.*"

This demonstrates *ahavat Yisrael* — *chasidut*.

In *Avot* V:22, ben Bag Bag states: "Study Torah again and again, for everything is contained in it." There is no need whatsoever to add or to detract, for Torah is all-inclusive. The Torah warns in Deuteronomy 4:2: "You shall not add unto the word which I command you, neither shall you diminish from it." In *Sanhedrin* 29a we learn in fact: "Anyone who adds [to the Torah] in effect diminishes it."

The Dubner Maggid illustrated this point with the following timely story:

> A Jew went to his neighbor and borrowed a spoon. The next day he returned and handed two spoons to his surprised neighbor. The borrower then explained: "Your spoon was pregnant and gave birth to a second spoon." The neighbor wondered about the sanity of his friend, but nevertheless accepted the two spoons. The same thing occurred again when his friend borrowed a fork and later returned two forks. A few days later, the borrowing neighbor appeared and asked to borrow his friend's beautiful silver candelabrum. The neighbor was quite happy to loan him his silver candelabrum, and eagerly anticipated receiving two in return! Several days passed and no word was heard from the borrower. Concerned, the neighbor called upon him and asked in some alarm: "Where is my silver candelabrum, my friend?" "Ah," replied the friend with a sad sigh, "your silver candelabrum, *nebach*, died." "What?" shouted the neighbor. "Are you crazy? How can a candelabrum die?" The friend then explained: "If you could accept the fact that spoons, forks and all the other things I borrowed could give birth to others of their kind, then surely you can see that it is also possible for spoons, forks and silver candelabra to die."

So too with one who attempts to add to the Torah: He will find that doing so detracts from its sanctity and leaves it open for others to diminish its teachings. A *chasid* is ever on guard to "make a fence for the Torah" (AVOT I:1).

And thus the attribute of *chasidut* — lovingkindness — permeates the teachings of *Pirkei Avot*, and through them guides us and inspires us to attain it.

Historical Background and Biographies of the Sages in Order of Their Reference in Pirkei Avot

Chapter I

ANSHEI KNESSET HA-GEDOLAH:
MEN OF THE GREAT ASSEMBLY

The *Anshei Knesset Ha-Gedolah*, an assembly of 120 great scholars, prophets and priests, was established by Ezra the Scribe, the High Priest and spiritual leader of the Jewish community, upon the return to *Eretz Yisrael* from exile in Babylonia. Ezra, assisted by Nechemiah, withstood the attacks of the Samaritans and "restored Torah to its proper position in Jewish life in *Eretz Yisrael*" (YOMA 69b). Among the first members of the *Anshei Knesset Ha-Gedolah* were the prophets Chaggai, Zechariah and Malachi, as well as Daniel, Chananiah, Mishael and Azariah (saved from death miraculously), Mordechai, Zerubavel and many others, who in this critical era of Jewish history instructed the people and organized Jewish religious services in much the same order and manner that we observe to this day. They prepared the order of prayer, including the *Shemoneh Esreh* (the eighteen blessings in the silent prayer; later a nineteenth blessing was added for protection against informers and tale-bearers, a common danger in the days preceding the destruction of the Second Temple). They assembled all the books of the Bible as we have them now, and decided to include the books of Ezekiel, the Twelve Minor Prophets, Daniel, the Book of Esther, the Books of Chronicles and the Books of Ezra and Nechemiah. They counted all the letters in their proper order and listed them so that scribes in future generations would be guided by these instructions and copy the

Biblical scrolls properly and accurately. They established the order of services for Sabbaths and Festivals, and the precise order of ceremonies to be followed in their observance.

The original scrolls were written in the ancient Hebrew script. The *Anshei Knesset Ha-Gedolah*, however, used what we call the Assyrian script, the one which is in use to this day and which was familiar then, to most of the people. They further instituted the custom of reading an appropriate chapter of the Prophets, on Sabbaths and Festivals, after the reading of the Torah. This reading, the *Haftarah*, would provide an opportunity to learn the writings of the Prophets. The prevalent spoken language in the region was Aramaic, and although there were Jews who could read and pray in Hebrew, many did not understand the meaning of the words. Hence, a *meturgeman* — a translator — was appointed, to explain in Aramaic the Hebrew text during the Torah reading.

It can be said of the *Anshei Knesset Ha-Gedolah* that they certainly put into practice in their own time that which they urged future generations to observe meticulously: "Raise up many students" (AVOT I:1).

SHIMON HA-TZADDIK

Shimon *Ha-Tzaddik* (the only one of our Talmudic Sages referred to as "*Ha-Tzaddik*" — the righteous or just) was the last of the *Anshei Knesset Ha-Gedolah*, and lived during the end of the two-hundred-year period of its jurisdiction, toward the close of the fourth century B.C.E. This was the period during which the reign of the Persian Empire came to an end with the rise of the Macedonian conqueror Alexander the Great. In *Yoma* 69a, it is related that Alexander, at the urging of the Cuthites, made his way to Jerusalem, intent on destroying the city and the Temple. Shimon, the High Priest, donned in his white priestly garments, set out together with a delegation of other priests, with torches in hand, to greet the conqueror.

As Alexander the Great approached Shimon, he immediately halted his horse, dismounted and bowed down to the High Priest. Turning to his amazed entourage, Alexander then explained, "On the night before every important battle, I saw a vision of this man offering me encouragement."

"If that is the case," Shimon said, "then what cause brings you here? Is it logical that the very House which prays for your victory and your welfare should be destroyed?"

"What wicked people urge that this be done?" inquired Alexander.

"The *Kutim* [Cuthites]," replied Shimon.

"They are now in your hands," declared Alexander. "Do with them as you wish."

When Alexander wanted his statue to be placed in the Temple, Shimon offered him an alternative that found favor in his eyes. "For a whole year," he promised, "we shall name every son born in Israel 'Alexander,' as a tribute to you." Alexander accepted the offer with pleasure, and to this day, "Alexander," "Sender," "Alec," and "Alex" all have as their source this incident with Shimon.

Shimon *Ha-Tzaddik* served as High Priest for forty years, inspiring his people with Torah, good will and kindness, setting an example for all to follow. He encouraged and supported Torah learning on a nationwide scale. Throughout all his years of service in the Temple, it is said, he was favored with Divine approval in the following way.

During the Yom Kippur Service, two goats were brought before the High Priest, one to be sacrificed to God and the other to be sent to Azazel, a mountain in the desert, symbolically bearing the sins of Israel. In order to determine which goat would be chosen for each function, the High Priest would draw tallies — one marked "to God" and one "to Azazel," the one in his right hand for the animal on his right, and the one in his left hand for the animal on his left. It is said of Shimon *Ha-Tzaddik* that during his forty years as High Priest, he always drew with his right hand the tally marked "to God" — a most favorable omen.

He predicted his own approaching death, explaining, "Every year on Yom Kippur, an old man dressed in white has accompanied me into the Holy of Holies, and has came out again with me. This year he was dressed in black. He came in with me, but did not go out with me." Within a week, Shimon *Ha-Tzaddik* died.

ANTIGNOS OF SOCHO

Antignos was a student of Shimon *Ha-Tzaddik*, and succeeded him as *Nasi*. During his administration, Greek influence upon the Jews was spreading rapidly, particularly among the upper classes. Antignos did his best to combat this influence, but he was relatively unsuccessful. His two students, Tzadok and Baytos, misunderstood or misinterpreted the injunction of their teacher: "Be not like the servants who serve their master for the sake of receiving a reward" (AVOT I:3), to mean that there exists no Divine reward and punishment, and thus there is no basis for the belief in the hereafter nor in the resurrection of the dead. They left Antignos, and founded two sects in the spirit of Hellenism, the *Tzadokim* (Sadducees) and the *Baytosim* (Bethusians), who created great controversy in their struggle against the *Perushim* (Pharisees, the traditionalists) for many years. Some of the wealthier Jews adopted their doctrines and removed themselves from the mainstream of Judaism, while others left the fold entirely.

YOSEI BEN YOEZER OF TZEREDAH
and YOSEI BEN YOCHANAN OF JERUSALEM

Following the leadership of Antignos were five successive "pairs" of scholars, the one serving as *Nasi* of the Sanhedrin and the other as Head of the Court and Deputy to the *Nasi*. They served through the entire period of the Hasmoneans, almost to the era of Roman domination. Greek rule over Israel continued to erode the unity of the people and there was widespread loathing of the growing influence of Hellenistic philosophy and its emphasis on physical pleasures and immorality. The Sages, especially the *Nasi* and Head of the Court, continued to oppose the heretics up until the destruction of the Temple in 70 C.E.

The "pairs" carried no title of "Rabbi" or "*Rabban*" (reserved later for the *Nasi*), but were simply called by their names and/or places of residence. The first such pair, Yosei ben Yoezer of Tzeredah and Yosei ben Yochanan of Jerusalem, were students of both Shimon *Ha-Tzaddik* and Antignos. Yosei ben Yoezer was a Priest, about whom was recorded the description: "the most righteous of *Kohanim*" (CHAGIGAH 18b). Both of these distinguished Sages were highly regarded as great scholars, and as leaders with impeccable integrity. Both were eulogized as men with all the finest qualities (SOTAH 47b). Despite their noble efforts, though, they were unable to withstand the double jeopardy of Greek domination and Sadducee-Hellenistic influence that led to the Hasmonean revolt in 167 B.C.E.

YEHOSHUA BEN PERACHIAH and NITTAI OF ARBEL

The second "pair," Yehoshua ben Perachiah and Nittai of Arbel (near Tiberias), served as *Nasi* and Head of the Court respectively during the reign of the Hasmoneans, in an Israel which was enjoying independence for the first time in over four hundred years. But the times were far from easy; the ongoing struggle for power between the Pharisees and the Sadducees reached even the High Priesthood, and Yochanan the High Priest, at the venerable age of 80, joined the Sadducees. In the wake of the struggle, King Alexander Yannai decimated the Sanhedrin of Pharisees and appointed Sadducees in their place. Yehoshua ben Perachiah consequently fled to Alexandria in Egypt, where a large Jewish community flourished, and a great synagogue had been established. Upon the death of

Yannai, Shimon ben Shatach called upon Yehoshua to return to *Eretz Yisrael*. In the context of the perilous times in which they lived, it is understandable that both of these Sages advised their fellow Jews to exercise great care in choosing their leaders, teachers, and friends.

YEHUDAH BEN TABBAI and SHIMON BEN SHATACH

The third "pair" of Sages, Yehudah ben Tabbai and Shimon ben Shatach, held office during the trying reign of King Alexander Yannai. Shimon ben Shatach, as *Nasi* of the Sanhedrin, made every effort to remove the Sadducees from the Sanhedrin, but King Yannai persisted and Yehudah ben Tabbai ultimately had to leave Israel and take refuge in Alexandria, as had Yehoshua ben Perachiah before him. Through the influence of his sister, Queen Shlomtzion, Shimon ben Shatach retained his position as *Nasi*, but when he ordered the King to stand trial before the Sanhedrin, he was forced to flee into hiding. Near the end of his reign, King Yannai recanted and Shimon was restored to his position. After the King's death, Queen Shlomtzion reigned and Shimon, her brother, was able to cleanse the entire Sanhedrin of Sadducees and restore the authority of Torah in Israel. He brought Yehudah ben Tabbai back from Alexandria and together they spread Torah study throughout the nation, assuring every Jewish child the opportunity to learn.

It is told of Shimon ben Shatach that, confronted with the growing prevalence of witchcraft in Ashkelon, he took bold action and had an entire band of eighty practitioners executed in one day. As a result, their families took revenge and bore false witness against Shimon's son, who was subsequently convicted and put to death. Eventually, Shimon ben Shatach was able to restore tranquillity to Israel; we read in *Ta'anit* 23a that the years under the authority of Queen Shlomtzion and her brother were among the most peaceful and bountiful for Israel.

An illustration of Shimon's sterling character is recorded in *Devarim Rabbah* 3:5. Shimon acquired a donkey from an Ishmaelite and as his students were admiring it, they discovered a valuable jewel in a bag hung from its neck. The students thereupon congratulated Shimon, quoting Proverbs 10:22: "The blessing of God will make one wealthy." Shimon, however, did not share their enthusiasm and responded, "I bought a donkey, not a valuable jewel." He returned the jewel to the Ishmaelite, who was overwhelmed with joy and cried out, "Blessed be the God of Shimon ben Shatach!"

SHEMAYAH and AVTALYON

Shemayah, the *Nasi* of the Sanhedrin, and Avtalyon, the Head of the Court, were the fourth "pair," and they continued the tradition received from their teachers Yehudah ben Tabbai and Shimon ben Shatach. Tractate *Gittin* 57b records that they were the descendants of converts whose genealogy led back to the Assyrian conqueror Sancheriv. They were held in high regard by the entire Jewish nation, as great teachers of Torah and as leaders who took a vital interest in the people and their problems. Unlike their predecessors, they studiously avoided becoming embroiled in the political struggles of the time, a time which witnessed "civil war" between the two brothers Hurkanos and Aristoblus, the sons of Queen Shlomtzion, who vied for the throne after her demise. The brothers called in the Roman authorities to choose between them, and the Romans slyly chose the weaker of the two, Hurkanos, thus helping to clear the way for Roman rule, which culminated in the destruction of the Second Temple.

Shemayah and Avtalyon rather concentrated their efforts upon strengthening the people internally, through their dedication to Torah living. Shemayah instructed the people: "Love work; and hate holding offices of authority; and do not seek intimacy with the governing officials" (AVOT I:10). Avtalyon, in the same vein, advised: "Be careful with your words, for you may incur the penalty of *galut* [exile]" (AVOT I:11). Both urged the populace not to meddle in the political struggle, lest they be exiled to Alexandria, as were Yehoshua ben Perachiah and Yehudah ben Tabbai. Dedication to Torah study was their goal for the nation.

Shemayah and Avtalyon followed a policy of charging their students a nominal amount for learning at their *beit midrash*. It is told that on one cold Friday during the winter month of Tevet snow had fallen, and as Shemayah and Avtalyon sat teaching they noticed a dark shadow on the skylight overhead. Upon examining the cause, they found a man lying on the roof, stretched out across the skylight, covered with snow and almost frozen. They immediately carried him down and brought him inside. As they revived him, they realized that it was none other than Hillel, who had not been able to come in because he had no money for the fee. Determined to learn nonetheless, he had climbed up to the skylight in order to hear the teachings of these two revered scholars. Hillel continued to learn from Shemayah and Avtalyon, and later succeeded them in leadership. In *Pesachim* 70b, the two are described as: "Wise Sages and great teachers."

HILLEL and SHAMMAI

The fifth and last of the "pairs," Hillel and Shammai, were *Nasi* and Head of the Court during the reign of Herod. Despite economic prosperity, the period was a perilous one for the Pharisees, who were waging a struggle to maintain leadership against Sadducee opposition. The Romans had already established a firm hold upon Israel, and although Herod the Edomite claimed Jewish descent, his ruthless murder of all descendants of the Hasmoneans estranged him from the Jewish people. Still standing today are remains of his many grandiose construction projects: the *Kotel* (the Western Wall), as well as the palaces at Herodion and Massada.

Born in Babylonia, Hillel arrived in Israel at the age of 40 to learn Torah from Shemayah and Avtalyon. Later he returned to Babylonia, where he continued to learn, supported by his brother Shevno who shared his earnings with Hillel. After the passing of Shemayah and Avtalyon, the sons of Beteira served briefly as *Nasi* and Head of the Court. In the face of many Halachic problems, they turned to Hillel and asked him to return to Israel. Hillel acceded to their request and returned, and, because of his renowned scholarship, was appointed *Nasi* of the Sanhedrin. He later appointed Shammai as Head of the Court and as associate *Nasi*. Hillel served in this capacity for forty years, and died at the age of 120. It is said that Hillel's lineage went back to King David, through Shefatiah ben Avital (the son of Avital and David) (KETUBBOT 62b).

Hillel's stature among his people, and in the generations that followed as well, was of the highest order. In *Sanhedrin* 11a the Sages pay tribute to his greatness: "After the passing of the last prophets — Chaggai, Zechariah and Malachi — there vanished the Holy Spirit from Israel. However, a *bat kol* [voice from Heaven] remained, and was heard on occasion. Once the Sages were gathered on the veranda of Guriah in Jericho, and a *bat kol* was heard saying: 'There is one present among you who is worthy to have the Holy Spirit of the Almighty shine upon him as on Moses our Teacher, except that this generation does not merit it.' All eyes then turned as one toward Hillel the Elder."

Hillel, a great educator, raised an entire generation of outstanding teachers and scholars who in turn trained others in his ways. In Tractate *Sukkah* 28a we read a remarkable account of Hillel's accomplishments: "Hillel the Elder had eighty outstanding students. Thirty of them were worthy to have the Holy Spirit of the Almighty shine upon them, as upon Moses our Teacher. Thirty of them were as worthy as Joshua, to have had the sun stand still for them as it did for him. Twenty of them were 'average' — the smallest [youngest] of them was [the great] Yochanan ben Zakkai, and the greatest of them all,

Yonatan ben Uziel." In Tractate *Shabbat* 30b, we are advised: "A person should always be modest and congenial like Hillel, and not somber and harsh like Shammai."

The Sages go on to relate the well-known incidents of the would-be converts to Judaism whom Shammai dismissed summarily, but whom Hillel welcomed and, with remarkable patience, set on the right path to Judaism. Hillel's patience is similarly illustrated by the oft-told story of the man who made a wager with his friend, insisting that he could make Hillel lose his famed patience and become angry. He approached Hillel one Friday when he was busy preparing for the Sabbath, asking him a series of foolish questions. Hillel concluded: "Better that you should lose 400 *zuzim*...than that Hillel should lose his temper" (SHABBAT 31a).

Hillel also introduced the adoption of two significant laws. The first was a *prozbul* — a declaration that one who has a note due on the Sabbatical year (in which debts are canceled) may collect the sum due him by depositing the note with the Court, and the practice is followed to this day. This practice encouraged the normal conduct of business, including extension of credit through loans and timely loans to the needy. The second law enabled the seller of a city dwelling to exercise the legal right to redeem his home within one year, by depositing his money with the Court if the buyer is not available. This law made possible the orderly transfer of property to the original owner, preventing the buyer from using devious means to block the required redemption by the seller.

In Tractate *Sofrim* (chapter 16, *mishnah* 9), it is recorded of Hillel: "He learned all that was possible from the scholars, including all the languages, all the sounds and ways of nature — the mountains, hills and valleys, the trees and the meadows, the sounds of wild and domestic animals, the sounds of 'spirits' and all parables.... All this for one supreme purpose, that is, in order to observe fully the verse: 'The Almighty was pleased for the sake of his righteousness to render the Torah increasingly great and glorious' (ISAIAH 42:21)."

SHAMMAI, Hillel's associate, was a devoted *tzaddik* who was meticulous in his observance of Torah, enjoying with a full heart the performance of mitzvot. He was particularly fond of the mitzvah of Sabbath observance. It was recorded about him that all week he prepared for the Sabbath. "If he saw a particularly fine cow," we read, "he designated it for the Sabbath. If, during the week, he found a nicer one, then that is the one that he chose for the Sabbath" (BEITZAH 16a). In all their work together, it is said that Hillel and Shammai differed on only three occasions — when Shammai appears to have judged too hastily the three prospective converts who then turned to Hillel with success. But it must be said in defense of Shammai that the three conditions set by the three candidates must have made them sound insincere and motivated by the wrong reasons: "Convert me on condition that you teach me the entire Torah while I stand on one foot"; "Convert me, but only to accept the written Torah"; and "Convert me so that I can be a High Priest" (SHABBAT 31a). Although Shammai is generally thought of as an uncompromising, cheerless person, his advice to "receive every person with a kindly countenance" (AVOT I:15) belies this description of him.

Yet there were different approaches, and these were reflected in the debates between the two schools of thought, *Beit Hillel* and *Beit Shammai*, for over one hundred years. Of the 316 Halachic controversies between them, in only 55 was *Beit Shammai* more lenient than *Beit Hillel*. Their debates comprised many philosophical issues, including the question of whether it was better to be born, or better not to be born! By a democratic vote it was decided that it was better that one not be born; but both schools of thought concluded that, in view of the fact that one has no choice in the matter, "he should examine his deeds carefully and act accordingly" (ERUVIN 13b). Upon the death of Hillel, his son Shimon served as *Nasi* briefly; but upon the death of Shammai, *Beit Shammai* waived the right to serve as Head of the Court, thus bringing to an end the reign of the "pairs," and instituting the rule of but one leader, the *Nasi* of the Sanhedrin. This position was held by Hillel's grandson, the noted *Rabban* Gamliel the Elder.

RABBAN GAMLIEL THE ELDER

Gamliel was the first to be designated *Rabban*, an Aramaic word meaning "our teacher" or "our master," a title reserved only for the descendants of Hillel (with one exception — the dedicated student of Hillel, *Rabban* Yochanan ben Zakkai). *Rabban* Gamliel served as *Nasi* and Head of the Court, initiating a practice which continued up to the decline of *Eretz Yisrael*, and the rise of Babylonia, as the center of Torah studies. *Rabban* Gamliel continued in the path of his famous grandfather Hillel, making significant legal innovations in urgent matters of the day within the framework of *Halachah*. The principle of "because of adjustment to the times and conditions," exemplified by Hillel in his *prozbul* amendment, thus applied as well to a number of *Rabban* Gamliel's concerns. For instance, he made conditions easier for granting a bill of divorce to a woman whose husband was missing, requiring but one witness. He corrected a custom that was a result of Greek influence: holding lavish, costly funerals, to the point where poor people often left their dead in the street because they could not afford the high cost of burial. *Rabban* Gamliel stipulated in his will that he be buried in a simple white shroud, whereupon everyone began to follow his example.

He was dearly loved by the people, and highly respected as a great scholar both in Torah learning and in general knowledge. His son Shimon reported that some five hundred students were studying the Greek language in the household of *Rabban* Gamliel in order to faciliate diplomatic contacts with the ruling authorities. "With the passing of *Rabban* Gamliel, the glory of the Torah was extinguished and cleanliness and purity vanished" (SOTAH 49a).

RABBAN SHIMON BEN GAMLIEL THE ELDER

The last of the chain of the house of Hillel to serve as *Nasi* during the Temple Era was *Rabban* Shimon. He had the misfortune to witness the deterioration and virtual disintegration of the Jewish community in *Eretz Yisrael* during the period of the uprising and the subsequent unsuccessful war against the powerful Roman legions. During *Rabban* Shimon's service, the office of High Priest became a prize to be auctioned to the highest bidder. The Talmud contains numerous references attesting to *Rabban* Shimon's great efforts to restore order in communal life; for example, we read in Tractate *Keritot* 8a of *Rabban* Shimon's ruling on the bringing of sacrificial doves to the Temple by women who have given birth — that one pair be considered sufficient in all cases, even in multiple births. The effect of this ruling was to reduce substantially the demand for doves and thus drastically lower their high cost.

Tractate *Sukkah* 53a describes *Rabban* Shimon's great love for the Temple. During the rejoicing and merriment of the *Simchat Beit Ha-Sho'evah*, we read, *Rabban* Shimon would perform unusual feats: He would toss into the air eight large, lit torches, and would juggle them so well that none touched the others. He would bow down deeply, balancing on his two thumbs, and kiss the ground of the Temple area.

Rabban Shimon and Rabbi Ishmael ben Elisha the High Priest were the first of the Ten Martyrs to be put to death by the Romans. *Rabban* Shimon left a son, *Rabban* Gamliel, later of Yavneh, whose daughter, Imma-Shalom, became the wife of the outstanding Sage, Rabbi Eliezer ben Hurkanos.

RABBAN SHIMON BEN GAMLIEL THE SECOND OF YAVNEH

This *Rabban* Shimon was the sixth generation in the lineage of Hillel, the son of *Rabban* Gamliel of Yavneh, who, after the execution of his father *Rabban* Shimon, escaped to Babylonia until after the conclusion of the war and the establishment of Yavneh as the center of learning. *Rabban* Shimon underwent a similar experience during and after the Bar Kochba uprising. He returned to *Eretz Yisrael* from Babylonia to assume the position of *Nasi*, but by then the new center of scholarship was in Usha in the Galilee, rather than in Yavneh. He made a supreme effort to restore cohesion within the Jewish community, but the harsh decrees issued by the Emperor Hadrian were still in effect, and there was widespread suffering. *Rabban* Shimon was privileged to witness the abatement of the edicts, however, and took the opportunity to spread Torah learning throughout the land.

He had acquired his learning from his father, *Rabban* Gamliel, and from the teaching and guidance of Rabbi Yosei. Rabbi Akiva's brilliant students were held in high regard by him, particularly Rabbi Shimon bar Yochai, to whom he compared himself as a fox to a lion. He reviewed with sorrow the many afflictions suffered by his people, and although it was fitting for the Jews to refrain from meat and wine after the destruction of the Temple, he declared that "one should not decree edicts of forbiddance that the populace cannot bear" (TOSEFTA SOTAH 15:1). He is quoted frequently in the Halachic literature — over one hundred times in the Mishnah alone — and was active in maintaining contact with the Jewish communities in Babylonia and elsewhere. His brilliant son, Rabbi Yehudah, listed his father as one of the three most modest and humble men in all history (BAVA METZIA 84b).

Chapter II

RABBI YEHUDAH HA-NASI (RABI)

Rabbi Yehudah *Ha-Nasi*, son of *Rabban* Shimon and the seventh generation in the lineage of Hillel, served as *Nasi* of the Sanhedrin with great distinction. Honored and respected by the entire population during his lifetime of public service, it was through his initiative that all the Sages of his time were gathered together to complete the codification of the Mishnah begun by Rabbi Akiva, and in part by *Rabban* Yochanan ben Zakkai, and continued by Rabbi Meir and his associates. Setting down the Oral Law in writing for the first time provided us with the Mishnah and its division into six major orders: *Zera'im, Mo'ed, Nashim, Nezikin, Kodashim,* and *Taharot* (163 tractates in all), which remain to this day the foundation of organized Talmudic study. The Mishnah was completed about 200 C.E.; the Babylonian Talmud was completed some three hundred years later. "*Rabi*" or "*Rebi*" was always the endearing term by which the Sages referred to Rabbi Yehudah *Ha-Nasi* in the Talmud.

He was born in Beit She'arim at a time when Hadrian's decree forbidding circumcision was still in force. His father, *Rabban* Shimon, defied the order and had his son circumcised. When the circumcised child was asked to be brought before the Roman Governor to a certain death, Antoninus' mother substituted her son for Yehudah, thus saving his life. Yehudah and Antoninus, who later became Emperor, became close friends and this relationship continued throughout their lives.

When the decrees were recalled, Rabbi Yehudah *Ha-Nasi* was enabled to continue, unhampered, his manifold activities for Torah and for the unity of his people. The Sanhedrin was moved from Usha and Shfaram to Beit She'arim, where it remained during the lifetimes of Rabbi Yehudah and his son, *Rabban* Gamliel. It is recorded in Tractate *Kiddushin* 72b that on the day that Rabbi Akiva died, *Rabi* was born; and that it was of him that it was said: "As the sun set, the sun then shone" (ECCLESIASTES 1:5).

Rabbi Yehudah was particularly anxious to learn from all the scholars of his generation, and most particularly from the five great students of Rabbi Akiva, the brilliant Rabbis Meir, Yehudah, Yosei, Shimon, and Elazar. About Rabbi Meir, *Rabi* acknowledged: "In the *beit midrash* I sat behind Rabbi Meir; had I sat where I could see his face, I would have learned even more" (ERUVIN 13b). He was opposed in principle to the extensive use of Aramaic as the spoken language in Israel, once remarking, "Why must we use this foreign language in *Eretz Yisrael?*" (BAVA KAMA 82b, 83). His Mishnah is written in perfect Hebrew; he was such a great Hebraist that even his servants were well-versed in the holy tongue.

There are numerous references to *Rabi* as *Rabbenu Ha-Kadosh* (our holy teacher), a sign of the high regard in which he was held by his colleagues as well as by the people. About him it was said, "From Moses until *Rabi*, we did not see Torah and greatness within one man" (GITTIN 59a). Rabbi Shimon ben Menasia declared that the great qualities of the righteous, enumerated by the Sages (beauty, strength, riches, honor, wisdom, old age, a hoary head, and children), "were all realized in Rabbi Yehudah *Ha-Nasi* and his sons" (AVOT VI:8). His outstanding student, Rav, paid him the greatest tribute: "If the Messiah is among the living, he must be like our holy *Rabi*" (SANHEDRIN 98b). *Rabi* lived out his last seventeen years in the Galilee hilltop town of Sepporis.

RABBAN GAMLIEL, SON OF RABBI YEHUDAH HA-NASI

Rabban Gamliel (the third) was appointed *Nasi* by his father, on his deathbed, with the instructions: "Conduct your *Nesi'ut* [Presidency] with great dignity and upon a high level. Exercise authority with your students" (KETUBBOT 103b). *Rabban* Gamliel served during the first part of the third century C.E. His teachings included emphasis on the necessity of an orderly life of gainful occupation along with Torah study, and sincere dedication to public service. His mentor was the outstanding scholar Rabbi Chiyya, whose guidance he followed; Rav (Rav Abba) was a student of his as well as of his father. The last *Nasi* to be listed in the Mishnah among the *Tanna'im, Rabban* Gamliel was succeeded by his son, *Rabban* Yehudah Nesiah.

RABBAN YOCHANAN BEN ZAKKAI AND HIS FIVE OUTSTANDING SCHOLARS

Rabban Yochanan, the only one of our Sages to merit the title *Rabban* despite the fact that he was not a descendant of Hillel, served as *Nasi* and lived to the age of 120. In his youth he was privileged to learn from Hillel, who predicted for this youngest of his eighty great students a career as "Father of all wisdom and a father for all the generations of Israel" (YERUSHALMI NEDA-RIM 5:5,6). About *Rabban* Yochanan the Sages noted admiringly, "He never ceased learning Scriptures, Mishnah, Talmud, laws and legends, special mystical instruction from terms used in the Torah, limitations imposed by the Sages, the use of principles of logic, astronomy, mathematical equivalents of the Hebrew letters and words, the whispers of the angels, of the spirits and of the palms [for even trees impart messages], parables of the foxes, and all things — great and small" (SUKKAH 28a).

He followed strictly the ways of Hillel in his conduct, displaying modesty, humility and friendship to everyone. "It was said of him, that no one that he encountered was the first to say 'Shalom,' not even the non-Jewish stranger in the market" (BERACHOT 17a). In the difficult years preceding the destruction of the Temple, *Rabban* Yochanan was a tower of strength to the people. After the execution of the *Nasi Rabban* Shimon, *Rabban* Yochanan carried on the vital work of leadership. During the war against Rome, *Rabban* Yochanan constantly urged that peace be sought, and that General Vespasian's request for a symbolic surrender — a spear or an arrow — be honored for the sake of peace. The extremist fanatics refused, and we read, in Tractate *Gittin* 56a,b, of how *Rabban* Yochanan, in anticipation of the destruction, summoned his nephew Abba Sikra, leader of the fanatics, and arranged with him to be carried out of Jerusalem for "burial" by his two trusted students, Eliezer and Yehoshua. Appearing before General Vespasian, *Rabban* Yochanan addressed him as "Your Majesty," whereupon Vespasian replied, "You are guilty of two violations: first of all, I am not a king; and secondly, why did you not come until now?" *Rabban* Yochanan answered both points — to the first he replied with the Biblical verse that Jerusalem would be turned over only to a king, and to the second, that the fanatics had not permitted him to leave Jerusalem (GITTIN 56a,b).

As the discussion progressed, a messenger suddenly appeared, announcing the death of the Emperor and the appointment of Vespasian as the new Emperor. Impressed by the prophetic wisdom of *Rabban* Yochanan, the new Emperor granted him three requests. Thereupon, *Rabban* Yochanan asked for 1) permission to establish a center for Torah study in Yavneh, 2) the restoration of the traditional chain of authority through *Rabban* Gamliel's appointment as *Nasi*, and 3) medical care for Rabbi Tzadok, who was dangerously ill as a result of his repeated fasting for many years prior to the destruction.

Rabbi Yosef and Rabbi Akiva later asked, "Why didn't *Rabban* Yochanan request that Jerusalem and the Temple be spared?" The answer given is that *Rabban* Yochanan, in his wisdom, realized that this request would not be granted, and that he would thereby stand to lose everything.

Rabban Yochanan brought all his surviving scholars to Yavneh and established a citadel for Torah and a means of restoring the shattered Jewish community of *Eretz Yisrael* as it groped toward reconstruction after the national tragedy. The last decade of his life was devoted to this holy work, and after his death, his five sterling students carried on this task as a new and great Sage appeared on the horizon: Rabbi Akiva. *Rabban* Yochanan had been proud of these five students, and described them in glowing terms: "Rabbi Eliezer ben Hurkanos is a cemented cistern which loses not a drop [of learning]; Rabbi Yehoshua ben Chananiah — happy is she who bore him; Rabbi Yosei *Ha-Kohen* — is truly pious; Rabbi Shimon ben Netanel is sin-fearing; Rabbi Elazar ben Arach is like a spring which ever increases its flow" (AVOT II:8).

Rabban Yochanan added: "If all the Sages of Israel were in one scale of the balance and Eliezer ben Hurkanos in the other, he would outweigh them all. Abba Shaul [however] said in his name: If all the Sages of Israel, including Eliezer ben Hurkanos, were in one scale of the balance, and Elazar ben Arach in the other, he would outweigh them all" (AVOT II:8). Each of these outstanding scholars contributed to the spread of Torah throughout Israel.

Rabbi Eliezer ben Hurkanos decided at the age of 22 to learn Torah, came to Jerusalem, and studied with *Rabban* Yochanan. Hurkanos, furious at what he saw as his son's desertion of his family, came to search for him in Jerusalem, intent on disinheriting him. Instead, upon seeing his son honored as a great scholar, he rewarded him richly. Rabbi Eliezer became a prominent teacher, and because of his amazing ability to retain what he learned from *Rabban* Yochanan, he was referred to as "Eliezer *Ha-Gadol*" (Eliezer the Great). His phenomenal erudition caused him to be so firm in his Halachic opinions that he refused to accept majority rulings when he felt they were incorrect. When this happened, he was then shunned by his fellow Sages, although many scholars learned in his yeshiva in Lod, and Rabbi Akiva was one of his great students. Rabbi Eliezer was married to Imma-Shalom, the daughter of the *Nasi Rabban* Gamliel of Yavneh. He lived to the age of 100. In the Mishnah we find over three hundred laws that are attributed to him, and many more in the *Baraitot*. It is told that when the Sages were visiting him at his deathbed they asked him a Halachic question, and he ruled "*Tahor*" (pure), thus passing away "in purity" (SANHEDRIN 68a).

Rabbi Yehoshua ben Chananiah, born in Jerusalem during the time of *Rabban* Gamliel the Elder, was from birth saturated with Torah. It is said that his mother would bring him in his cradle to the *beit midrash* so that he could hear the words of Torah. He later learned from *Rabban* Yochanan and was a very close friend of Rabbi Eliezer, although on occasion they differed on Halachic rulings. He was a Levite and served as a chanter in the Temple. Accompanying *Rabban* Yochanan to Yavneh, he served there as the Head of the Court and, like his teacher, mastered a great deal of general knowledge, which he used to great advantage in his discussions with Roman dignitaries, including the Emperor himself.

He was a noted astronomer, expert in calculation of the holidays. Once a controversy arose between the better-informed Yehoshua and the *Nasi*, *Rabban* Gamliel, as to the exact date of Yom Kippur. In order to demonstrate his own authority, *Rabban* Gamliel ordered Rabbi Yehoshua to appear in his weekday garb on the very day which Rabbi Yehoshua had calculated to be Yom Kippur. Although Yehoshua obeyed, the *Nasi*'s colleagues were greatly vexed at his behavior and deposed him, replacing him with the 18-year-old Elazar ben Azariah. Later, all were reconciled, the *Nasi* was restored to his post, Rabbi Elazar was appointed Head of the Court and Rabbi Yehoshua left and established his yeshiva in the Galilee town of Peki'in.

Like many of the other Sages, Rabbi Yehoshua refrained from earning his living from Torah; he was a blacksmith and lived in poverty.

Convinced that the mighty Roman Empire could not be defeated, he advised caution to those who wanted to wage war, citing a parable: "A lion, while eating from the meat of his kill, got a bone stuck in his throat and called out: 'Whoever will remove the bone shall be rewarded amply.' In response, a heron with a long bill stuck its head into the lion's great mouth and removed the bone. 'Please pay me the reward as you promised!' requested the heron, whereupon the lion roared, 'Away with you! It is enough of a reward that henceforth you can boast that your head was in the lion's mouth and you removed it in peace'" (BERESHIT RABBAH 64:8).

Rabbi Yosei Ha-Kohen, designated by *Rabban* Yochanan as "truly pious," is praised even more profusely in *Avot d'Rabbi*

Natan, as "the most pious in that generation." His sincere and dedicated character is reflected in his words: "Let all your deeds be done in the name of Heaven" (AVOT II:12). In Tractate *Chagigah* 14b, it is related that Rabbi Yosei *Ha-Kohen* and Rabbi Yehoshua ben Chananiah were strolling along and discussing mysticism. As they began to talk about the matter of the blazing chariot (*ma'aseh ha-merkavah*) in Ezekiel, the skies suddenly clouded over, an unusual occurrence in *Eretz Yisrael* in the summer, and something like a large bow appeared in the heavens as angels hovered overhead to hearken to their words. Later, when they related this incident to *Rabban* Yochanan, he blessed them both with great enthusiasm.

Rabbi Shimon ben Netanel, praised by *Rabban* Yochanan as "sin-fearing," was a priest who was known for his devotion to service and prayer. He stressed the importance of prayer recited at the proper time and with care, suppliance and devotion. Gentle and loving as well as sin-fearing, he cautioned that self-criticism, while helpful for the improvement of character, should not be carried to extremes. "Do not be wicked in your own esteem," he warned (AVOT II:13). He was the son-in-law of *Rabban* Gamliel the Elder.

Rabbi Elazar ben Arach, the most brilliant of *Rabban* Yochanan's five outstanding students, outshone all the others in his response to his teacher's two questions as to "which is the right way to which a man should cling" and "what is the evil way from which a man should distance himself" (AVOT II:9). His answer was the most acceptable because it was thorough and all-embracing. "A good heart" was his first answer, and "an evil heart" his second. His brilliance is illustrated in other matters as well. In Tractate *Chagigah* 14b, it is recorded that when Rabbi Elazar, in the company of his teacher and with his approval, began a discourse on the mysticism surrounding the blazing chariot, a fire descended from the heavens and encircled all the trees, which in turn began to sing Psalms. *Rabban* Yochanan then kissed Rabbi Elazar on the forehead, declaring: "Blessed is the Almighty who has granted such a son to our father Abraham...and blessed is Abraham to have had such a son." Clearly the study of mysticism was encouraged by *Rabban* Yochanan.

When he lost his very talented son and sat mourning, *Rabban* Yochanan's students tried to comfort him, but to no avail. Then, it is told, "Rabbi Elazar came and recited an apt parable: 'There was once a very distinguished man to whom the king entrusted a precious, valuable object. Each day the man watched over and cared for it with great concern and responsibility, knowing he must return the object in the perfect condition in which he had received it. You, as well, my teacher, have raised a son who was a great scholar, as pure and without sin as he was when you received him. You have served the King well, and returned His gift without blemish.' *Rabban* Yochanan responded, 'Elazar, my son, you have comforted me'" (AVOT D'RABBI NATAN 14:1).

After the passing of *Rabban* Yochanan, while all the other scholars remained in Yavneh, Rabbi Elazar succumbed to the urging of his wealthy wife and moved to the resort town of Emmaus, and there, isolated from his Torah learning, he lapsed into forgetfulness. His colleagues later prayed for him, and, we learn, "Elijah came and restored his learning" (YALKUT KOHELET § 973).

In *Avot* IV:14, we read: "Rabbi Nehorai says: Go into voluntary exile to a place where there is Torah, and do not say that it will follow you." This is actually attributed to Rabbi Elazar, because of his personal experience. "We learned: 'His name is not Nehorai...rather is his name Elazar ben Arach'" (SHABBAT 147b).

RABBI TARFON

A priest both from his mother's and his father's side, Rabbi Tarfon served in the Temple and lived until fifty years after its destruction. He learned Torah from *Rabban* Gamliel the Elder, as well as from *Rabban* Yochanan ben Zakkai. He was quite wealthy, very generous with *tzedakah*, and friendly toward everyone; the people held him in very high regard. In *Yerushalmi Yevamot* 4:12 and *Yerushalmi Horayot* 3:2, we read: "Rabbi Tarfon is the father of all Israel," and "Rabbi Tarfon is the *Rabban* of all Israel." Regarded as one of the outstanding Sages of Yavneh, he founded his yeshiva in the town of Lod, as did Rabbi Eliezer.

Rabbi Yehudah *Ha-Nasi* related: "Rabbi Tarfon could be properly called 'a mound of nuts'! When a person takes one nut from a mound, the rest roll down upon it. So it is when a student asks a question of Rabbi Tarfon — a mound of related information from Torah, Mishnah, *Halachah* and *Aggadah* descends upon him and he leaves filled with blessings and a wealth of knowledge" (AVOT D'RABBI NATAN 18:1).

Rabbi Tarfon's concern for others was legendary; it is said that once, when a bride passed his house, he invited her in and had his wife bathe her, perfume her, and dress her in fine clothes. During a famine, he used a "legal mechanism" to provide food and sustenance to three hundred women by "marrying" them so that they would be eligible to eat from *terumah* (the obligatory offering of produce to a priest, permitted to be eaten only by the priestly family) (YERUSHALMI YEVAMOT 4:12).

He held his gifted student, Rabbi Akiva, in very high esteem, declaring, "Anyone who parts from you, it is as if he parts from his life" (TOSEFTA MIKVA'OT, end of chapter 1). In his council in Lod was adopted the *halachah*, accepted to this day, that a Jew is required to sacrifice his life only in circumstances where he is forced to commit any one of three violations: "idolworship, forbidden relations, and murder" (SANHEDRIN 74a).

HILLEL, *see page 140*.

Chapter III

AKAVIA BEN MAHALALEL

Akavia ben Mahalalel, a contemporary of *Rabban* Gamliel the

Elder and *Rabban* Yochanan ben Zakkai, lived for sixty years preceding the destruction of the Temple and some ten years afterwards. He learned Torah from Shemayah and Avtalyon and from Hillel. He was known as an erudite scholar and a sin-fearing person. That he was a man of principle is indicated by the fact that, although he was offered the position of Head of the Court if he would but recant on four Halachic matters in which he differed from the Sages, he refused the offer; he did not want to give the impression that he recanted because of his desire for personal gain. Nevertheless, upon his deathbed, he demonstrated his scrupulous integrity by instructing his son to recant on these four matters, explaining that while his son heard the ruling from a minority (himself), the Sages had heard their version from a majority. Avtalyon himself had heard his view from other Sages (a majority), and therefore maintained his opinions (EDUYOT, MISHNAH 5:6,7).

His statement in *Avot* III:1 is recited at every funeral: "Know whence you came, and where you are going, and before Whom you are destined to render a strict accounting," which is itself based upon a statement in Ecclesiastes 12:1: "Remember your Creator." The word *Borecha* (your Creator) is used in three senses: *Be'ercha* — your source; *Borcha* — the pit to which you go; and *Borecha* — your Creator, to Whom you will give an account (MIDRASH RABBAH VAYIKRA 18:1).

RABBI CHANINA

Rabbi Chanina served as Deputy to the High Priests, as we learn from the discussion recorded in *Yoma* 39a, on the question of a High Priest who is disqualified from serving on Yom Kippur. Living in an era of great upheaval, he witnessed the deterioration of Jewish life in *Eretz Yisrael*, the baseless hatred, strife and dissension that led to the destruction of the Second Temple. After the destruction, he became a reliable source of information on conduct in the Temple, for those who had not merited to see the Service with their own eyes. He also related many miracles that had occurred in connection with the Menorah during his service in the Temple. Pained and saddened by the terrible conflicts of his time and the personal and national tragedies he had witnessed, he preached peace to all. His statement in *Avot* III:2 — "Pray for the welfare of the government, since were it not for the fear of it, men would swallow each other alive" — reflects these feelings, as do statements in *Sifri Naso* 42:6: "'And He shall bring upon you peace' (NUMBERS 6:26) — in your coming in and going out, and with all persons. Rabbi Chanina...says: 'And He shall bring upon you peace' — in your household"; "Rabbi Chanina says: 'Great is peace, for it is equated with Creation.'" He is listed in *Megillat Ta'anit* as a martyr: "On the 25th of Sivan *Rabban* Shimon ben Gamliel, Rabbi Ishmael, and Rabbi Chanina, Deputy to the Priests, were executed."

RABBI CHANINA (CHANANIAH) BEN TERADYON

Rabbi Chanina ben Teradyon lived during the difficult period of Hadrian's harsh decrees, an oppressive time which followed Bar Kochba's disastrous uprising against the Romans. Despite Roman decrees against teaching Torah, Rabbi Chanina conducted a prominent yeshiva in Sichni. He was well-known as a *tzedakah* collector and as a communal leader. To combat the dearth of study that resulted from the Roman decree, he taught his classes in public; Torah learning, he wanted to stress, should not be left to the few but should be widespread. His close friend Rabbi Yosei ben Kisma warned him that the Romans would not tolerate this practice and would surely "burn you together with the *sefer Torah*" (AVODAH ZARAH 18a).

This is precisely what happened — Rabbi Yosei's grim warning proved prophetic. The Romans arrested Rabbi Chanina and executed him with great cruelty: they wrapped a Torah scroll around him and set it on fire. To increase his suffering, they put moist wool around his heart, to delay his death. It is recorded that his daughter wept, "Father — woe that I should see you in this condition!" But Rabbi Chanina consoled her: "The One Who will avenge the honor of the Torah will avenge me as well." His students called out to him through the flames, "Rabbi, what do you see?" Rabbi Chanina replied, "The scrolls are burning, but the letters continue to float in the air." His executioner, overwhelmed by the enormity of Rabbi Chanina's courage and faith, requested, "Rabbi, if I make the fire stronger and remove the moist wool, thereby mercifully hastening death, will you take me with you to the world Above?" Rabbi Chanina agreed, whereupon the executioner performed his compassionate deed, leapt into the pyre himself and died with Rabbi Chanina. A Heavenly voice was heard saying: "Rabbi Chanina...and his executioner are both welcome to the world Above." Rabbi Yehudah *Ha-Nasi* wept, saying, "One may earn his share in the World-to-Come within an hour [for doing a good deed] and another may do so only after many, many years" (AVODAH ZARAH 18a).

Rabbi Chanina's wife and son also were executed and one of his daughters was sent to a house of ill repute. She was later rescued by her brother-in-law, Rabbi Meir, who was married to Bruriah, her sister. His courageous act of rescue forced Rabbi Meir to seek refuge in Babylonia from Roman wrath.

RABBI SHIMON BAR (BEN) YOCHAI

Rabbi Shimon, one of the five outstanding students of Rabbi Akiva, was among the survivors of Bar Kochba's revolt against Rome. As a young man, he studied at Kerem B'Yavneh, and later he spent thirteen years studying with Rabbi Akiva at his yeshiva in Bnei Brak. We learn from the *Yerushalmi Sanhedrin* 1:2 that in those times it was customary for the *Rosh Yeshiva* to designate his successor. *Rabban* Yochanan ben Zakkai had appointed Rabbi Eliezer and Rabbi Yehoshua; Rabbi Yehoshua appointed Rabbi Akiva; and Rabbi Akiva appointed both Rabbi Meir and Rabbi Shimon. He commented: "If Rabbi Meir sat in the head seat, Rabbi Shimon's face would pale." Rabbi

Akiva comforted Rabbi Meir for having to share the office, saying: "It is sufficient for you if I and your Creator know well your talents." There was great mutual regard and respect between teacher and student, and Rabbi Shimon used to tell his students: "My sons, observe my conduct and act accordingly, for these are the ways I learned from Rabbi Akiva" (GITTIN 67a).

Both Rabbi Shimon and his son suffered the consequences of words spoken hastily and without caution in those perilous times. It is related that at a gathering Rabbi Yehudah praised the Romans, declaring: "They have improved the markets, repaired the roads, and opened bathhouses." Rabbi Yosei made no comment, but Rabbi Shimon responded in anger: "All that they have done was done for their own needs and benefit. They improved the markets and placed therein harlots; they repaired the roads in order to collect more tolls; and they opened bathhouses for their own gratification." A certain Yehudah, who was the son of a convert, was sitting nearby; later he repeated this discussion to his family and friends — and it eventually reached Roman ears. The Governor decreed: "Rabbi Yehudah, who praised us, shall be raised in stature. Rabbi Yosei, who was silent, shall be exiled to Sepporis. And Rabbi Shimon, who insulted us and our achievements, shall be put to death."

Rabbi Shimon and his son Elazar fled into hiding in a cave near Peki'in in Upper Galilee. Miraculously, a carob tree and a fresh-water spring were nearby, and from these they were sustained for the twelve years that they remained in hiding, studying Torah together. It is said that Elijah the Prophet appeared at their cave and informed them when it was safe for them to leave. As they walked through the Galilee together, watching the people at work in their fields, Rabbi Shimon turned to his son and remarked, "What a pity these people are wasting their time farming, rather than devoting themselves to spiritual matters." Whereupon they were ordered from the Heavens above to return to their cave for another year. The year passed, and once again they walked together through the countryside. Soon they came upon an old man carrying two bunches of fragrant greens. "What are you going to do with these?" they inquired. "I am going to honor the Sabbath," was the reply. "And why do you need two bunches?" they asked. "One for *zachor* [remember] and one for *shamor* [observe]," was the prompt answer. Rabbi Shimon, moved and gratified, turned to his son, remarking, "Do you see how our people love the mitzvot?" (SHABBAT 33b, 34a). Both were now reconciled to the normal conduct of life combined with the observance of mitzvot.

Rabbi Shimon played a leading role in the communal life of Israel, and on occasion represented the people in dealing with the Romans. To him is attributed authorship of the *Sifri* and the *Zohar*. In the Mishnah alone there are 323 laws recorded in his name. His yeshiva was located in Meron, north of Safed; Rabbi Yehudah *Ha-Nasi* was his favorite student. Rabbi Shimon died at the age of 80, and was buried on Mount Meron, as was his son Elazar. To this day, hundreds of thousands of visitors come to their grave sites on *Lag Ba-Omer*, the anniversary of his death, to recite special prayers, dance and sing, light torches, and pay their respects to these two great *tzaddikim*. His famous statement (SHABBAT 118b): "If only Israel were to observe two consecutive Sabbaths properly, the Redemption would come immediately," is as meaningful today as it was in his time.

RABBI CHANINA (CHANANIAH) BEN CHACHINAI

One of Rabbi Akiva's gifted students, Rabbi Chanina was among those who were privileged to learn from their teacher not only the regular curriculum of Torah studies but also the hidden mystical truths contained in the flaming chariot of Ezekiel and what are called in the Talmud the "secrets of Creation" (CHAGIGAH 14b). Together with his close friend Rabbi Shimon bar Yochai, he spent thirteen years at Rabbi Akiva's yeshiva in Bnei Brak.

It is told that during this time Rabbi Shimon kept in close contact with his family, but Rabbi Chanina did not. One day word reached Rabbi Akiva that Rabbi Chanina's daughter was about to be married, and that her father was not taking any part in the wedding arrangements. Rabbi Akiva took this to heart and, with sensitivity, subsequently announced: "Anyone who has a daughter to marry off should leave in order to do so." Rabbi Chanina understood, and set off for the home he had not seen for many years. But over the course of time he had forgotten exactly where it was; in his searchings, he arrived at the local well, where people were drawing water, and heard someone address a young girl as *"Bat Chanina"* (the daughter of Chanina). He followed her home, and as he entered, unannounced, his wife saw him and immediately fell dead. Rabbi Chanina prayed: "Master of the Universe, is this the reward for this pious woman who waited thirteen years for her husband?" Immediately his prayer was answered and she was restored to life. About her it was said: "The expression in Genesis, 'I shall create a helpmate for man,' refers to a wife like Rabbi Chanina's" (BERESHIT RABBAH 17:3). He is listed as one of the Ten Martyrs executed by the Romans; at his death he was ninety-five years old.

RABBI NECHUNIA BEN HA-KANAH

Rabbi Nechunia was a student of *Rabban* Yochanan ben Zakkai, and was held in high esteem by his colleagues. Because he lived to a ripe old age, his students would inquire of him: "To what do you attribute your longevity?" His response was as follows: "I never sought honor at the expense of my friends; I never retired for the night with a person's curse upon me; and money matters never concerned me" (MEGILLAH 28a). A similar question was put to him by "young" Akiva, whereupon Rabbi Nechunia, regarding the query as disrespectful, ordered the "youngster" away. Akiva, from the vantage point of a palm tree, then posed another question to Rabbi Nechunia: "Why does the Torah state 'one sheep,' when the word used [*keves*] is the singular form for 'sheep,' and it is clear that one is meant?" Rabbi Nechunia, impressed by the question, replied, "'One sheep' means one special sheep for a sacrifice." Recognizing Akiva as a scholar, he then answered Akiva's question about his longevity. "All my life," he explained, "I refused to accept gifts, as it is written, 'One who despises gifts will live long' (PROVERBS 14:27); I never sought honor, and money matters were of no concern to me" (MEGILLAH 28a). Like some of his colleagues, he too delved into the hidden secrets of mysticism; he is known to have composed the daily prayer *Ana b'Cho'ach*, which contains mystical titles for the Almighty.

RABBI CHALAFTA BEN DOSA OF KFAR CHANANIAH

Rabbi Chalafta was a student of Rabbi Meir, and it is he whom Rabbi Meir quoted on Halachic matters in *Bava Metzia* 94a. He was the father of two great scholars, Rabbi Yosei and Rabbi Shimon. His village, Kfar Chananiah, is located in Western Galilee; Rabbi Chalafta and his two sons are buried there. In *Avot* III:6, he emphasizes the accompaniment of the Divine Presence whenever and wherever Jews are engaged in the study of Torah.

RABBI ELAZAR BEN YEHUDAH OF BARTOTA

Rabbi Elazar was the student of Rabbi Yehoshua ben Chananiah, and was a close associate of Rabbi Akiva. A ruling in Rabbi Elazar's name is quoted by *Rabban* Shimon ben Gamliel and Rabbi Shimon bar Yochai in Mishnah *Orlah* 1:4. His statement in *Avot* III:7 sets the principle of *tzedakah*: that what one gives is only that which the Almighty has loaned to him, for both we and what we have are His. Because he practiced what he preached to such an extent, it is told that *tzedakah*-collectors would avoid him, not wanting to cause him to give away all that he had. But on one occasion, he caught up with them and insisted that they tell him the cause for which they were collecting. When he heard that the collection was for the marriage of two orphans, he immediately gave them all the money in his possession, which in fact he had intended to be for his own daughter's trousseau. We read that thereupon his house was filled with wheat, a wonder merited only by a true *tzaddik* (TA'ANIT 24a).

RABBI DOSTAI BEN RABBI YANNAI

Rabbi Dostai was a devoted student of Rabbi Meir, whom he quoted repeatedly. His talents lay more in the realm of *Aggadah* — homiletic exposition — than in *Halachah*. He was an accomplished speaker whose keen sense of humor delighted his students and his audience; a number of his witty sayings are recorded in the Talmud.

"Why does the man pursue the woman?" his students inquired. Rabbi Dostai (perhaps with a twinkle in his eye) replied, "Take, for example, a person who loses a very valuable object — who looks for whom? Obviously, the man looks for the lost object [his rib]" (NIDDAH 31b). To his students' question: "Why aren't the hot springs of Tiberias in Jerusalem?" his apt answer was: "So that the pilgrims who come up to Jerusalem on the Festivals won't say, 'If the trip was only for the purpose of bathing in the hot springs — it would have been sufficient!'" (PESACHIM 8b). Both the Jerusalem and the Babylonian Talmud relate his experiences on his trips to Babylonia.

RABBI MEIR

Rabbi Meir, the most brilliant of all of Rabbi Akiva's outstanding students, was the dominant personality in *Eretz Yisrael* in the middle of the second century C.E. Neither his place of birth nor his parentage is recorded. In Tractate *Gittin* 56a, it is related that the Emperor Nero had converted to Judaism and one of his descendants was the Torah genius Rabbi Meir. Others say that Meir — "one who enlightens" — was not his name, but rather a description of his erudition and of the "light" which Rabbi Meir cast for his and all the future generations. He received his Rabbinical ordination from Rabbi Akiva, but because he and four of his fellow students were actually considered too young for ordination at the time, Rabbi Yehudah ben Babba later ordained all five, for which "crime" he was executed by the Romans (all aspects of religious observance were subject to the death penalty). Rabbi Meir, Rabbi Yehudah, Rabbi Yosei, Rabbi Shimon and Rabbi Elazar, the surviving remnant of Rabbi Akiva's 24,000 students (who, we are told, "were lost because they did not give proper respect to each other" — a possible hint and censor cover for "lost in the war with Bar Kochba against the Roman enemy"), are credited with saving Torah in a most critical period in Jewish history.

Rabbi Meir played a great part in the final composition of the Mishnah, according to Rabbi Akiva — Rabbi Meir's own Mishnah laid the foundation for the final form assembled by Rabbi Yehudah *Ha-Nasi*. The Sages agreed: "Where there is no source ascribed to a particular *mishnah*, it may be assumed to be that of Rabbi Meir." It is recorded that Rabbi Meir was a great teacher and a spellbinding speaker. His technique was one from which teachers in every generation could learn. He divided his presentation into three parts: one third *Halachah*, one third *Aggadah*, and one third parables. About him it was reported that he used no less than three hundred parables about the fox.

According to many sources, he was both inspired and inspiring. "Anyone who has seen the unforgettable Rabbi Meir in the *beit ha-midrash*," it is recorded, "it was as if he were taking great mountains and smashing them one into the other" (SANHEDRIN 24a).

Rabbi Meir earned his living as an expert scribe; he was reputed to know the entire Torah by memory. It is said that once, on Purim, when he was stranded in a city outside of *Eretz Yisrael* and there was no *Megillah* to read, he sat down and promptly wrote the entire *Megillah* from memory (MEGILLAH 18b).

In this troubled era, Rabbi Meir bore a substantial share of sorrow and disappointment. One of his dearest and most beloved teachers, Rabbi Elisha ben Avuyah, strayed from Judaism and, while others shunned him, Rabbi Meir continued to befriend him and learn from him, convincing him in the end to return to his faith (TOSAFOT, CHAGIGAH 15:1 FROM THE YERUSHALMI). When some of his colleagues criticized him for his continued association, others replied: "He [Rabbi Meir] found a pomegranate, has eaten its contents and has disposed of the peelings."

Yalkut Shimoni, Mishlei 31, relates the well-known, sorrowful episode in the life of Rabbi Meir and his wife Bruriah, who was known as an outstanding scholar in her own right. While Rabbi Meir was lecturing at the *beit midrash* after *minchah* (the afternoon prayer service) on the Sabbath, his two sons died at home. Later, Rabbi Meir returned home and inquired: "Where are our two sons? I did not see them in the *beit midrash*." Bruriah remained silent and handed him his wine cup; he chanted *Havdalah* (the blessings recited at the close of the Sabbath) and then again asked where his sons were. Bruriah explained their absence somehow and gave her husband supper. When he was finished, she asked him: "Rabbi, I have a question. Someone gave me a valuable object for safekeeping — must I return it?" "Of course," replied Rabbi Meir. "You must return it." She remarked, "If not for your reply, I would have hesitated [to act in this manner]." Tenderly she took his hand and led him to the other room where his two sons lay dead. He wept and cried out, "My sons — my teachers!" Whereupon Bruriah said: "But did you not say that we are obligated to return valuable objects to their owner?" He replied sadly: "The Almighty has given; the Almighty has taken. May the Name of the Almighty be blessed" (JOB 1:21).

As related above, Bruriah and her sister were daughters of the martyr, Rabbi Chanina ben Teradyon. Her sister had been taken by the Romans to a house of ill repute, and Rabbi Meir, risking his life, offered a large sum of money to the guard if he would release the girl. "If there is any trouble," Rabbi Meir assured the hesitant guard, "cry out: 'God of Meir, save me,' and you will be saved." For further assurance, Meir threw a stone at a pack of threatening dogs who were approaching, shouting: "God of Meir, save me!" The dogs ran away immediately, and the guard was thereby convinced of the truth of Rabbi Meir's words, and Rabbi Meir saved his sister-in-law. Nevertheless, as a result of this daring rescue, he was forced to flee and seek refuge in Babylonia (AVODAH ZARAH 18a). He lived out his years in exile. Before his death, he expressed his desire to be buried in *Eretz Yisrael*, but until that would become possible, he wanted his coffin to be temporarily buried at the seashore, where he would lie near the very waters that also washed the shores of *Eretz Yisrael*. (YERUSHALMI KILA'IM 9:3).

RABBI CHANINA BEN DOSA

"A voice from Heaven calls out daily: 'The entire world is sustained because of the merit of my son Chanina; yet my son Chanina suffices with a measure of carob from the eve of one Sabbath to the eve of the next'" (TA'ANIT 24b). This is one of the many quotations in the Talmud that testify to the piety and righteousness of Rabbi Chanina, to whom the entire community looked when aid was needed. Rabbi Chanina learned from *Rabban* Yochanan ben Zakkai, who recognized the unique qualities of his gifted student. In Tractate *Berachot* 34b, it is recorded that *Rabban* Yochanan's son became critically ill, and that the anguished father turned to Chanina with a plea: "Chanina, my son, please pray for mercy for my sick son." Accordingly, Chanina placed his head between his knees and prayed for the welfare of the ailing boy, who recovered immediately. *Rabban* Yochanan's wife, astonished that her husband's prayers would presumably be unanswered while Chanina's were heeded, asked: "Is Chanina more important than you?" Replied *Rabban* Yochanan: "You see, there is a difference between us. Chanina is like a faithful servant to a king — he can enter at any time [to care for sundry matters];

whereas I am like a minister before a king [who enters when summoned on matters of state]."

A similar incident is recorded about Rabbi Chanina's prayer for another ailing son — this time the son of *Rabban* Gamliel. Even as *Rabban* Gamliel's messengers approached him, it is said, Rabbi Chanina informed them of the boy's instant recovery. Amazed, they recorded the exact time of Rabbi Chanina's report and upon their return, found that the boy had indeed recovered at that precise moment (BERACHOT 34b).

Distressed by the fact that a poisonous snake frequented their house of study, Rabbi Chanina's students told him of the problem. It is said that Rabbi Chanina immediately proceeded to the snake's hole and placed his foot over it, whereupon the snake bit him, and died instantly. Rabbi Chanina brought the dead snake to the *beit midrash* and declared: "It is not the snake that kills, but rather the sin that kills" (the snakebite is the punishment). From then on it was said: "Woe unto the person bitten by the snake, and woe to the snake 'bitten' [touched] by Rabbi Chanina" (BERACHOT 33a).

Upon his death, his colleagues sadly commented: "With the demise of Rabbi Chanina there ceased to be righteous people of his stature" (SOTAH 49a). His way of life was typified by his teachings, in which he urged his students to concentrate on the performance of good deeds which are pleasing both to man and to the Almighty.

RABBI DOSA BEN HARKINAS

Rabbi Dosa ben Harkinas merited great longevity; he lived before, during and after the lifetime of *Rabban* Yochanan ben Zakkai, who himself lived to the age of 120. The Sages came to him for advice on many occasions; one involved the controversy between Rabbi Yehoshua ben Chananiah and *Rabban* Gamliel of Yavneh, regarding the fixing of the correct date for Yom Kippur. Rabbi Dosa advised that Rabbi Yehoshua concede to the *Nasi*'s opinion, for otherwise, he said, "one can question authority all the way back to Moshe *Rabbenu*" (ROSH HASHANAH, MISHNAH 2:9).

Another incident involved Rabbi Yehoshua, Rabbi Elazar and Rabbi Akiva. We learn of Rabbi Dosa's advanced age and of his great wealth by the story of their visit to him: He seated them on "seats of gold," it is said, and then recalled fond memories from distant times. About Rabbi Yehoshua, he remembered how his mother would bring his cradle to the *beit midrash* so that the infant Yehoshua would hear words of Torah. About Rabbi Elazar, he recalled his father Azariah well, saying that he was the ninth generation from Ezra, "and his eyes were just like those of Ezra" (YERUSHALMI 1:6).

To Rabbi Akiva he declared: "You are the great Akiva ben Yosef, whose fame is spread from one end of the world to the other? May there be many more like you in Israel" (YEVAMOT 16a).

RABBI ELAZAR HA-MODA'I

Rabbi Elazar, a student of *Rabban* Yochanan ben Zakkai, was from the town of Modi'in, home of the Hasmoneans. His talents in *Aggadah* were such that *Rabban* Gamliel once stated: "We most certainly need [Rabbi Elazar] Ha-Moda'i, who can centralize ideas into one place" (CHULLIN 92a).

Rabbi Elazar was the uncle of Bar Kochba and prayed and fasted in Beitar for the success of his nephew's ill-fated uprising against Rome. The following is told about his death: For three-and-a-half years, Hadrian laid siege to the stronghold of Beitar without success, and finally decided to withdraw his forces. At that crucial point, a renegade Cuthite approached him and told him that as long as Rabbi Elazar lived, Beitar could not be conquered. He offered to bring about Rabbi Elazar's death, and Hadrian, eager for victory, readily agreed.

The Cuthite planned his action with great cunning. He sneaked into Beitar through the sewage ducts, and approached the praying Rabbi Elazar, pretending to whisper into his ear.

Bar Kochba's soldiers seized the Cuthite who then "confessed" that he had passed information to Rabbi Elazar regarding the surrender of the city. Bar Kochba immediately questioned his uncle, who explained that he had been praying and heard nothing. But Bar Kochba suspected him of betrayal, and in anger kicked him, killing Rabbi Elazar on the spot. It is said that Bar Kochba was punished greatly for this: Beitar fell, and its thousands of casualties included Bar Kochba himself, whose body was found encircled by the poisonous snake that had caused his death.

RABBI ISHMAEL (BEN ELISHA)

In his youth, Rabbi Ishmael was captured and taken prisoner to Rome. It is recorded that Rabbi Yehoshua ben Chananiah, on a visit to Rome, heard that a bright young Jewish boy was being held captive there. Concerned, he approached the prison and in order to determine the truth of what he had heard, called out in the direction of Ishmael's window part of a sentence from the prophet Isaiah. The young Ishmael promptly completed the verse, whereupon Rabbi Yehoshua collected and paid a large ransom to free the youth. He then took him back to *Eretz Yisrael*, taught him, and produced a great scholar.

Rabbi Ishmael also learned from Rabbi Eliezer, and was a colleague of Rabbi Akiva. It is Rabbi Ishmael who established the thirteen principles of logic which are the foundation of Torah learning and interpretation and which we recite in our daily prayers. A well-organized scholar, he laid down several other rules for Torah study which were to enlighten students for the generations to come: "The Torah speaks in the language of men" (BERACHOT 31b); "There is not necessarily a chronological sequence in the Torah" (PESACHIM 6b); "Whenever there is a repetition in the Torah, there is something new to be learned therefrom" (SOTAH 3a).

In Tractate *Nedarim* 66a, an incident is recorded which is typical of Rabbi Ishmael. A man vowed that he would not wed his niece, because of her unattractive appearance. When Rabbi Ishmael heard of this, he took the girl into his household and the womenfolk "made her beautiful." He then brought her back to her uncle, and inquired: "Is it against this beauty that you vowed?" "Certainly not," replied the overjoyed uncle and promptly married her. Rabbi Ishmael wept and declared: "All the daughters of Israel are beautiful. It is only poverty which detracts from their appearance." When Rabbi Ishmael passed away, it is said that all the daughters of Israel mourned him, saying: "We weep for our patron, Rabbi Ishmael" (NEDARIM 66a).

RABBI AKIVA BEN YOSEF

In Tractate *Menachot* 29b, we read that Rav reports in the name of Rabbi Yehudah: "When Moses our Teacher went up to Heaven, he found the Almighty, blessed be He, sitting and affixing crowns to the letters of the Torah. Said Moses: 'Who prevents you from presenting the Torah as it is [without affixing the crowns on the letters, especially since we humans would not understand their significance in any case]?' Answered the Almighty: 'There is one person in the coming generations, Akiva ben Yosef by name, who is destined to explain every line and sign that I make in the Torah.' Moses requested: 'Master of the Universe, please show him to me.' Came the reply: 'Proceed to his time and place.' Moses took his place in Rabbi Akiva's classroom, in the eighth row, and listened to the discussion — but he could not understand what was being said, and he despaired. Just then a student asked: 'What is your source?' And Rabbi Akiva replied: 'It is the *Halachah* given to Moses on Sinai.' Then was Moses comforted. He returned to the Almighty and immediately declared: 'Master of the Universe, You have a person as great as that and You choose to give the Torah through me?' Came the answer: 'It is not for you to question.' Continued Moses: 'You have shown me his learning of Torah — now, please, show me his reward.' Moses looked upon the scene where the martyred Rabbi Akiva's flesh was being cut with iron combs by the Roman executioners (as meat in a butcher shop is cut). He asked in wonder: 'Master of the Universe, is this the proper reward for great Torah learning?' Replied the Almighty: 'Silence. It is not for you to question.'"

This rich and meaningful Talmudic account imparts the essence of the life and influence of Rabbi Akiva, one of the most outstanding scholars and leaders in all of Jewish history. His beginnings were extremely humble and he retained his inherent humility throughout the 120 years of his life. His name is linked with the redeemers of Judaism and of Torah learning in all generations, from Moses to Ezra, to Hillel, to *Rabban* Yochanan ben Zakkai — each of whom lived for 120 years and during critical periods in our history, in which they provided the necessary leadership and guidance that would nurture Torah learning. It is said that Rabbi Akiva's father, Yosef, was a convert who did not provide his son Akiva with any formal education, but was nevertheless privileged to appreciate his son's great achievements.

Akiva, a widower, was inspired to start learning Torah at the age of forty, together with his young son. While he was working as a shepherd, caring for the flocks of the wealthy Kalba Savua in Jerusalem, his master's daughter Rachel observed his kindness and humility and fell in love with him. Recognizing his potential greatness, she offered to marry him on the condition that he go and study Torah.

Their marriage took place despite the stubborn disapproval of Kalba Savua, who immediately disowned his daughter. Stripped of her wealth, they struggled to eke out a living, as described in *Ketubbot* 62b and 63a. We read that they slept on straw, which would become entangled in Rachel's beautiful hair, and as Akiva picked the straw from her hair he vowed to her that the day would come when he would purchase for her a gold brooch — called "A Jerusalem of Gold."

Rachel's vision of her husband's greatness proved true indeed; he learned at the yeshivot of Rabbi Yehoshua ben Chananiah and of Rabbi Eliezer ben Hurkanos, who had been students of *Rabban* Yochanan ben Zakkai. Within twelve years, Akiva himself had acquired 12,000 students. Then, upon returning home, he overheard an elderly person speaking harshly to Rachel, saying: "What kind of life is this for you? You are a living widow — your husband has been away learning for twelve years already." Rachel retorted with pride: "And I wish that he would learn for another twelve years." Rabbi Akiva, hearing Rachel, turned around without entering the house and went back for further study.

After twenty-four years, Rabbi Akiva had already acquired 24,000 students throughout the land, and he was returning to Jerusalem. By now his fame had spread far and wide. As his wife prepared to greet him, her neighbors offered her clothing that was more attractive than her worn-out garments, but she refused, quoting: "A *tzaddik* knows well the soul of his favored ('cow')" (PROVERBS 12:10). As her revered husband approached, she ran forward and fell to the ground to kiss his feet. Not realizing who she was, his students hastened to remove her, but Rabbi Akiva intervened, declaring emotionally: "Leave her! All that is mine and that is yours — my Torah learning and yours — are truly hers."

Kalba Savua, in the meantime, had regretted disowning his daughter, and when he heard that a great scholar had arrived in Jerusalem, he hastened to meet with him in order to have his vow annulled. Rabbi Akiva listened to his request, and then inquired: "If your son-in-law had been a scholar, would you have made such a vow?" "Certainly not," replied Kalba Savua. "If he had known even one sentence, I would have accepted him as a son-in-law." Rabbi Akiva declared: "Your vow is annulled. I am your son-in-law." Family unity was restored.

Throughout the Talmud, there are six references to Rabbi Akiva's having acquired great wealth. Active as both a collector and donor of *tzedakah*, he set an example of proper conduct for his many students. His maxim that Torah study must of necessity lead to mitzvot and acts of lovingkindness was borne out in his own behavior.

This truth is illustrated by an incident in which Rabbi Akiva visited a student who had become ill. When he saw the neglected state of the patient and his surroundings, he cleaned the room, washed his student, and fed him. The student, much refreshed and encouraged, joyously declared: "My teacher, you have restored me to life!" When Rabbi Akiva returned to the *beit midrash*, he taught: "One who fails to visit the sick — it is as if he sheds blood" (NEDARIM 40a).

Rabbi Akiva was known not only for his great erudition in Judaic studies but for his knowledge of science, medicine, agriculture, and languages as well. He was proficient in the study of mysticism, that which is termed *Pardes* (an orchard) in Tractate *Chagigah* 14b. There we read of four who "entered the orchard," but only one was to benefit from its fruit. Elisha ben Avuyah was "injured" (lost faith); ben Azzai died; ben Zoma found it too intensive and suffered thereby; and only Rabbi Akiva entered the study in peace and left it in peace.

Rabbi Akiva was much influenced by a third teacher, Nachum *Ish Gamzo*, whose total faith and resulting optimism were moving and impressive under the difficult circumstances prevailing in those days of harsh Roman domination. Nachum *Ish Gamzo* was known for his statement: *"Gam zo l'tovah,"* which means that whatever God does is ultimately for the best. Rabbi Akiva demonstrated the wisdom of this philosophy with the following incident: Once he set out on a journey, taking with him a donkey, a rooster and a candle. Arriving at a city, he was denied lodging, so he camped outside in the countryside. As he settled down, a strong wind blew and extinguished the candle. Rabbi Akiva told himself: "Whatever God does, He does for the best." Next came a cat and ate the rooster. Rabbi Akiva repeated the thought. Then came the greatest calamity of all: a lion attacked and devoured his donkey. Undaunted, he declared aloud, "Whatever God does, He does for the best."

Rabbi Akiva then slept, and the next morning he learned that during the night bandits had attacked the city, robbing and murdering the inhabitants. He reflected: "Had my candlelight been seen, or had my rooster crowed and my donkey brayed, the bandits surely would have discovered me and killed me as well. Verily, whatever God does, He does for the best" (BERACHOT 60b).

An active supporter of the extended struggle against Rome (132-135 C.E.), Rabbi Akiva aided Bar Kochba with funds and the recruiting of soldiers among his own students, who were possibly decimated in the ill-fated uprising. A period of semi-mourning for them is observed between Pesach and Shavuot.

In defiance of the Romans and despite the warnings of friends, he continued to hold his classes in public. To those who thought his behavior foolhardy, he explained with a parable: A fox was strolling along a river bank, and noticed that the fish were swimming hurriedly downstream. The fox asked them: "From what danger are you fleeing?" Replied the fish: "From the fishing nets that the people are casting." Offered the fox: "Why don't you come ashore and we can live together in peace, as did your forefathers and mine?" Scoffed the fish in derision: "And you are said to be the wisest of animals? Not only are you not wise, but you are an outright fool! If, in our own natural habitat, we are afraid, how much more so would we fear for our lives on dry land — where we cannot possibly survive!" (BERACHOT 61b). Rabbi Akiva thus tried to demonstrate that remaining in his own "natural habitat" — Torah — was the only choice.

Shortly thereafter, he was arrested and jailed in Caesaria. On Yom Kippur he was executed with the cruelty and violence typical of the Romans. In front of his students and colleagues, his flesh was torn with iron combs. As death approached and it came time to say the *Shema*, his students cried out: "Our teacher, even to this degree [of suffering]?" Replied Rabbi Akiva: "All my life I have recited in my prayer of *Shema*: 'And you shall love the Lord your God...with all your *soul*...' and I always wondered when I could possibly observe this mitzvah properly. Now my opportunity has come. Shall I not observe it?" He recited the *Shema*, drawing out the last word until his soul was taken Heavenward.

Rabbi Akiva left his mark on his generation and those that followed. He had written a Mishnah (putting the Oral Law into writing — lest it be forgotten during those years of terror when learning was forbidden), which was supplemented by his student Rabbi Meir, and finally codified by Rabbi Yehudah *Ha-Nasi*. Rabbi Akiva's five youngest students, whom he had ordained before they were of the proper age, were again ordained by Rabbi Yehudah ben Babba, who suffered a martyr's death for this deed. These great students spread Torah throughout the entire Land of Israel. In both the Jerusalem and the Babylonian Talmud, there are altogether some 614 references to Rabbi Akiva in *Halachah, Aggadah*, parables, and cogent statements.

RABBI ELAZAR BEN AZARIAH

Rabbi Elazar ben Azariah was a great scholar and the son of a great scholar. Held in high regard as a community leader as well, he was said to be a tenth-generation descendant of Ezra. At the age of eighteen he was considered sufficiently erudite to be the unanimous choice of the Sages to replace the *Nasi* Gamliel, who was removed as a result of his having shown disrespect for Rabbi Yehoshua ben Chananiah on three occasions. (After a reconciliation between *Rabban* Gamliel and Rabbi Yehoshua, however, *Rabban* Gamliel was restored to his former position.)

Tractate *Berachot* 28a relates that Rabbi Elazar, conscious of his extreme youth, prayed for some gray hair to appear in his beard, and that his prayer was granted. His classic commentary in the *Haggadah* refers to his youth: "It is as if I were 70 years of age...."

He was among the outstanding Sages at Yavneh, but in his later years he moved to Sepporis in the Galilee. He was aptly described by his student Isi ben Yehudah as a "container of all that was pleasant" (GITTIN 16a), and by Rabbi Yehudah *Ha-Nasi* as a "'merchant's store' of all knowledge."

RABBI ELAZAR (BEN) CHISMA

A student of Rabbi Yehoshua and Rabbi Akiva, Rabbi Elazar Chisma was prominent among the Sages of Yavneh. Although he was particularly proficient in science and mathematics, he nevertheless considered these disciplines to be but supplements to Torah study (AVOT III:18). It is said that *Rabban* Gamliel, on a sea voyage with Rabbi Yehoshua, marveled at the latter's knowledge of astronomy; whereupon Rabbi Yehoshua declared: "If you think I have great knowledge, you should surely recognize the vast scientific knowledge of Rabbi Elazar and Rabbi Yochanan ben Gudgada, who can calculate even the drops in the sea — and both of them are starving." Upon his return, *Rabban* Gamliel immediately summoned the two scholars and offered them positions in Yavneh. Both refused, declaring humbly that they were not worthy of the honor. *Rabban* Gamliel chided them, saying: "You think I am giving you honors? Not at all! I am rather giving you servitude, for one who serves the public need is perforce a servant to the public" (HORAYOT 10a-b).

Although Rabbi Elazar was a brilliant scholar, he was not trained to lead the congregation. Once, when visiting a community, he was invited to be the *chazan* (cantor), and in great embarrassment he pleaded ignorance, never having performed in this capacity. Some rude congregants made derogatory remarks about him which caused him much sorrow, and he immediately went to Rabbi Akiva and related his experience to him. Rabbi Akiva took him in hand and taught him what he didn't know. Some time later, when Rabbi Elazar was visiting that same community, he was invited once again to lead the congregation, and he led them admirably. They responded: "Rabbi Elazar *'nechsam'* [was strengthened]." This may explain the name "Chisma," which is from the same Hebrew root; or "Chisma" may have been his father's name.

Chapter IV

BEN ZOMA and BEN AZZAI

Ben Zoma and ben Azzai shared many similar attributes. Both were called Shimon, and both learned Torah with an unmatched avidity that apparently absorbed them entirely. Neither married, and both died at an early age. Despite the fact that both were great scholars associated with the Sages of Yavneh, the giants of Torah — Rabbi Yehoshua, Rabbi Tarfon, Rabbi Elazar ben Azariah, and Rabbi Akiva — neither received Rabbinical ordination, and both were known by the names of their respective fathers, rather than by their own first names.

Both were popular lecturers renowned for their ability to expound on verses of the Torah with legends and homiletic interpretations. An example of this technique is provided in the Pesach *Haggadah*, wherein Rabbi Elazar ben Azariah quotes ben Zoma on the verse in Deuteronomy 16:3: "So that you shall remember the day of your Exodus from Egypt all the days of your life." "The 'days of your life' refers to mentioning the Exodus during our daily prayers, when we recite the *Shema*. 'All the days...' refers to the nights for mentioning the Exodus" (in prayers and in reciting the *Haggadah*) (BERACHOT 12b).

About ben Zoma it was said: "Whoever sees ben Zoma in his dream, it is said to be a good omen for acquiring wisdom" (BERACHOT 57b).

Both ben Azzai and ben Zoma joined Rabbi Akiva and Rabbi Elisha ben Avuyah in the study of mysticism, with disastrous results. Ben Zoma "delved deeply and was injured." Ben Azzai "delved deeply and died" (CHAGIGAH 14b). "Rabbi Yehoshua told his students: 'The other day I passed ben Zoma on the street and he failed to greet me. I fear he is not long for this world.' Shortly thereafter, he passed away" (CHAGIGAH 15a).

Even though ben Azzai was a student and close associate of Rabbi Akiva, he differed with him philosophically on occasion. Rabbi Akiva declared that the commandment: "You shall love your fellowman as yourself," was the most comprehensive principle in the Torah; ben Azzai claimed that the concept of the creation of man and his exalted position in God's world was of greater significance (TOSEFTA BERACHOT 7:7).

Ben Azzai stated: "Any Jew who does not observe the mitzvah to 'be fruitful and multiply,' it is as though he were shedding blood and diminishing the image [of the Almighty]." His students pointed out: "You preach well and yet you yourself do not observe what you preach." Ben Azzai acknowledged the inconsistency, remarking sadly: "What can I do? My soul is totally absorbed with Torah. The world will perforce be maintained by others" (YEVAMOT 63b). In Tractate *Ketubbot* 63a, it is recorded that ben Azzai was engaged to Rabbi Akiva's daughter, who, following in her mother's footsteps, encouraged him to study more Torah. The marriage was apparently never consummated; a quotation from *Tosafot* in *Yevamot* states that they were married and later divorced. His perfect piety was acknowledged in *Berachot* 17b: "Whoever sees ben Azzai in his dream, it is a good omen for acquiring piety."

RABBI LEVITAS, "MAN OF YAVNEH"

As his designation indicates, Rabbi Levitas was one of the Sages of Yavneh, and he studied under the tutelage of Rabbi Yehoshua ben Chananiah. His statement (AVOT IV:4) emphasizing the importance of humility is the only *mishnah* bearing his name, although there are other references to Rabbi Levitas in the Rabbinic literature.

RABBI YOHANAN BEN BEROKA

Rabbi Yochanan, one of the Sages of Yavneh and an outstanding student of Rabbi Yehoshua, is mentioned over ten times in the Mishnah. It is related that he and his close friend, Rabbi Elazar (ben) Chisma, went to Peki'in to make a call upon their Rabbi, who was then residing there. Knowing that they had come from Yavneh, Rabbi Yehoshua inquired: "Whose Sabbath [whose turn to preach] was it?" They replied, "That of Rabbi

Elazar ben Azariah." "And what new message did he deliver?" asked Rabbi Yehoshua. Not wanting it to appear that they followed a teacher other than their own, they replied: "We drink from the springs of our teacher, Rabbi Yehoshua." "Nevertheless," he insisted,"I want to hear." Whereupon they related Rabbi Elazar's interpretation of the commandment that men, women, and children are all required to attend the *Hakhel* assembly during Sukkot in a Sabbatical year — "the men to learn, the women to hear, and the children to bring reward to those who brought them" (CHAGIGAH 3a). Declared Rabbi Yehoshua, "You brought a beautiful jewel with you, and you wished to hide it?"

Rabbi Yochanan is known for his support for women's rights. He interpreted the commandment to "be fruitful and multiply" as being incumbent upon both men and women (to be equally responsible and hence share the reward of the mitzvah) (YEVAMOT 65b). To his credit is a ruling that unmarried daughters, upon the demise of their father, must be supported by the heirs (KETUBBOT 49a). He is also recorded as cautioning against desecration of the Name of God that could occur during times of turmoil and crisis.

RABBI ISHMAEL BEN RABBI YOCHANAN (BEN BEROKA)

Rabbi Ishmael, the son of a distinguished scholar, became a distinguished scholar in his own right. He learned from his father and from the Sages in Yavneh, and he was a close associate of *Rabban* Shimon ben Gamliel the *Nasi*, whose *beit midrash* in Usha, in the Galilee, he frequented. His opinions are recorded in the Mishnah only three times, but appear many times in the *Tosefta* and in the *Baraitot*.

RABBI TZADOK

Rabbi Tzadok is a mystical figure who lived during one of the most tragic eras of our people. Anticipating the destruction of our Temple forty years prior to the event, he fasted constantly, subsisting on a single fig from one Sabbath to the next, in the vain hope that thus he would help to avert the tragedy. *Rabban* Yochanan ben Zakkai said of him that, "if there had been one more like Rabbi Tzadok, Jerusalem could never have been conquered" (MIDRASH RABBAH EICHAH 1:5). One of the three requests granted *Rabban* Yochanan by Emperor Vespasian was the provision of a doctor to cure the ailing Rabbi Tzadok.

From the days of Hillel, he had been a prominent scholar, and after the destruction of the Temple he continued his association with *Rabban* Gamliel in Yavneh, and was highly regarded.

In Tractate *Kiddushin* 32b, it is related that Rabbi Tzadok, in the exalted company of Rabbi Eliezer and Rabbi Yehoshua, attended a dinner for the son of *Rabban* Gamliel. The *Nasi* himself served these three distinguished personalities and Rabbi Eliezer, uncomfortable about it, asked his colleagues: "Is it proper that the *Nasi* should be serving *us*?" Rabbi Tzadok remarked: "If the Holy One, blessed be He, sends the winds and the rain and makes produce grow, thereby preparing a table of food for each person, should then the *Nasi* not serve us?"

RABBI YOSEI (BEN CHALAFTA)

Rabbi Yosei (or Yosi) was one of the five outstanding students of Rabbi Akiva who spread Torah learning in Israel during and after the oppression and evil decrees of the Romans. He was ordained by Rabbi Yehudah ben Babba along with Rabbi Meir, Rabbi Yehudah, Rabbi Shimon and Rabbi Elazar, and he was teacher and adviser to Rabbi Yehudah *Ha-Nasi*.

So meticulous was he in regard to his conduct and his avoidance of all controversy that he proved very effective in settling the conflicts of others, in particular the one involving Rabbis Meir and Natan with *Rabban* Shimon the *Nasi* (HORAYOT 13b).

Rabbi Yosei established his yeshiva in Sepporis, after having spent lengthy periods learning and teaching at Yavneh and

Usha. As was customary among the Sages then, he too was an artisan, a tanner by trade. His general knowledge was considerable and he even wrote a book on the history of the Jewish people, from Adam to the Bar Kochba uprising against the Romans, entitled *Seder Olam* (YEVAMOT 82b).

Rabbi Yosei was among the few of our Sages who, it is said, merited an occasional visit from Elijah the Prophet. As Rabbi Yosei himself related, he was once walking in Jerusalem, and entered a crumbling, disintegrating house in order to recite his prayers in private. When he walked out, he found waiting for him Elijah, who proffered the following three pieces of advice: "Never enter a wrecked structure; one may pray on the roadway; on the roadway one should recite the shortened version of the prayer" (BERACHOT 3a).

Rabbi Yosei was extremely proud of his five scholarly sons: Rabbis Ishmael, Elazar, Chalafta, Avtilas, and Menachem. "I have planted five cedars in Israel," he would declare (SHABBAT 118b).

Rabbi Yosei's famous discussion with a Roman matron is often quoted. The matron inquired: "In how many days did your God create the world?" "In six days," replied Rabbi Yosei. "And what has He been doing ever since?" posed the matron. "Making matches," answered Rabbi Yosei. "That's all?" scoffed the matron with a derisive laugh. "Why, I can do the same!" Immediately, it is said, she ordered her thousand manservants and her thousand maidservants to form two rows, whereupon she commanded: "Marry each other!" The next morning they all came to her crying and complaining — one with a broken leg, another blinded, and others with bruises and various injuries. She called upon Rabbi Yosei and acknowledged: "Great is your God. There is none like Him." Rabbi Yosei added: "Making matches is as difficult for God as the splitting of the Sea of Reeds" (BERESHIT RABBAH 68:4).

Over eight hundred Halachic rulings and declarations are found throughout the Mishnah and *Tosefta* in the name of Rabbi Yosei. When he died in Sepporis, it is said, "The rainspouts of Sepporis 'wept' with blood" (MO'ED KATAN 25b).

RABBI ISHMAEL BEN RABBI YOSEI

Rabbi Ishmael, Rabbi Yosei's devoted son, carried on his father's tradition in Sepporis. Both Torah study and comradeship comprised his close association with Rabbi Yehudah *Ha-Nasi*. Rabbi Ishmael idolized his father, and is quoted as saying: "Just as is the difference between gold and dust, so is the difference between my generation and the generation of my father" (YERUSHALMI GITTIN 10:7). But Rabbi Yehudah *Ha-Nasi* added: "Blessed is the generation, that both of you are in it" (YERUSHALMI MEGILLAH 4:1).

Serving as a judge in Sepporis, Rabbi Ishmael was extremely careful and scrupulous with regard to his conduct, lest there be even a shadow of a doubt about his impartiality. He took great pride in his achievements in Bible study, declaring: "I could write the entire Torah by heart [should it become necessary]" (YERUSHALMI MEGILLAH 4a).

RABBI YONATAN

Rabbi Yonatan was the devoted student of Rabbi Ishmael and, like his teacher, concentrated on Bible study. He is mentioned but once in the Mishnah, where he stresses the necessity of Torah study under any and all conditions, whether one is rich or poor. In the *Mechilta* on Exodus and in the *Sifri* on Numbers (an integral part of the teachings of Rabbi Ishmael), in contrast to the didactic instruction of Rabbi Akiva on every letter of the Torah, Rabbi Yonatan favored a more simplistic approach: "The Torah speaks in the language and [with the] concepts of the people" (SIFRI NASO 2:38).

RABBI ELIEZER BEN YA'AKOV

Rabbi Eliezer, one of Rabbi Akiva's surviving students, settled in Usha in the Galilee, to continue his studies and teaching. His Halachic rulings and opinions are recorded in several tractates in the Mishnah. In *Pirkei Avot* IV:11, he urges the performance of mitzvot and kind deeds.

In character with his teachings, Rabbi Eliezer is recorded as having performed the following act of kindness: Once a blind man came to Usha, and immediately Rabbi Eliezer seated him by his side and gave him his attention. The people of the town, following suit, lavished so much *tzedakah* upon this blind man that he wondered: "To what do I owe your generosity?" They replied: "When we noted the attention given you by Rabbi Eliezer, we knew you were worthy." The blind man then offered a prayer for Rabbi Eliezer: "You have performed an act of lovingkindness to one who is seen but cannot see. May He Who sees but cannot be seen grant you lovingkindness in return" (YERUSHALMI, END OF PE'AH).

A midrashic interpretation was given by Rabbi Eliezer to the verse in Hosea 2:1 in which Israel is likened unto sand "which cannot be measured nor counted." Rabbi Eliezer commented: "If one makes a substantial hole in the sand, he returns the next morning and finds the hole completely filled. So is it with Israel — in the time of David many fell, but in Solomon's time their numbers were restored" (PESIKTA D'RAV KAHANA 18.2). This was a consolation to the people in the context of the overwhelming losses suffered as a result of Bar Kochba's uprising (and can surely be applied to our time as well).

RABBI YOCHANAN HA-SANDLAR

Rabbi Yochanan Ha-Sandlar is reported to have come to *Eretz Yisrael* from Alexandria. The word *Ha-Sandlar* could indicate either that he was from Alexandria or that he was a shoemaker. Others attribute his name to the following incident involving the resolution of a Halachic question about the legitimacy of a particular case of levirate marriage (in which a symbolic ceremony involving a shoe is central). It is said that Rabbi Yochanan passed under the window of Rabbi Akiva's jail cell in Caesaria, pretending to be a peddler with a pack of shoes. Loudly peddling his wares, he managed to insert his question in the midst of his peddler's cries. Rabbi Akiva is reported to have answered the question in an equally clever fashion.

Rabbi Yochanan and the other remaining disciples of Rabbi Akiva met together in the Valley of Rimon to establish the order of the calendar. It was on this occasion that Rabbi Yochanan made his declaration that is quoted in *Pirkei Avot* IV:11: "Every assembly which is for the sake of Heaven [a noble purpose], will in the end endure."

During the period of Rome's harsh decrees, Rabbi Yochanan and his friend Rabbi Elazar ben Shammua decided to go to Netzivin in Babylonia, to study at the yeshiva of Rabbi Yehudah ben Beteira. When they crossed the northern border of *Eretz Yisrael* and reached Sidon, they burst into tears and decided to return immediately, declaring: "Living in *Eretz Yisrael* is equal to all the mitzvot in the Torah" (SIFRI R'EI 80:4).

RABBI ELAZAR BEN SHAMMUA

Rabbi Elazar was one of the five outstanding disciples of Rabbi Akiva, who, along with his colleagues, spread Torah throughout Israel during some of its darkest days. He is mentioned many times in the Mishnah; every reference to Rabbi Elazar is to Rabbi Elazar ben Shammua. He had set out with Rabbi Yochanan Ha-Sandlar on the way to Babylonia, but upon reaching Sidon changed his mind and returned to *Eretz Yisrael*, along with Rabbi Yochanan. His many students included Rabbi Yehudah *Ha-Nasi*, who reported: "When Rabbi Elazar taught, we had to squeeze in six to each *ammah* [18-inch space]" (ERUVIN 53a).

In *Kohelet Rabbah* 11:2, it is related that Rabbi Elazar was walking along the seashore, and noticed a shipwreck out at sea. Only one survivor reached the shore, naked and hungry. Rabbi Elazar assisted him, clothed him, and fed him. This man ultimately became Emperor, and during his reign issued harsh and evil decrees against the Jews. Sent by his people to plead on their behalf and to try to influence the Emperor, Rabbi Elazar approached him. The Emperor was so moved by the sight of his rescuer, that he canceled the decrees and rewarded Rabbi Elazar handsomely.

It is said of Rabbi Elazar that he loved his students dearly and took a personal interest in each and every one of them, as is evident in his statement in *Avot* IV:12: "Let the honor of your student be as dear to you as your own." One of his favorite students was Rabbi Yosef of Babylonia, who reported seeing his teacher, with tears streaming down his cheeks, declare with joy: "Blessed are you, my wise scholars, to whom the words of Torah are dearer than all else" (MENACHOT 18a). Peace and tranquillity were beloved to him: "Great is peace, for our prophets emphasized its benefits to all creation" (SIFRI NASO 6:26). Because he merited to live to a ripe old age, Rabbi Elazar's students were interested in his formula for longevity. He obliged them, confiding: "In all my days I was careful to be respectful of the congregation; I was never late to a class, so as not to disturb the students who were already seated; and I never lifted up my hands [to bestow the priestly blessing] without first reciting the benediction" (SOTAH 30a).

RABBI YEHUDAH BAR ILLAI

Rabbi Yehudah bar Illai was one of the five students of Rabbi Akiva who carried on after his death and after the deaths of virtually all the great scholars of the period. He lived in Usha and spread Torah throughout the Galilee. He had studied with Rabbi Tarfon, who referred to him as "my son," as well as with his father, Rabbi Illai. Among the attainments of his scholarship was the foundation for the *Sifra*, on Leviticus. Honored on all occasions as "first among speakers," he is referred to throughout the Mishnah, and the Halachic ruling is generally in accordance with his opinion. References to Rabbi Yehudah are always to Rabbi Yehudah bar Illai. Until his appointment as "head of the house of the *Nasi*," he lived in very humble circumstances, sharing his one cloak with his wife, and refusing offers of aid. So well-known was he for his lovingkindness that the Sages generalized: "Wherever a reference is made to *ish chasid*, it is either Rabbi Yehudah ben Babba, the martyr, or Rabbi Yehudah bar Illai" (BAVA KAMA 103b).

We mentioned earlier the unfortunate incident in which during a conversation Rabbi Yehudah praised Rome, Rabbi Yosei remained silent, and Rabbi Shimon bar Yochai spoke ill of the Romans, resulting in Rabbi Yosei's exile to Sepporis and Rabbi Shimon's thirteen years of hiding.

It is told of Rabbi Yehudah that although he was reluctant to leave his Torah studies for state occasions, he would leave them in honor of a wedding. "He would grasp a myrtle twig," we read, "and dance before the bride, chanting, '*Kallah, kallah* — beautiful and graceful bride'" (as today we dance before the bride) (KETUBBOT 17a).

Rabbi Yehudah enjoyed many fertile years of Torah teaching; he outlived most of his colleagues and was a light unto the younger generation that followed.

RABBI NEHORAI — RABBI NECHEMIAH

It is generally accepted that the personality known as "Rabbi Nehorai" was Rabbi Nechemiah. The description *Nehorai* ("light-giving") is an apt title for the man of whom it was said: "He was a light to the students of *Halachah*" (SHABBAT 147a). An associate of Rabbi Yehudah in Usha, he is mentioned in the Talmud and in the Midrash, together with Rabbi Yehudah or alone, over two hundred times. He differed with Rabbi Yehudah on the issue of teaching one's son a trade. While Rabbi Yehudah warned: "Whoever does not teach his son a trade, it is as if he were teaching him to steal" (KIDDUSHIN 30b), Rabbi Nechemiah insisted: "I put aside all trades in the world, and I shall teach my son only Torah, for one eats from its fruits in this world, but the principal remains for the World-to-Come — which is not the case with any other trade" (KIDDUSHIN 82b).

Rabbi Nechemiah lived in poverty all his life, eking out a meager living from his work as a potter. He was one of the students of Rabbi Akiva who gathered in the Valley of Rimon to set the calendar, and later settled in Usha to spread Torah. He was the compiler of the *Tosefta*, according to the teachings of Rabbi Akiva (SANHEDRIN 86a). Particularly proficient in *Aggadah* and Midrash, his interests also extended to mysticism, and he studied the mysteries of the prophet Ezekiel's chariot (SHABBAT 80b).

RABBI YANNAI

Rabbi Yannai lived at the end of the second century C.E., and was the distinguished student of Rabbi Yehudah *Ha-Nasi*, later becoming a member of his *Beit Din*. A descendant of Eli the High Priest, he was held in high regard by the entire community.

To Rabbi Yannai is credited the establishment of an innovative yeshiva in Achbra, a Galilee village near Sepporis, in which the students, in addition to their Torah study, worked in Rabbi Yannai's orchards, thereby earning their livelihood. He studied the Scriptures deeply, and eagerly sought midrashic commentary which would enlarge his knowledge of Torah. It is reported that he was puzzled by the connection of tale-bearing and leprosy (its punishment), until the following incident occurred and shed light on the matter: One day he overheard a peddler's cries: "Who wants a tablet for long life?" Rabbi Yannai beckoned to the peddler, who mumbled, "No, Rabbi, this is not for one of your stature." Intrigued, Rabbi Yannai insisted that the peddler show him his product, whereupon the peddler took out a book of Psalms and read: "Who is the person who loves life...guard your tongue from saying evil things...abandon the bad and do only what is good" (34:13). Upon hearing this verse, Rabbi Yannai suddenly understood clearly how to resolve what had been bothering him, and he was very grateful to the peddler for inadvertently clarifying the matter: for the word for "saying evil things" is *motzi-ra*, which resembles the word for "leper" — *metzora* (VAYIKRA RABBAH 16:2).

Some of the outstanding scholars of the first generation of *Amora'im* were students of Rabbi Yannai, including Rabbi Yochanan and Rabbi Shimon ben Lakish (Reish Lakish). Out of deep respect and honor he was called "Rabbi Yannai *Rabbah* (great)." He lived to an old age, and always observed the custom of dressing in his finest and going out to welcome the Sabbath, singing: "Enter, O Sabbath bride!" (SHABBAT 119a). (The song is recited to this day in our Sabbath eve prayers.)

RABBI MATIA BEN CHARASH

Rabbi Matia ben Charash was a student of Rabbi Eliezer ben Hurkanos and of Rabbi Elazar ben Azariah. Like Rabbi Yehudah ben Beteira and Rabbi Chananiah, he too left Israel to establish a yeshiva abroad. Rabbi Matia founded his yeshiva in Rome, and there developed scholars of note, establishing a significant reputation in the growing Jewish community in Rome as well as among the Romans themselves. His teachings also spread to *Eretz Yisrael*, and his advice which is recorded in *Avot* IV:15 — "Be the first to greet every man" (as a sign of respect and good relations) — is particularly applicable to Jewish communities which are surrounded by a non-Jewish majority, as was the case in Rome. He was buried in *Eretz Yisrael*.

RABBI YA'AKOV (BEN KURSHAI)

Rabbi Ya'akov was a student of Rabbi Meir and a teacher of Rabbi Yehudah *Ha-Nasi*. He is mentioned in the Mishnah and extensively in the *Baraitot*. His kindness was demonstrated in the role he played in the dispute between Rabbis Meir and Natan and the *Nasi, Rabban* Shimon ben Gamliel, on Halachic matters, wherein the former plotted to demonstrate the *Nasi*'s ignorance on the Tractate *Uktzin*, a very difficult subject. Rabbi Ya'akov, in order to caution the *Nasi* and save him from humiliation, sat by his open window beforehand and "reviewed" aloud the Tractate *Uktzin*. The *Nasi* understood the hint, and came fully prepared. The plotters were later punished by the Sages. Whenever Rabbi Ya'akov is mentioned in the sources, the reference is to Rabbi Ya'akov ben Kurshai. One of his well-known remarks is the oft-quoted: "Anyone without a wife lives without benefit, without assistance, without happiness, without blessings, and without forgiveness" (BERESHIT RABBAH 17:1).

RABBI SHIMON BEN ELAZAR

Rabbi Shimon was a dedicated student and disciple of Rabbi Meir, about whom he said: "The staff of Rabbi Meir was in my hand, and it taught me knowledge and understanding" (YERUSHALMI MO'ED KATAN 3:5). He was a close friend and associate of Rabbi Yehudah *Ha-Nasi*; and he outlived both his teacher and his friend. In *Pirkei Avot* he cautions sensitivity and consideration for the feelings of others (AVOT IV:23). He taught in *Derech Eretz Rabbah* 4.6: "A person should always strive to be as flexible [and bending] as a reed, rather than as hard as a cedar."

The above statement may reflect a very embarrassing experience which he once brought upon himself. As he was returning from a visit to his teacher in Migdal Eder, he proceeded along the seashore, filled with pride and self-satisfaction over the Torah study he had accomplished. One of the local residents passed and greeted him: "Shalom to you, Rabbi." Taken aback momentarily by the fellow's unappealing countenance, Rabbi Shimon cried out thoughtlessly: "My, how ugly you are! Are there others in your town just as ugly?" Shocked and hurt, the man retorted: "I will never forgive you, unless you go to my Maker and tell Him how ugly was the product of His hand." Realizing what a terrible thing he had done, Rabbi Shimon followed the man in the direction of his village, pleading for forgiveness — but in vain, for the man was adamant. Thus they reached the outskirts of the village, where a delegation came out to greet Rabbi Shimon, calling: "Rabbi, Rabbi, welcome!" "Just whom are you calling 'Rabbi, Rabbi'?" scoffed the man. "Why, the one behind you," they replied. "May there be no more like him in Israel!" he responded tersely, and then related to them the entire story. Noting that Rabbi Shimon was filled with regret and pleading for forgiveness, they urged the man to forgive him. He finally agreed, on condition that Rabbi Shimon agree never to make such remarks again.

Rabbi Shimon later commented that being as flexible and bending (humble) as a reed had its compensation, for the reed merited to be the source of the quill with which are written scrolls, *tefillin* and *mezuzot*.

SHMUEL HA-KATAN

Shmuel Ha-Katan (the small) lived in very humble circumstances. When he died, at a ripe old age, he left neither family, property, nor belongings. He had never received Rabbinical ordination; some felt that he was on such a high spiritual level that it would have been superfluous. His piety, modesty, and humility were legendary; it is said that the reason for his appellation "*ha-katan*" was that, in his extraordinary humility, he always made "little" of himself. Others offered an even more complimentary explanation: This Shmuel was but a bit "smaller" than the great prophet Shmuel. This evaluation is substantiated by an incident related in *Sanhedrin* 11a: "Once the Sages were gathered on a veranda in Yavneh, when suddenly a voice was heard from Heaven: 'There is one present here who is worthy that the *Shechinah* should dwell with him, but alas — his generation is not worthy of him.' All eyes turned to Shmuel Ha-Katan. When he died, they mourned: 'Pious one, humble one, a true likeness of Hillel.'"

At the request of *Rabban* Gamliel of Yavneh, Shmuel Ha-Katan composed the nineteenth blessing of the daily silent prayer, against heretics and slanderers. This blessing was composed in response to threats of the heretical Jewish sects active in his time, such as the Sadducees, early Christians and others.

It is told that *Rabban* Gamliel once convened a meeting of seven Sages in order to calculate the leap year — and, through apparent misunderstanding, eight appeared. *Rabban* Gamliel immediately requested: "Would whoever is here uninvited please leave." Shmuel Ha-Katan rose immediately, saying: "I am the one. I did not come to calculate the leap year with you; I simply came to learn how the mitzvah is done." *Rabban* Gamliel, knowing full well that Shmuel Ha-Katan was not the intruder, but was simply trying to prevent another's shame, responded kindly: "Sit, my son, sit with us. It is fitting that all of the required years be calculated by you" (SANHEDRIN 11a).

ELISHA BEN AVUYAH

Elisha ben Avuyah is surely one of the most tragic personalities among the Sages. He is one of the four who "entered the orchard" — the intense study of mysticism — delving into the account of Creation, the meaning of Ezekiel's chariot, the prophet Ezekiel himself, etc., and was thereby spiritually injured, ultimately abandoning the faith. His loyal student, Rabbi Meir, continued to study with his misguided teacher, hoping to help restore his faith and his stature as a great scholar. It is recorded that once, on the Sabbath, while Elisha rode his horse Rabbi Meir walked beside him and learned from him. As they reached the limit of the distance permitted to walk on the Sabbath, it was Elisha who reminded his student: "You have now reached the *techum Shabbat*. It is time for you to return." Rabbi Meir responded: "It is now time for *you* to 'return,' as well." "It is too late for me," replied Elisha sadly. Rabbi Meir then quoted Psalms to prove that the gates of repentance are always open. He then took his teacher to thirteen synagogues and had children cite similar quotations for him, but to no avail.

Nevertheless, Rabbi Meir refused to lose faith in his beloved teacher. It is told that as Elisha lay on his deathbed, he asked Rabbi Meir: "Will I be accepted in Heaven?" "You most certainly will be accepted," Rabbi Meir assured him. Elisha then wept, and died. Rabbi Meir felt joy, declaring: "Elisha died in repentance." Although Rabbi Meir was criticized by some of his colleagues for maintaining his relationship with Elisha, others admired his perseverance, explaining: "He [Rabbi Meir] found a pomegranate, has eaten its contents and has disposed of the peelings" (CHAGIGAH 15b). Most of Elisha's Halachic opinions are recorded as "Others declare..."

RABBI YOSEI BAR YEHUDAH

Rabbi Yosei bar Yehudah was a contemporary of Rabbi Yehudah *Ha-Nasi*, at the close of the second century C.E. He is described as a native of Kfar Ha-Bavli, a village not readily identifiable, but thought to be in the Galilee, which was the center of Torah study during that era. His comments in *Avot* IV:20 are the only ones that appear in the Mishnah. They indicate a respect for the Sages and an encouragement to follow their wise teachings, in preference to the younger scholars then appearing on the scene.

RABBI ELIEZER (OR ELAZAR) HA-KAPPAR

Rabbi Eliezar Ha-Kappar, one of the last of the *Tanna'im*, was also a contemporary of Rabbi Yehudah *Ha-Nasi*. He died before the birth of his son, who was called Eliezer bar Kappara in his memory. One of his pupils was the outstanding Sage, Rabbi Yehoshua ben Levi, who praised Rabbi Eliezer: "It is from him that I received answers to all of my questions" (CHULLIN 56b). Elsewhere he refers to Rabbi Eliezer as "the great one" (AVODAH ZARAH 43a). In addition to Rabbi Eliezer's comments in *Pirkei Avot* IV:21-22, he is also quoted in *Megillah* 29a, in which he expresses his enduring faith. "All the synagogues and *battei midrash* of Babylonia (and in the entire Diaspora) will one day be reestablished in *Eretz Yisrael*."

RABBI MEIR, *see page 163.*
RABBI SHIMON BAR (BEN) YOCHAI, *see page 158.*
RABBI YEHUDAH HA-NASI (RABI), *see page 146.*

Chapter V

YEHUDAH BEN TEIMA

Although Yehudah ben Teima's comments appear only once in *Pirkei Avot* V:20,21, they are much-loved and often-quoted:

"Be strong as a leopard, light as an eagle, swift as a deer, and mighty as a lion, to do the will of your Father Who is in Heaven. He used to say: The impudent is destined for Gehinnom and the shamefaced is destined for *Gan Eden*. May it be Your will, O Lord our God, that You rebuild Your city speedily in our days, and grant us our portion in Your Torah.

"He used to say: At five years of age [one is ready] for the study of Torah; at ten for the study of Mishnah; at thirteen, for the fulfillment of mitzvot; at fifteen, for the study of Talmud; at eighteen, for marriage; at twenty, for a career; at thirty, for strength; at forty, for understanding; at fifty, for giving counsel; at sixty, to reach old age; at seventy, the hoary head; at eighty, for strength in old age; at ninety, in decline; at one hundred, it is as if he had died and passed away and departed from this world."

In *Avot d'Rabbi Natan*, 41:11, Rabbi Yehudah states: "If you have done even a tiny injustice to your friend, let it be in your eyes like a major thing. If you have done to your friend a great deed, let it be in your eyes as a mere nothing. If your friend has done for you a very small favor, let it be in your eyes as if he had done a great thing. And if your friend has done you a grave injustice, let it be in your eyes as a small thing."

The Talmud pays tribute to him in *Chagigah* 14a: "The Sages interpreted 'the stay and the staff (ISAIAH 3:1) as follows: the stay are the masters of the Bible, and the staff are the masters of the Mishnah — like Rabbi Yehudah ben Teima and his associates."

BEN BAG BAG and BEN HEI HEI

Ben Bag Bag and Ben Hei Hei are the pseudonyms of two Sages who lived at the time of Hillel the Elder, about a century before the destruction of the Temple. Their names were kept secret to protect them from informers. It is said that they were converts, and some associate the two with those whom Hillel had converted. Their appellations can be explained as follows: The letters *beit* and *gimmel* in Hebrew stand for *ben ger* (son of a convert); the letter *hei* refers to Abraham and Sarah, to whose original names was added the *hei* at the time of Abraham's circumcision.

The comments of both Sages (AVOT V:22-23) are recorded in Aramaic, the widespread spoken language of the era throughout the Middle East; it is also the language of both the Babylonian and Jerusalem Talmud. It was customary in *Eretz Yisrael* then, when some of the scholars lectured publicly in Hebrew, to have an official translator (a *meturgeman*) present so that the people would understand.

The message of the two Sages — that the Torah contains all knowledge; that the more one studies, the more he realizes how much more there is to learn; and that the ultimate reward is related to the effort expended — reflects the teachings of Hillel.

Chapter VI

RABBI YEHOSHUA BEN LEVI

Rabbi Yehoshua was born in Lod and learned there from the Sages. At this time (about 200 C.E.) the Mishnah had already been assembled and completed by Rabbi Yehudah *Ha-Nasi*, and the *Tosefta-Baraitot* completed by Rabbi Chiyya. Rabbi Yehoshua was among the outstanding personalities in the first and second generations of *Amora'im*, along with Rabbi Chiyya, Rav, and Rabbi Yannai. While Rabbi Yehoshua's expertise was in *Aggadah* and homiletics, he was nevertheless involved in Halachic controversies. Countless quotations by him or attributed to him are found throughout both the Jerusalem and Babylonian Talmud, as well as in the *midrashim*. He was wealthy, and very active in public affairs as well as in *tzedakah*.

On one occasion, it is said, Rabbi Yehoshua, in the company of Rabbi Chiyya, appeared before the Roman Governor in Caesaria. As they entered, the Governor rose to honor them. His associates were astounded and asked in disdain: "For these

Jews you rise?" "Yes," replied the Governor, "for, as they entered, I saw the countenance of angels" (YERUSHALMI BERACHOT 6:5).

Exemplary in his piety, he fasted both on *Tisha B'Av* (the Ninth of Av) and on the next day as well, because, although the destruction began on the ninth, most of the Temple burned on the tenth of Av. He lived to a good old age and attributed his longevity to following the advice he gave his students: "One should always rise early, in order to be among the first ten in the synagogue, for even if one hundred come after him, his reward is as much as all of them" (BERACHOT 47b); and "Be among the first in the synagogue in the morning, and among the last to leave after the evening prayer. In this way you will merit length of days." It was he who instituted the recitation of the *Shema* prayer in bed before going to sleep for the night.

It is said that his great piety and humility merited him close contact with the prophet Elijah. Numerous tales are recorded of their conversations: Once, as they stood by the cave of Rabbi Shimon bar Yochai, Rabbi Yehoshua asked Elijah: "When is the Messiah coming?" "Go and ask him," was the reply. "But where can I find him?" "At the Roman Gate," was the answer. "How will I know him?" wondered Rabbi Yehoshua. Elijah declared: "The one who is bandaging the sick — that is the Messiah." Rabbi Yehoshua rushed to the gate, identified the Messiah and inquired anxiously: "When is the master coming?" "Today!" was the ready reply. But the day passed and the Messiah did not arrive, whereupon Rabbi Yehoshua returned to Elijah, claiming: "The Messiah is a liar — he said he would come today, and he did not come." Elijah explained: "You apparently did not understand him. He said: *'Today'* — that is true — but *today*, only if you follow all God's commandments!" (SANHEDRIN 98a).

On another occasion Rabbi Yehoshua accompanied Elijah on a journey, during which he witnessed four strange incidents that defied explanation. When Elijah explained all the incidents, in each case the facts were entirely different than what they appeared to be, and thus Rabbi Yehoshua understood that mankind cannot possibly comprehend the ways of the Almighty upon this earth.

Rabbi Yehoshua was one of the very few, in all our sources, who is said to have entered *Gan Eden* while still living. The incident is described in *Ketubbot* 77b. When the time came for Rabbi Yehoshua to die, the Angel of Death was instructed to grant him a last wish. Rabbi Yehoshua requested that he be shown his place in *Gan Eden*. The Angel agreed, and as they proceeded, Rabbi Yehoshua made another request: "Please let me hold your knife. It makes me nervous." The Angel of Death complied. Upon reaching their destination, the Angel lifted Rabbi Yehoshua to the height of the wall in order to show him his place in *Gan Eden*, whereupon Rabbi Yehoshua immediately leapt over the wall, directly into *Gan Eden*, vowing, "I swear that I shall not return!" The Angel, still holding on to Rabbi Yehoshua's coattails, complained to the Almighty, who replied: "If ever he has made a previous vow and asked that it be annulled, then he must leave." Rabbi Yehoshua stayed! The Angel then demanded: "Please, give me back my knife." But Rabbi Yehoshua absolutely refused. Came a voice from Heaven: "Return the knife to the Angel of Death, for the benefit of those whose time has come to leave the world."

RABBI SHIMON BEN MENASIA

Rabbi Shimon was a contemporary of Rabbi Yehudah *Ha-Nasi*. He and his close associate, Rabbi Yosei ben Ha-Meshullam, headed a group called the "Holy Congregation," whose daily schedule consisted of three parts: one third Torah study, one third prayer, and one third work. (Others have explained that the division consisted of Torah study during the winter, and work during the summer.) He is mentioned but once in the Mishnah, but repeatedly in the *Tosefta*.

He had two explanations for the *halachah* that treating the seriously ill (*pikuach nefesh*) takes precedence over Sabbath observance. He interpreted the injunction: "And you shall observe the Sabbath because it is holy to you" (EXODUS 31:14) to mean: "To you the Sabbath is turned over, but you are not to be turned over to the Sabbath" (your good health comes first) (MECHILTA, KI TISSA). In a *baraita* he adds: "It is worthwhile that one Sabbath be violated for a sick person, in order to enable him to observe many more Sabbaths."

RABBI YOSEI BEN KISMA

Rabbi Yosei was a contemporary of Rabbi Chanina ben Teradyon, who was one of the Ten Martyrs executed after the Bar Kochba uprising. Rabbi Yosei, in contrast, kept a low profile during this precarious period so as not to call the attention of the Romans to his teaching. He taught Torah in Caesarea, and preached peace and the avoidance of controversy. On one occasion, in a synagogue in Tiberias, he witnessed an argument between two Rabbis that was so heated it resulted in the accidental tearing of a Torah scroll. The peace-loving Rabbi Yosei ben Kisma declared in dismay: "I fear that one day this synagogue will be a place of idol worship." And so it later became (YEVAMOT 96b).

In *Pirkei Avot* VI:9, Rabbi Yosei rejects an offer of gold and silver, preferring to remain in a place where there is Torah rather than enjoy riches offered him in a place without Torah, for, he explains, "in the hour of man's departure, neither silver nor gold nor precious stones and pearls accompany him, but Torah and good deeds alone, as it is said... (PSALMS 119:72): 'The Torah of Your mouth is better unto me than thousands of gold and silver.'"

RABBI MEIR, *see page 163.*
RABBI SHIMON BAR (BEN) YOCHAI, *see page 158.*

RABBI CHANANIA BEN AKASHIA

Rabbi Chanania ben Akashia was the author of the *mishnah* at the end of Tractate *Sukkot*: "The Holy One, blessed be He, desired to bestow favor upon Israel; hence He gave them Torah and commands in large number, as it is said (ISAIAH 42:21): 'The Almighty was pleased for the sake of His righteousness to render the Torah increasingly great and glorious.'" This quote concludes each of the six chapters of *Pirkei Avot*.

פרקי אבות
PIRKEI AVOT

with English translation by
Samson Krupnick

This mishnah, and the concluding mishnah at the end of the chapter, are customarily recited before and after each chapter when *Pirkei Avot* is recited.

All Israel have a share in the World-to-Come, as it is said (ISAIAH 60:21): "Your people, all of them righteous, shall inherit the world forever; they are the flower of My plantings, the work of My hands, wherein I glory" (SANHEDRIN 10b).

CHAPTER I

1 Moses received the Torah from Sinai, and handed it down to Joshua, Joshua to the Elders, the Elders to the Prophets, and the Prophets handed it down to the Men of the Great Assembly. They declared three things: Be cautious in judgment; raise up many students; and make a fence for the Torah.

2 Shimon *Ha-Tzaddik* was of the last survivors of the Great Assembly. He used to say: On three things the world stands: on the Torah, on the Service of the Almighty, and on acts of lovingkindness.

3 Antignos of Socho received the tradition from Shimon *Ha-Tzaddik*. He used to say: Be not like the servants who serve their master for the sake of receiving a reward, but be like servants who serve their master not for the sake of receiving a reward; and let the fear of Heaven be upon you.

כָּל יִשְׂרָאֵל יֵשׁ לָהֶם חֵלֶק לָעוֹלָם הַבָּא, שֶׁנֶּאֱמַר (ישעיהו ס, כא) וְעַמֵּךְ כֻּלָּם צַדִּיקִים לְעוֹלָם יִירְשׁוּ אָרֶץ נֵצֶר מַטָּעַי מַעֲשֵׂה יָדַי לְהִתְפָּאֵר (סנהדרין י, ב).

פרק א

א מֹשֶׁה קִבֵּל תּוֹרָה מִסִּינַי וּמְסָרָהּ לִיהוֹשֻׁעַ וִיהוֹשֻׁעַ לִזְקֵנִים וּזְקֵנִים לִנְבִיאִים וּנְבִיאִים מְסָרוּהָ לְאַנְשֵׁי כְנֶסֶת הַגְּדוֹלָה: הֵם אָמְרוּ שְׁלֹשָׁה דְבָרִים, הֱווּ מְתוּנִים בַּדִּין וְהַעֲמִידוּ תַלְמִידִים הַרְבֵּה וַעֲשׂוּ סְיָג לַתּוֹרָה.

ב שִׁמְעוֹן הַצַּדִּיק הָיָה מִשְּׁיָרֵי כְנֶסֶת הַגְּדוֹלָה. הוּא הָיָה אוֹמֵר, עַל-שְׁלֹשָׁה דְבָרִים הָעוֹלָם עוֹמֵד, עַל הַתּוֹרָה וְעַל הָעֲבוֹדָה וְעַל גְּמִילוּת חֲסָדִים.

ג אַנְטִיגְנוֹס אִישׁ סוֹכוֹ קִבֵּל מִשִּׁמְעוֹן הַצַּדִּיק. הוּא הָיָה אוֹמֵר, אַל-תִּהְיוּ כַעֲבָדִים הַמְשַׁמְּשִׁין אֶת-הָרַב עַל-מְנָת לְקַבֵּל פְּרָס, אֶלָּא הֱווּ כַּעֲבָדִים הַמְשַׁמְּשִׁין אֶת-הָרַב שֶׁלֹּא עַל-מְנָת לְקַבֵּל פְּרָס וִיהִי מוֹרָא שָׁמַיִם עֲלֵיכֶם.

4 Yosei ben Yoezer of Tzeredah and Yosei ben Yochanan of Jerusalem received the tradition from them. Yosei ben Yoezer of Tzeredah says: Let your house be a meeting place for scholars, and cover yourself with the dust of their feet, and drink in their words with thirst.

5 Yosei ben Yochanan of Jerusalem says: Let your house be wide open, and let the poor be members of your household. Do not engage in gossip with a woman. This they said even regarding a man's own wife; how much more so of his neighbor's wife. From this source the Sages concluded: Whoever gossips with a woman brings trouble upon himself, and he neglects the study of Torah, and in the end will inherit Gehinnom.

6 Yehoshua ben Perachiah and Nittai of Arbel received the tradition from them. Yehoshua ben Perachiah says: Provide yourself with a teacher; acquire for yourself a companion; and judge every person favorably.

7 Nittai of Arbel says: Keep a distance from a wicked neighbor; and do not associate with an evil person; and do not give up your belief in retribution.

8 Yehudah ben Tabbai and Shimon ben Shatach received the tradition from them. Yehudah ben Tabbai says: In the function of judge do not act the part of the counsels; and while the litigants stand before you let them be as guilty in your eyes; but when they depart from you, let them be innocent in your eyes, once they have submitted to the judgment.

ד יוֹסֵי בֶּן־יוֹעֶזֶר אִישׁ צְרֵדָה וְיוֹסֵי בֶּן־יוֹחָנָן אִישׁ יְרוּשָׁלַיִם קִבְּלוּ מֵהֶם. יוֹסֵי בֶּן־יוֹעֶזֶר אִישׁ צְרֵדָה אוֹמֵר, יְהִי בֵיתְךָ בֵּית וַעַד לַחֲכָמִים וֶהֱוֵה מִתְאַבֵּק בַּעֲפַר רַגְלֵיהֶם וֶהֱוֵה שׁוֹתֶה בַצָּמָא אֶת־דִּבְרֵיהֶם.

ה יוֹסֵי בֶּן־יוֹחָנָן אִישׁ יְרוּשָׁלַיִם אוֹמֵר, יְהִי בֵיתְךָ פָּתוּחַ לִרְוָחָה וְיִהְיוּ עֲנִיִּים בְּנֵי בֵיתֶךָ וְאַל־תַּרְבֶּה שִׂיחָה עִם הָאִשָּׁה, בְּאִשְׁתּוֹ אָמְרוּ קַל וָחֹמֶר בְּאֵשֶׁת חֲבֵרוֹ. מִכַּאן אָמְרוּ חֲכָמִים כָּל־הַמַּרְבֶּה שִׂיחָה עִם הָאִשָּׁה גּוֹרֵם רָעָה לְעַצְמוֹ וּבוֹטֵל מִדִּבְרֵי תוֹרָה וְסוֹפוֹ יוֹרֵשׁ גֵּיהִנֹּם.

ו יְהוֹשֻׁעַ בֶּן־פְּרַחְיָה וְנִתַּאי הָאַרְבֵּלִי קִבְּלוּ מֵהֶם. יְהוֹשֻׁעַ בֶּן־פְּרַחְיָה אוֹמֵר, עֲשֵׂה לְךָ רַב וּקְנֵה לְךָ חָבֵר וֶהֱוֵה דָן אֶת־כָּל־הָאָדָם לְכַף זְכוּת.

ז נִתַּאי הָאַרְבֵּלִי אוֹמֵר, הַרְחֵק מִשָּׁכֵן רָע וְאַל־תִּתְחַבֵּר לָרָשָׁע וְאַל־תִּתְיָאֵשׁ מִן־הַפּוּרְעָנוּת.

ח יְהוּדָה בֶּן טַבַּאי וְשִׁמְעוֹן בֶּן שָׁטַח קִבְּלוּ מֵהֶם. יְהוּדָה בֶּן־טַבַּאי אוֹמֵר, אַל־תַּעַשׂ עַצְמְךָ כְּעוֹרְכֵי הַדַּיָּנִין וּכְשֶׁיִּהְיוּ בַּעֲלֵי הַדִּין עוֹמְדִים לְפָנֶיךָ יִהְיוּ בְעֵינֶיךָ כִּרְשָׁעִים וּכְשֶׁנִּפְטָרִים מִלְּפָנֶיךָ יִהְיוּ בְעֵינֶיךָ כְּזַכָּאִין כְּשֶׁקִּבְּלוּ עֲלֵיהֶם אֶת־הַדִּין.

9 Shimon ben Shatach says: Be persistent and thorough in examining the witnesses; and be careful with your words, lest through them they learn to falsify.

10 Shemayah and Avtalyon received the tradition from them. Shemayah says: Love work; and hate holding offices of authority; and do not seek intimacy with the governing officials.

11 Avtalyon says: Wise scholars, be careful with your words, for you may incur the penalty of *galut* [exile] and be exiled to a place of evil waters, and the students who follow you may drink from them with the result that the Name of Heaven would be profaned.

12 Hillel and Shammai received the tradition from them. Hillel says: Be of the disciples of Aaron, loving peace and pursuing peace, loving your fellow men and bringing them nearer to the Torah.

13 He used to say: He who covets a name will lose his name; and he who does not add to his knowledge decreases it; and he who does not study is deserving of death; and he who makes improper use of the crown of Torah shall pass away.

14 He used to say: If I am not for myself, who will be for me? And if I care only for myself, what am I? And if not now, then when?

Chapter I 205

ט שִׁמְעוֹן בֶּן־שָׁטָח אוֹמֵר, הֱוֵה מַרְבֶּה לַחֲקוֹר אֶת־הָעֵדִים וֶהֱוֵה זָהִיר בִּדְבָרֶיךָ שֶׁמָּא מִתּוֹכָם יִלְמְדוּ לְשַׁקֵּר.

י שְׁמַעְיָה וְאַבְטַלְיוֹן קִבְּלוּ מֵהֶם. שְׁמַעְיָה אוֹמֵר, אֱהַב אֶת־הַמְּלָאכָה וּשְׂנָא אֶת־הָרַבָּנוּת וְאַל־תִּתְוַדַּע לָרָשׁוּת.

יא אַבְטַלְיוֹן אוֹמֵר, חֲכָמִים הִזָּהֲרוּ בְּדִבְרֵיכֶם שֶׁמָּא תָחוֹבוּ חוֹבַת גָּלוּת וְתִגְלוּ לִמְקוֹם מַיִם הָרָעִים וְיִשְׁתּוּ הַתַּלְמִידִים הַבָּאִים אַחֲרֵיכֶם וְיָמוּתוּ וְנִמְצָא שֵׁם שָׁמַיִם מִתְחַלֵּל.

יב הִלֵּל וְשַׁמַּאי קִבְּלוּ מֵהֶם. הִלֵּל אוֹמֵר, הֱוֵה מִתַּלְמִידָיו שֶׁל־אַהֲרֹן אוֹהֵב שָׁלוֹם וְרוֹדֵף שָׁלוֹם אוֹהֵב אֶת־הַבְּרִיּוֹת וּמְקָרְבָן לַתּוֹרָה.

יג הוּא הָיָה אוֹמֵר, נְגִיד שְׁמָא אֲבַד שְׁמֵהּ וּדְלָא מוֹסִיף יָסֵף וּדְלָא יַלִּיף קְטָלָא חַיָּב וּדְאִשְׁתַּמֵּשׁ בְּתָגָא חֲלָף.

יד הוּא הָיָה אוֹמֵר, אִם אֵין אֲנִי לִי מִי לִי וּכְשֶׁאֲנִי לְעַצְמִי מָה אֲנִי וְאִם לֹא עַכְשָׁו אֵימָתַי.

15 Shammai says: Make your study of Torah a fixed activity; say little but do much; and receive every person with a kindly countenance.

16 *Rabban* Gamliel says: Provide yourself with a teacher, and liberate yourself of doubt, and do not give excess tithes through guesswork.

17 Shimon his son says: All my life I have grown up among the Sages, and I have found nothing better for the physical welfare of a person than silence; and the teaching and study of Torah are not the most important things, but rather the practice of Torah; and whoever speaks too much brings about sin.

18 *Rabban* Shimon ben Gamliel says: By virtue of three things does the world endure: truth and justice, and peace, as it is said (ZECHARIAH 8:16): "…administer the judgment of truth and peace within your gates."

Rabbi Chanania ben Akashia says: The Holy One, blessed be He, desired to bestow favor upon Israel; hence He gave them Torah and commands in large number, as it is said (ISAIAH 42:21): "The Almighty was pleased for the sake of His righteousness to render the Torah increasingly great and glorious" [SUKKOT].

טו שַׁמַּאי אוֹמֵר, עֲשֵׂה תוֹרָתְךָ קֶבַע אֱמֹר מְעַט וַעֲשֵׂה הַרְבֵּה וֶהֱוֵה מְקַבֵּל אֶת־כָּל־הָאָדָם בְּסֵבֶר פָּנִים יָפוֹת.

טז רַבָּן גַּמְלִיאֵל אוֹמֵר, עֲשֵׂה לְךָ רַב וְהִסְתַּלֵּק מִן הַסָּפֵק וְאַל־תַּרְבֶּה לְעַשֵּׂר אֲמָדוֹת.

יז שִׁמְעוֹן בְּנוֹ אוֹמֵר, כָּל־יָמַי גָּדַלְתִּי בֵּין הַחֲכָמִים וְלֹא מָצָאתִי לַגּוּף טוֹב מִשְּׁתִיקָה וְלֹא הַמִּדְרָשׁ עִקָּר אֶלָּא הַמַּעֲשֶׂה, וְכָל־הַמַּרְבֶּה דְבָרִים מֵבִיא חֵטְא.

יח רַבָּן שִׁמְעוֹן בֶּן־גַּמְלִיאֵל אוֹמֵר, עַל־שְׁלֹשָׁה דְבָרִים הָעוֹלָם קַיָּם עַל הָאֱמֶת וְעַל הַדִּין וְעַל־הַשָּׁלוֹם שֶׁנֶּאֱמַר אֱמֶת וּמִשְׁפַּט שָׁלוֹם שִׁפְטוּ בְּשַׁעֲרֵיכֶם.

❁ ❁ ❁

רַבִּי חֲנַנְיָא בֶּן־עֲקַשְׁיָא אוֹמֵר, רָצָה הַקָּדוֹשׁ בָּרוּךְ הוּא לְזַכּוֹת אֶת־יִשְׂרָאֵל לְפִיכָךְ הִרְבָּה לָהֶם תּוֹרָה וּמִצְווֹת. שֶׁנֶּאֱמַר יְיָ חָפֵץ לְמַעַן צִדְקוֹ יַגְדִּיל תּוֹרָה וְיַאְדִּיר.

CHAPTER II

1 *Rabi* [*Yehudah Ha-Nasi*] says: Which is the right course that a man should choose for himself? That which brings credit to one who adopts it, and brings him respect from men. And be as careful with a minor commandment as with a major one, for you do not know the reward given for the commandments. Balance the loss sustained in the performance of a commandment against its reward, and the gain derived from a sin against the loss it entails. Consider three things and you will not fall into committing sin: Know what is above you — a seeing eye, a listening ear, and that all your deeds are recorded in the Book.

2 *Rabban* Gamliel, the son of Rabbi Yehudah *Ha-Nasi*, says: The study of Torah together with an occupation is an excellent thing, for the effort in both areas averts sin. While all study of Torah which is not combined with work ultimately must fail and is

פרק ב

א רַבִּי אוֹמֵר, אֵיזוֹ הִיא דֶרֶךְ יְשָׁרָה שֶׁיָּבוֹר לוֹ הָאָדָם כָּל-שֶׁהִיא תִפְאֶרֶת לְעוֹשֶׂהָ וְתִפְאֶרֶת לוֹ מִן הָאָדָם, וֶהֱוֵה זָהִיר בְּמִצְוָה קַלָּה כְּבַחֲמוּרָה שֶׁאֵין אַתָּה יוֹדֵעַ מַתַּן שְׂכָרָן שֶׁל-מִצְוֹת, וֶהֱוֵה מְחַשֵּׁב הֶפְסֵד מִצְוָה כְּנֶגֶד שְׂכָרָהּ וּשְׂכַר עֲבֵרָה כְּנֶגֶד הֶפְסֵדָהּ. הִסְתַּכֵּל בִּשְׁלֹשָׁה דְבָרִים וְאֵין אַתָּה בָא לִידֵי עֲבֵרָה, דַּע מַה-לְמַעְלָה מִמְּךָ עַיִן רוֹאָה וְאֹזֶן שׁוֹמַעַת וְכָל-מַעֲשֶׂיךָ בַּסֵּפֶר נִכְתָּבִים:

ב רַבָּן גַּמְלִיאֵל בְּנוֹ שֶׁל-רַבִּי יְהוּדָה הַנָּשִׂיא אוֹמֵר, יָפֶה תַלְמוּד תּוֹרָה עִם דֶּרֶךְ אֶרֶץ שֶׁיְּגִיעַת שְׁנֵיהֶם מַשְׁכַּחַת עָוֹן וְכָל-תּוֹרָה שֶׁאֵין עִמָּהּ מְלָאכָה סוֹפָהּ בְּטֵלָה וְגוֹרֶרֶת עָוֹן וְכָל-הָעוֹסְקִים

conducive to sin. And all those who work for the community [should] do so only for the sake of Heaven, for the merit of their fathers will sustain them and their righteousness will endure forever. "As for you [says God], I credit to you a great reward, as if you had accomplished it all."

3 Be cautious with the ruling authorities, for they do not befriend a man except for their own interests; they appear as friends when it is to their advantage, but they do not support a man when he is in distress.

4 He used to say: Do His will as you would do your own will, so that He may do your will as He does His will. Put aside your will for the sake of His will, so that He may set aside the will of others before your will. Hillel says: Do not set yourself apart from the community; and do not rely on yourself alone until the day of your death; do not judge your fellowman until you have been in his position; do not say of anything that it cannot possibly be heard, for eventually it will be heard; do not say: "When I shall have leisure time I shall study," for you may never have leisure time.

5 He used to say: An ignorant man cannot be sin-fearing, nor can an unlearned man be pious; a timid man will not learn, and an impatient man cannot teach; and not everyone who is absorbed with business acquires wisdom; and in a place where there are no men, strive to be a man.

עִם־הַצִּבּוּר יִהְיוּ עוֹסְקִים עִמָּהֶם לְשֵׁם שָׁמַיִם שֶׁזְּכוּת אֲבוֹתָם מְסַיַּעְתָּם וְצִדְקָתָם עוֹמֶדֶת לָעַד וְאַתֶּם מַעֲלֶה אֲנִי עֲלֵיכֶם שָׂכָר הַרְבֵּה כְּאִלּוּ עֲשִׂיתֶם.

ג הֱווּ זְהִירִין בָּרָשׁוּת שֶׁאֵין מְקָרְבִין לוֹ לְאָדָם אֶלָּא לְצֹרֶךְ עַצְמָן נִרְאִין כְּאוֹהֲבִין בִּשְׁעַת הֲנָאָתָן וְאֵין עוֹמְדִין לוֹ לְאָדָם בִּשְׁעַת דָּחֳקוֹ.

ד הוּא הָיָה אוֹמֵר, עֲשֵׂה רְצוֹנוֹ כִּרְצוֹנְךָ כְּדֵי שֶׁיַּעֲשֶׂה רְצוֹנְךָ כִּרְצוֹנוֹ. בַּטֵּל רְצוֹנְךָ מִפְּנֵי רְצוֹנוֹ כְּדֵי שֶׁיְּבַטֵּל רְצוֹן אֲחֵרִים מִפְּנֵי רְצוֹנֶךָ. הִלֵּל אוֹמֵר, אַל־תִּפְרֹשׁ מִן־הַצִּבּוּר וְאַל־תַּאֲמִין בְּעַצְמְךָ עַד יוֹם מוֹתְךָ וְאַל־תָּדִין אֶת־חֲבֵרְךָ עַד שֶׁתַּגִּיעַ לִמְקוֹמוֹ וְאַל־תֹּאמַר דָּבָר שֶׁאִי אֶפְשָׁר לִשְׁמוֹעַ שֶׁסּוֹפוֹ לְהִשָּׁמַע וְאַל־תֹּאמַר לִכְשֶׁאֶפָּנֶה אֶשְׁנֶה שֶׁמָּא לֹא תִפָּנֶה.

ה הוּא הָיָה אוֹמֵר, אֵין בּוּר יְרֵא חֵטְא וְלֹא עַם הָאָרֶץ חָסִיד וְלֹא הַבַּיְשָׁן לָמֵד וְלֹא הַקַּפְּדָן מְלַמֵּד וְלֹא כָּל־הַמַּרְבֶּה בִסְחוֹרָה מַחְכִּים וּבַמָּקוֹם שֶׁאֵין אֲנָשִׁים הִשְׁתַּדֵּל לִהְיוֹת אִישׁ.

6 He also saw a skull floating on the surface of the water. He said to it: Because you have drowned others, you were drowned, and in the end those who have drowned you will themselves be drowned.

7 He used to say: The more flesh, the more worms in the grave; the more property, the more concern; the more wives, the more superstition; the more maidservants, the more lewdness; the more menservants, the more theft; but the more Torah study, the more life; the more study, the more wisdom; the more counsel, the more understanding; the more *tzedakah*, the more peace. One who has acquired a good name — has acquired it for himself; one who has acquired the words of Torah — has acquired for himself the life of the World-to-Come.

8 *Rabban* Yochanan ben Zakkai received the tradition from Hillel and Shammai. He used to say: If you have learned much Torah, do not take credit for yourself, for this is the purpose for which you were created. *Rabban* Yochanan ben Zakkai had five disciples, namely: Rabbi Eliezer ben Hurkanos, Rabbi Yehoshua ben Chananiah, Rabbi Yosei *Ha-Kohen*, Rabbi Shimon ben Netanel, and Rabbi Elazar ben Arach. He used to enumerate their merits: Rabbi Eliezer ben Hurkanos is a cemented cistern which loses not a drop; Rabbi Yehoshua ben Chananiah — happy is she who bore him; Rabbi Yosei *Ha-Kohen* — is truly pious; Rabbi Shimon ben Netanel is sin-fearing; Rabbi Elazar ben Arach is like a spring which ever increases its flow. He used to say: If all the Sages of Israel were in one scale of the balance and Eliezer ben Hurkanos in the other, he would outweigh

ו אַף הוּא רָאָה גֻלְגֹּלֶת אַחַת שֶׁצָּפָה עַל-פְּנֵי הַמָּיִם. אָמַר לָהּ, עַל דְּאַטִיפְתְּ אַטִיפוּךְ וְסוֹף מְטַיְפָיִךְ יְטוּפוּן.

ז הוּא הָיָה אוֹמֵר, מַרְבֶּה בָשָׂר מַרְבֶּה רִמָּה, מַרְבֶּה נְכָסִים מַרְבֶּה דְאָגָה, מַרְבֶּה נָשִׁים מַרְבֶּה כְשָׁפִים, מַרְבֶּה שְׁפָחוֹת מַרְבֶּה זִמָּה, מַרְבֶּה עֲבָדִים מַרְבֶּה גָזֵל, מַרְבֶּה תוֹרָה מַרְבֶּה חַיִּים, מַרְבֶּה יְשִׁיבָה מַרְבֶּה חָכְמָה, מַרְבֶּה עֵצָה מַרְבֶּה תְבוּנָה, מַרְבֶּה צְדָקָה מַרְבֶּה שָׁלוֹם. קָנָה שֵׁם טוֹב קָנָה לְעַצְמוֹ, קָנָה לוֹ דִבְרֵי תוֹרָה קָנָה לוֹ חַיֵּי הָעוֹלָם הַבָּא.

ח רַבָּן יוֹחָנָן בֶּן-זַכַּאי קִבֵּל מֵהִלֵּל וּמִשַּׁמַּאי. הוּא הָיָה אוֹמֵר, אִם לָמַדְתָּ תּוֹרָה הַרְבֵּה אַל-תַּחֲזִיק טוֹבָה לְעַצְמָךְ, כִּי לְכָךְ נוֹצָרְתָּ. חֲמִשָּׁה תַלְמִידִים הָיוּ לוֹ לְרַבָּן יוֹחָנָן בֶּן-זַכַּאי. וְאֵלּוּ הֵן: רַבִּי אֱלִיעֶזֶר בֶּן-הוֹרְקָנוֹס וְרַבִּי יְהוֹשֻׁעַ בֶּן-חֲנַנְיָה וְרַבִּי יוֹסֵי הַכֹּהֵן וְרַבִּי שִׁמְעוֹן בֶּן-נְתַנְאֵל וְרַבִּי אֶלְעָזָר בֶּן-עֲרָךְ: הוּא הָיָה מוֹנֶה שְׁבָחָם. רַבִּי אֱלִיעֶזֶר בֶּן-הוֹרְקָנוֹס בּוֹר סוּד שֶׁאֵינוֹ מְאַבֵּד טִפָּה רַבִּי יְהוֹשֻׁעַ בֶּן-חֲנַנְיָא אַשְׁרֵי יוֹלַדְתּוֹ רַבִּי יוֹסֵי חָסִיד רַבִּי שִׁמְעוֹן בֶּן-נְתַנְאֵל יְרֵא חֵטְא וְרַבִּי אֶלְעָזָר בֶּן עֲרָךְ מַעְיָן הַמִּתְגַּבֵּר. הוּא הָיָה אוֹמֵר, אִם יִהְיוּ כָּל-חַכְמֵי יִשְׂרָאֵל בְּכַף מֹאזְנַיִם, וֶאֱלִיעֶזֶר בֶּן-הוֹרְקָנוֹס בְּכַף שְׁנִיָּה מַכְרִיעַ אֶת כֻּלָּם: אַבָּא שָׁאוּל אוֹמֵר מִשְּׁמוֹ, אִם יִהְיוּ כָּל-חַכְמֵי יִשְׂרָאֵל בְּכַף מֹאזְנַיִם,

them all. Abba Shaul [however] said in his name: If all the Sages of Israel were in one scale of the balance, including Eliezer ben Hurkanos, and Elazar ben Arach in the other, he would outweigh them all.

9 He said to them: Go and see which is the right way to which a man should cling. Rabbi Eliezer says: A good eye. Rabbi Yehoshua says: A good friend. Rabbi Yosei says: A good neighbor. Rabbi Shimon says: One who has good foresight. Rabbi Elazar says: A good heart. He said to them: I prefer the words of Elazar ben Arach to yours, for your words are all included in his. He said to them: Go and see what is the evil way from which a man should distance himself. Rabbi Eliezer says: An evil eye. Rabbi Yehoshua says: A bad friend. Rabbi Yosei says: A bad neighbor. Rabbi Shimon says: One who borrows and does not repay, regardless of whether he borrows from man or from God, as it is said (PSALMS 37:21): "The wicked borrows and repays not; but the righteous deals graciously and gives." Rabbi Elazar says: An evil heart. He said to them: I prefer the words of Elazar ben Arach to yours, for your words are included in his.

10 They each said three things: Rabbi Eliezer says: Let the honor of your friend be as dear to you as your own; do not be easily provoked to anger; and repent one day before your death. And warm yourself beside the fire of the Sages; but beware of their glowing coals lest you burn yourself, for their bite is as the bite of a fox, their sting is as the deadly sting of a scorpion, and their hiss is the hiss of a snake, and all their words are like coals of fire.

וְרַבִּי אֱלִיעֶזֶר בֶּן־הוֹרְקָנוֹס אַף עִמָּהֶם, וְרַבִּי אֶלְעָזָר בְּכַף שְׁנִיָּה מַכְרִיעַ אֶת כֻּלָּם.

ט אָמַר לָהֶם, צְאוּ וּרְאוּ אֵיזוֹ הִיא דֶּרֶךְ יְשָׁרָה שֶׁיִּדְבַּק בָּהּ הָאָדָם. רַבִּי אֱלִיעֶזֶר אוֹמֵר עַיִן טוֹבָה. רַבִּי יְהוֹשֻׁעַ אוֹמֵר, חָבֵר טוֹב. רַבִּי יוֹסֵי אוֹמֵר שָׁכֵן טוֹב. רַבִּי שִׁמְעוֹן אוֹמֵר הָרוֹאֶה אֶת־הַנּוֹלָד. רַבִּי אֶלְעָזָר אוֹמֵר לֵב טוֹב. אָמַר לָהֶם, רוֹאֶה אֲנִי אֶת־דִּבְרֵי אֶלְעָזָר בֶּן־עֲרָךְ, שֶׁבִּכְלָל דְּבָרָיו דִּבְרֵיכֶם. אָמַר לָהֶם, צְאוּ וּרְאוּ אֵיזוֹ הִיא דֶּרֶךְ רָעָה שֶׁיִּתְרַחֵק מִמֶּנָּה הָאָדָם, רַבִּי אֱלִיעֶזֶר אוֹמֵר עַיִן רָעָה. רַבִּי יְהוֹשֻׁעַ אוֹמֵר חָבֵר רַע. רַבִּי יוֹסֵי אוֹמֵר שָׁכֵן רַע, רַבִּי שִׁמְעוֹן אוֹמֵר הַלֹּוֶה וְאֵינוֹ מְשַׁלֵּם, אֶחָד הַלֹּוֶה מִן־הָאָדָם כְּלֹוֶה מִן הַמָּקוֹם, שֶׁנֶּאֱמַר לֹוֶה רָשָׁע וְלֹא יְשַׁלֵּם וְצַדִּיק חוֹנֵן וְנוֹתֵן. רַבִּי אֶלְעָזָר אוֹמֵר לֵב רַע. אָמַר לָהֶם, רוֹאֶה אֲנִי אֶת־דִּבְרֵי אֶלְעָזָר בֶּן־עֲרָךְ, שֶׁבִּכְלָל דְּבָרָיו דִּבְרֵיכֶם.

י הֵם אָמְרוּ שְׁלֹשָׁה דְּבָרִים. רַבִּי אֱלִיעֶזֶר אוֹמֵר, יְהִי כְבוֹד חֲבֵרְךָ חָבִיב עָלֶיךָ כְּשֶׁלָּךְ וְאַל־תְּהִי נוֹחַ לִכְעוֹס וְשׁוּב יוֹם אֶחָד לִפְנֵי מִיתָתְךָ וֶהֱוֵה מִתְחַמֵּם כְּנֶגֶד אוּרָן שֶׁל־חֲכָמִים וֶהֱוֵה זָהִיר בְּגַחַלְתָּן שֶׁלֹּא תִכָּוֶה, שֶׁנְּשִׁיכָתָן נְשִׁיכַת שׁוּעָל וַעֲקִיצָתָן עֲקִיצַת עַקְרָב וּלְחִישָׁתָן לְחִישַׁת שָׂרָף וְכָל־דִּבְרֵיהֶם כְּגַחֲלֵי אֵשׁ.

11 Rabbi Yehoshua says: The evil eye, the evil impulse, and the hatred of mankind put a man out of the world.

12 Rabbi Yosei says: Let the property of your friend be as dear to you as your own; and prepare yourself for the study of Torah, for it does not come to you by inheritance; and let all your deeds be done in the name of Heaven.

13 Rabbi Shimon says: Be careful in reciting the *Shema* and in prayer [*Shemoneh Esreh*], and when you pray, do not make your prayer a routine function but rather a plea for mercy and favor before God, as it is said (JOEL 2:13): "For He is gracious and merciful, slow to anger and abundant in kindness, and relenting of evils"; and do not be wicked in your own esteem.

14 Rabbi Elazar says: Be diligent to study Torah; and know what to answer the unbeliever; and know before Whom you toil, and Who is your Employer — to be trusted to pay you the reward for your labor.

15 Rabbi Tarfon says: The day is short; and the task is great; and the workmen are lazy; and the reward is great; and the Employer is insistent.

יא רַבִּי יְהוֹשֻׁעַ אוֹמֵר, עַיִן הָרַע וְיֵצֶר הָרַע וְשִׂנְאַת הַבְּרִיּוֹת מוֹצִיאִין אֶת־הָאָדָם מִן־הָעוֹלָם.

יב רַבִּי יוֹסֵי אוֹמֵר, יְהִי מָמוֹן חֲבֵרְךָ חָבִיב עָלֶיךָ כְּשֶׁלָּךְ וְהַתְקֵן עַצְמְךָ לִלְמוֹד תּוֹרָה שֶׁאֵינָהּ יְרֻשָּׁה־לָךְ וְכָל־מַעֲשֶׂיךָ יִהְיוּ לְשֵׁם שָׁמָיִם.

יג רַבִּי שִׁמְעוֹן אוֹמֵר, הֱוֵה זָהִיר בִּקְרִיאַת שְׁמַע וּבִתְפִלָּה וּכְשֶׁאַתָּה מִתְפַּלֵּל אַל־תַּעַשׂ תְּפִלָּתְךָ קֶבַע אֶלָּא רַחֲמִים וְתַחֲנוּנִים לִפְנֵי הַמָּקוֹם, שֶׁנֶּאֱמַר כִּי־חַנּוּן וְרַחוּם הוּא אֶרֶךְ אַפַּיִם וְרַב־חֶסֶד וְנִחָם עַל־הָרָעָה. וְאַל־תְּהִי רָשָׁע בִּפְנֵי עַצְמֶךָ.

יד רַבִּי אֶלְעָזָר אוֹמֵר, הֱוֵה שָׁקוּד לִלְמוֹד תּוֹרָה וְדַע מַה־שֶּׁתָּשִׁיב לְאֶפִּיקוּרוֹס וְדַע לִפְנֵי מִי אַתָּה עָמֵל וּמִי הוּא בַּעַל מְלַאכְתְּךָ שֶׁיְּשַׁלֶּם לְךָ שְׂכַר פְּעֻלָּתֶךָ.

טו רַבִּי טַרְפוֹן אוֹמֵר, הַיּוֹם קָצֵר וְהַמְּלָאכָה מְרֻבָּה וְהַפּוֹעֲלִים עֲצֵלִים וְהַשָּׂכָר הַרְבֵּה וּבַעַל הַבַּיִת דּוֹחֵק.

16 He used to say: It is not up to you to complete the work; yet you are not free to evade it. If you have studied much Torah, much reward will be given to you, and your Employer is faithful to reward you for your work; and know that the reward of the righteous will be in the time to come.

CHAPTER III

1 Akavia ben Mahalalel says: Reflect upon three things and you will not come into the grip of sin: Know whence you came, and where you are going, and before Whom you are destined to render a strict accounting. Whence you came — from a malodorous drop; where you are going — to a place of dust, worms, and vermin; and before Whom you are destined to render a strict accounting — before the Supreme King of kings, the Holy One, blessed be He.

טז הוּא הָיָה אוֹמֵר, לֹא עָלֶיךָ הַמְּלָאכָה לִגְמוֹר וְלֹא־אַתָּה בֶן־חוֹרִין לְהִבָּטֵל מִמֶּנָּה. אִם לָמַדְתָּ תּוֹרָה הַרְבֵּה נוֹתְנִין לְךָ שָׂכָר הַרְבֵּה וְנֶאֱמָן הוּא בַּעַל מְלַאכְתְּךָ שֶׁיְּשַׁלֵּם לְךָ שְׂכַר פְּעֻלָּתֶךָ וְדַע שֶׁמַּתַּן שְׂכָרָן שֶׁל־צַדִּיקִים לֶעָתִיד לָבוֹא.

פרק ג

א עֲקַבְיָא בֶּן־מַהֲלַלְאֵל אוֹמֵר, הִסְתַּכֵּל בִּשְׁלֹשָׁה דְבָרִים וְאֵין אַתָּה בָא לִידֵי עֲבֵרָה, דַּע מֵאַיִן בָּאתָ וּלְאָן אַתָּה הוֹלֵךְ וְלִפְנֵי מִי אַתָּה עָתִיד לִתֵּן דִּין וְחֶשְׁבּוֹן. מֵאַיִן בָּאתָ מִטִּפָּה סְרוּחָה, וּלְאָן אַתָּה הוֹלֵךְ לִמְקוֹם עָפָר רִמָּה וְתוֹלֵעָה, וְלִפְנֵי מִי אַתָּה עָתִיד לִתֵּן דִּין וְחֶשְׁבּוֹן לִפְנֵי מֶלֶךְ מַלְכֵי הַמְּלָכִים הַקָּדוֹשׁ בָּרוּךְ הוּא.

2 Rabbi Chanina, the Deputy of the High Priests, says: Pray for the welfare of the government, since were it not for the fear of it, men would swallow each other alive. Rabbi Chananiah ben Teradyon says: When two sit together and no words of Torah are exchanged between them, this is a session of the scoffers, as it is said: (PSALMS 1:1) "...nor did he sit in the company of the scoffers." But when two sit together and interchange words of Torah, the *Shechinah* abides with them, as it is said (MALACHI 3:16): "Then they that feared the Lord spoke often one to another; and the Lord hearkened and heard it, and a book of remembrance was written before Him, for those who revered the Lord and who thought upon His name." This verse refers to two people; how do we know that even if a single person engages himself in the study of Torah, that the Holy One, blessed be He, will grant him a reward? Because it is said (LAMENTATIONS 3:28): "Although he will sit alone and keeps his silence, yet He has placed it [the reward] upon him."

3 Rabbi Shimon says: If three have eaten at one table and have not exchanged words of Torah over it, it is as though they had partaken of meal offerings made to the dead, as it is said (ISAIAH 28:8): "For all tables are full of vomit and filthiness so that there is no place clean." But if three have eaten at one table and have exchanged words of Torah over it, it is as though they had eaten from the table of God, as it is said (EZEKIEL 41:22): "And he said to me, 'This is the table that is before the Lord!'"

ב רַבִּי חֲנִינָא סְגַן הַכֹּהֲנִים אוֹמֵר, הֱוֵה מִתְפַּלֵּל בִּשְׁלוֹמָהּ שֶׁל־מַלְכוּת, שֶׁאִלְמָלֵא מוֹרָאָהּ, אִישׁ אֶת־רֵעֵהוּ חַיִּים בְּלָעוֹ. רַבִּי חֲנַנְיָה בֶּן תְּרַדְיוֹן אוֹמֵר, שְׁנַיִם שֶׁיּוֹשְׁבִין וְאֵין בֵּינֵיהֶן דִּבְרֵי תוֹרָה הֲרֵי זֶה מוֹשַׁב לֵצִים, שֶׁנֶּאֱמַר וּבְמוֹשַׁב לֵצִים לֹא יָשָׁב. אֲבָל שְׁנַיִם שֶׁיּוֹשְׁבִין וְיֵשׁ בֵּינֵיהֶם דִּבְרֵי תוֹרָה שְׁכִינָה בֵּינֵיהֶם, שֶׁנֶּאֱמַר אָז נִדְבְּרוּ יִרְאֵי יְיָ אִישׁ אֶל־רֵעֵהוּ, וַיַּקְשֵׁב יְיָ וַיִּשְׁמָע וַיִּכָּתֵב סֵפֶר זִכָּרוֹן לְפָנָיו לְיִרְאֵי יְיָ וּלְחֹשְׁבֵי שְׁמוֹ. אֵין לִי אֶלָּא שְׁנַיִם, מִנַּיִן אֲפִלּוּ אֶחָד שֶׁיּוֹשֵׁב וְעוֹסֵק בַּתּוֹרָה, שֶׁהַקָּדוֹשׁ בָּרוּךְ הוּא קוֹבֵעַ לוֹ שָׂכָר, שֶׁנֶּאֱמַר יֵשֵׁב בָּדָד וְיִדֹּם כִּי נָטַל עָלָיו.

ג רַבִּי שִׁמְעוֹן אוֹמֵר, שְׁלשָׁה שֶׁאָכְלוּ עַל שֻׁלְחָן אֶחָד וְלֹא אָמְרוּ עָלָיו דִּבְרֵי תוֹרָה כְּאִלּוּ אָכְלוּ מִזִּבְחֵי מֵתִים, שֶׁנֶּאֱמַר כִּי כָּל־שֻׁלְחָנוֹת מָלְאוּ קִיא צֹאָה בְּלִי מָקוֹם. אֲבָל שְׁלשָׁה שֶׁאָכְלוּ עַל שֻׁלְחָן אֶחָד וְאָמְרוּ עָלָיו דִּבְרֵי תוֹרָה כְּאִלּוּ אָכְלוּ מִשֻּׁלְחָנוֹ שֶׁל־מָקוֹם, שֶׁנֶּאֱמַר וַיְדַבֵּר אֵלַי זֶה הַשֻּׁלְחָן אֲשֶׁר לִפְנֵי יְיָ.

4 Rabbi Chanania ben Chachinai says: He who is awake at night, or travels on the road alone, or turns his heart to idle thoughts, sins against his own soul.

5 Rabbi Nechunia ben Ha-Kanah says: He who takes upon himself the yoke of Torah will be relieved of the yoke of government and the yoke of worldly affairs, but he who casts off the yoke of the Torah will be burdened with the yoke of government and the yoke of worldly affairs.

6 Rabbi Chalafta of Kfar Chananiah says: When ten sit together and occupy themselves with the Torah, the *Shechinah* abides among them, as it is said (PSALMS 82:1): "God stands in the congregation of the Almighty." And whence do we know that the same applies even to five? Because it is said (AMOS 9:6): "...and He has founded His band upon the earth." And whence do we learn that the same applies even to three? Because it is said (PSALMS 82:1): "...He judges in the midst of the judges." And whence do we know that the same applies even to two? Because it is said (MALACHI 3:16): "Then they that feared the Lord spoke often one to another, and the Lord hearkened and heard it." And whence do we know that the same applies even to one? Because it is said (EXODUS 20:21): "In every place where I cause My Name to be remembered, I will come to you and bless you."

7 Rabbi Elazar of Bartota says: Give to Him what is His, for you and all that you have are His. And thus King David said (CHRONICLES I 29:14): "For all things

ד רַבִּי חֲנַנְיָא בֶּן־חֲכִינַאי אוֹמֵר, הַנֵּעוֹר בַּלַּיְלָה וְהַמְהַלֵּךְ בַּדֶּרֶךְ יְחִידִי וְהַמְפַנֶּה לִבּוֹ לְבַטָּלָה — הֲרֵי זֶה מִתְחַיֵּב בְּנַפְשׁוֹ.

ה רַבִּי נְחוּנְיָא בֶּן־הַקָּנָה אוֹמֵר, כָּל־הַמְקַבֵּל עָלָיו עוֹל תּוֹרָה מַעֲבִירִין מִמֶּנּוּ עוֹל מַלְכוּת וְעוֹל דֶּרֶךְ אֶרֶץ וְכָל־הַפּוֹרֵק מִמֶּנּוּ עוֹל תּוֹרָה נוֹתְנִין עָלָיו עוֹל מַלְכוּת וְעוֹל דֶּרֶךְ אָרֶץ.

ו רַבִּי חֲלַפְתָּא אִישׁ כְּפַר חֲנַנְיָה אוֹמֵר, עֲשָׂרָה שֶׁיּוֹשְׁבִין וְעוֹסְקִין בַּתּוֹרָה שְׁכִינָה שְׁרוּיָה בֵינֵיהֶם, שֶׁנֶּאֱמַר אֱלֹהִים נִצָּב בַּעֲדַת־אֵל. וּמִנַּיִן אֲפִילוּ חֲמִשָּׁה, שֶׁנֶּאֱמַר וַאֲגֻדָּתוֹ עַל־אֶרֶץ יְסָדָהּ. וּמִנַּיִן אֲפִילוּ שְׁלשָׁה, שֶׁנֶּאֱמַר בְּקֶרֶב אֱלֹהִים יִשְׁפֹּט. וּמִנַּיִן אֲפִילוּ שְׁנַיִם, שֶׁנֶּאֱמַר אָז נִדְבְּרוּ יִרְאֵי יְיָ אִישׁ אֶל־רֵעֵהוּ וַיַּקְשֵׁב יְיָ וַיִּשְׁמָע, וְגוֹ'. וּמִנַּיִן אֲפִילוּ אֶחָד, שֶׁנֶּאֱמַר בְּכָל־הַמָּקוֹם אֲשֶׁר אַזְכִּיר אֶת־שְׁמִי אָבוֹא אֵלֶיךָ וּבֵרַכְתִּיךָ.

ז רַבִּי אֶלְעָזָר אִישׁ בַּרְתּוֹתָא אוֹמֵר, תֶּן לוֹ מִשֶּׁלּוֹ, שֶׁאַתָּה וְשֶׁלְּךָ שֶׁלּוֹ, וְכֵן בְּדָוִד הוּא אוֹמֵר כִּי־מִמְּךָ הַכֹּל וּמִיָּדְךָ נָתַנּוּ לָךְ. רַבִּי שִׁמְעוֹן אוֹמֵר,

come of You, and of Your own have we given You." Rabbi Shimon says: He who travels along a road studying, and interrupts his studies and says: "How beautiful is this tree!" or "How fine is that field!" — the Torah regards it as if he had sinned against his own soul.

8 Rabbi Dostai ben Rabbi Yannai says in the name of Rabbi Meir: He who forgets even a single word of his studies, Scripture regards it as though he had sinned against his soul; for it is said (DEUTERONOMY 4:9): "Only take heed to yourself, and guard your soul diligently, lest you forget the things which your eyes have seen." One might suppose that this applies even if his studies had been too hard for him. The Torah therefore states (DEUTERONOMY 4:9): "...and lest they depart from your heart all the days of your life"; accordingly he is guilty of sinning against his soul only if he sits down and deliberately removes them from his heart.

9 Rabbi Chanina ben Dosa says: Anyone whose fear of sin precedes his wisdom, his wisdom shall endure; but he whose wisdom precedes his fear of sin, his wisdom will not endure. He used to say: Anyone whose deeds exceed his wisdom, his wisdom shall endure; but he whose wisdom exceeds his deeds, his wisdom will not endure.

10 He used to say: He who is pleasing to his fellow men is pleasing also to God; but he who is not pleasing to his fellowmen is also displeasing to God. Rabbi Dosa ben Harkinas says: Morning sleep, and

הַמְהַלֵּךְ בַּדֶּרֶךְ וְשׁוֹנֶה וּמַפְסִיק מִמִּשְׁנָתוֹ וְאוֹמֵר: מַה נָּאֶה אִילָן זֶה וּמַה נָּאֶה נִיר זֶה, מַעֲלֶה עָלָיו הַכָּתוּב כְּאִלּוּ מִתְחַיֵּב בְּנַפְשׁוֹ.

ח רַבִּי דוֹסְתַּאי בַּר יַנַּאי מִשּׁוּם רַבִּי מֵאִיר אוֹמֵר, כָּל־הַשּׁוֹכֵחַ דָּבָר אֶחָד מִמִּשְׁנָתוֹ מַעֲלֶה עָלָיו הַכָּתוּב כְּאִלּוּ מִתְחַיֵּב בְּנַפְשׁוֹ, שֶׁנֶּאֱמַר רַק הִשָּׁמֶר לְךָ וּשְׁמֹר נַפְשְׁךָ מְאֹד פֶּן־תִּשְׁכַּח אֶת־הַדְּבָרִים אֲשֶׁר־רָאוּ עֵינֶיךָ. יָכוֹל אֲפִילוּ תָּקְפָה עָלָיו מִשְׁנָתוֹ, תַּלְמוּד לוֹמַר וּפֶן־יָסוּרוּ מִלְּבָבְךָ כֹּל יְמֵי חַיֶּיךָ, הָא אֵינוֹ מִתְחַיֵּב בְּנַפְשׁוֹ עַד שֶׁיֵּשֵׁב וִיסִירֵם מִלִּבּוֹ.

ט רַבִּי חֲנִינָא בֶּן דּוֹסָא אוֹמֵר, כָּל שֶׁיִּרְאַת חֶטְאוֹ קוֹדֶמֶת לְחָכְמָתוֹ חָכְמָתוֹ מִתְקַיֶּמֶת, וְכָל שֶׁחָכְמָתוֹ קוֹדֶמֶת לְיִרְאַת חֶטְאוֹ אֵין חָכְמָתוֹ מִתְקַיֶּמֶת. הוּא הָיָה אוֹמֵר, כָּל שֶׁמַּעֲשָׂיו מְרֻבִּין מֵחָכְמָתוֹ חָכְמָתוֹ מִתְקַיֶּמֶת, וְכָל שֶׁחָכְמָתוֹ מְרֻבָּה מִמַּעֲשָׂיו אֵין חָכְמָתוֹ מִתְקַיֶּמֶת.

י הוּא הָיָה אוֹמֵר, כָּל שֶׁרוּחַ הַבְּרִיּוֹת נוֹחָה הֵימֶנּוּ רוּחַ הַמָּקוֹם נוֹחָה הֵימֶנּוּ, וְכָל שֶׁאֵין רוּחַ הַבְּרִיּוֹת נוֹחָה הֵימֶנּוּ אֵין רוּחַ הַמָּקוֹם נוֹחָה הֵימֶנּוּ. רַבִּי דוֹסָא בֶּן הַרְכִּינָס אוֹמֵר, שֵׁנָה שֶׁל שַׁחֲרִית, וְיַיִן שֶׁל

midday wine, children's talk, and sitting in the meeting places of the ignorant — put a man out of the world.

11 Rabbi Elazar of Modi'in says: He who profanes the sacred objects and neglects the festivals, and humiliates his fellowman in public, and violates the covenant of our father Abraham (peace be upon him) and misinterprets the Torah in a manner contrary to the *Halachah*, even though he may have Torah knowledge and good deeds, he will have no share in the World-to-Come.

12 Rabbi Ishmael says: Be amenable with a superior, and kindly to the young, and receive all men with cheerfulness.

13 Rabbi Akiva says: Jesting and levity accustom a man to lewdness. The tradition is a protective fence about the Torah; tithes are a protective fence to wealth; vows are a fence for abstinence; a fence for wisdom is silence.

14 He used to say: Beloved is man, for he was created in His image; still greater was the expression of this love in that it was made known to him that he was created in His image, as it is said (GENESIS 9:6): "In the image of God did He create man." Beloved are Israel, for they are called the children of God; still greater was the expression of this love in that it was made known to them that they are called the children of God, as it is said (DEUTERONOMY 14:1): "You are the children of the Lord your God." Beloved

צָהֳרִים, וְשִׂיחַת הַיְלָדִים, וִישִׁיבַת בָּתֵּי כְנֵסִיּוֹת שֶׁל עַמֵּי הָאָרֶץ מוֹצִיאִין אֶת הָאָדָם מִן הָעוֹלָם:

יא רַבִּי אֶלְעָזָר הַמּוֹדָעִי אוֹמֵר, הַמְחַלֵּל אֶת־הַקֳּדָשִׁים וְהַמְבַזֶּה אֶת־הַמּוֹעֲדוֹת וְהַמַּלְבִּין פְּנֵי חֲבֵרוֹ בָּרַבִּים וְהַמֵּפֵר בְּרִיתוֹ שֶׁל־אַבְרָהָם אָבִינוּ וְהַמְגַלֶּה פָנִים בַּתּוֹרָה שֶׁלֹּא כַהֲלָכָה, אַף עַל פִּי שֶׁיֵּשׁ בְּיָדוֹ תוֹרָה וּמַעֲשִׂים טוֹבִים, אֵין לוֹ חֵלֶק לָעוֹלָם הַבָּא.

יב רַבִּי יִשְׁמָעֵאל אוֹמֵר, הֱוֵה קַל לְרֹאשׁ וְנוֹחַ לְתִשְׁחֹרֶת וֶהֱוֵה מְקַבֵּל אֶת־כָּל־הָאָדָם בְּשִׂמְחָה.

יג רַבִּי עֲקִיבָא אוֹמֵר, שְׂחוֹק וְקַלּוּת רֹאשׁ מַרְגִּילִין אֶת־הָאָדָם לְעֶרְוָה. מָסֹרֶת סְיָג לַתּוֹרָה, מַעְשְׂרוֹת סְיָג לָעֹשֶׁר, נְדָרִים סְיָג לִפְרִישׁוּת, סְיָג לַחָכְמָה שְׁתִיקָה.

יד הוּא הָיָה אוֹמֵר, חָבִיב אָדָם שֶׁנִּבְרָא בְּצֶלֶם, חִבָּה יְתֵרָה נוֹדַעַת לוֹ שֶׁנִּבְרָא בְּצֶלֶם, שֶׁנֶּאֱמַר כִּי בְּצֶלֶם אֱלֹהִים עָשָׂה אֶת־הָאָדָם. חֲבִיבִין יִשְׂרָאֵל שֶׁנִּקְרְאוּ בָנִים לַמָּקוֹם, חִבָּה יְתֵרָה נוֹדַעַת לָהֶם שֶׁנִּקְרְאוּ בָנִים לַמָּקוֹם, שֶׁנֶּאֱמַר בָּנִים

are Israel, for to them was given a precious instrument; still greater was the expression of this love in that it was made known to them that to them was given a precious instrument with which the world was created, as it is said (PROVERBS 4:2): "For I give you good doctrine; forsake not my Torah."

15 Everything is foreseen; yet freedom of choice is given; and the world is judged with goodness; yet the judgment of all is according to the predominance of man's kindly deeds.

16 He used to say: All is given on pledge, and a net is spread out over all the living. The shop is open; the merchant extends credit, the ledger is open and the hand records; whosoever wishes to borrow, many come and borrow; but the collectors make their appointed rounds each day, and take payment from man whether or not he realizes it; for they have good authority on which to rely, since the judgment is a judgment of truth; and all is ready for the festive banquet.

17 Rabbi Elazar ben Azariah says: Where there is no Torah, there is no proper conduct; where there is no proper conduct, there is no Torah. Where there is no wisdom, there is no reverence for God; where there is no reverence for God, there is no wisdom. Where there is no knowledge, there is no understanding; where there is no understanding, there is no knowledge. Where there is no bread, there is no Torah; where there is no Torah, there is no bread. He used to say: One whose wisdom exceeds

אַתֶּם לַיְיָ אֱלֹהֵיכֶם. חֲבִיבִין יִשְׂרָאֵל שֶׁנִּתַּן לָהֶם כְּלִי
חֶמְדָּה, חִבָּה יְתֵרָה נוֹדַעַת לָהֶם שֶׁנִּתַּן לָהֶם כְּלִי
חֶמְדָּה שֶׁבּוֹ נִבְרָא הָעוֹלָם שֶׁנֶּאֱמַר כִּי לֶקַח טוֹב
נָתַתִּי לָכֶם תּוֹרָתִי אַל־תַּעֲזֹבוּ.

טו הַכֹּל צָפוּי וְהָרְשׁוּת נְתוּנָה. וּבְטוֹב
הָעוֹלָם נָדוֹן. וְהַכֹּל לְפִי רֹב הַמַּעֲשֶׂה.

טז הוּא הָיָה אוֹמֵר, הַכֹּל נָתוּן בְּעֵרָבוֹן.
וּמְצוּדָה פְרוּשָׂה עַל־כָּל־הַחַיִּים. הַחֲנוּת
פְּתוּחָה וְהַחֶנְוָנִי מַקִּיף, וְהַפִּנְקָס פָּתוּחַ וְהַיָּד
כּוֹתֶבֶת, וְכָל הָרוֹצֶה לִלְווֹת יָבֹא וְיִלְוֶה. וְהַגַּבָּאִין
מַחֲזִירִין תָּדִיר בְּכָל־יוֹם וְנִפְרָעִין מִן הָאָדָם מִדַּעְתּוֹ
וְשֶׁלֹּא מִדַּעְתּוֹ וְיֵשׁ לָהֶם עַל מַה שֶּׁיִּסְמֹכוּ. וְהַדִּין דִּין
אֱמֶת וְהַכֹּל מְתֻקָּן לִסְעוּדָה.

יז רַבִּי אֶלְעָזָר בֶּן־עֲזַרְיָה אוֹמֵר. אִם אֵין תּוֹרָה,
אֵין דֶּרֶךְ אֶרֶץ, אִם אֵין דֶּרֶךְ אֶרֶץ אֵין תּוֹרָה.
אִם אֵין חָכְמָה אֵין יִרְאָה, אִם אֵין יִרְאָה אֵין חָכְמָה.
אִם אֵין בִּינָה אֵין דַּעַת, אִם אֵין דַּעַת אֵין בִּינָה. אִם אֵין
קֶמַח, אֵין תּוֹרָה, אִם אֵין תּוֹרָה, אֵין קֶמַח. הוּא הָיָה
אוֹמֵר, כָּל שֶׁחָכְמָתוֹ מְרֻבָּה מִמַּעֲשָׂיו לְמָה הוּא דוֹמֶה,

his deeds, to what is he compared? To a tree whose branches are many, but whose roots are few, and the wind comes and uproots it and overturns it upon its top, as it is said (JEREMIAH 17:6): "For he shall be like a lone tree in the desert, and shall not see when good comes; but shall inhabit the parched soil in the wilderness, a salt-saturated land which is uninhabitable." But he whose deeds exceed his wisdom, to what is he compared? To a tree whose branches are few, but whose roots are many; even if all the winds of the world come and blow upon it, they cannot move it from its place, as it is said (JEREMIAH 17:8): "For he shall be as a tree planted by the waters, that spreads out its roots to the stream of water, and shall not see that the heat comes, and its leaves are ever fresh and green; and shall not be troubled in the year of drought; neither shall it cease from bearing fruit.

18 Rabbi Elazar (ben) Chisma says: The laws regarding the sacrifices of birds and of the beginning of woman's unclean period are important precepts of *Halachah*; but astronomy and geometry are condiments to wisdom.

לְאִילָן שֶׁעֲנָפָיו מְרֻבִּין וְשָׁרָשָׁיו מוּעָטִין, וְהָרוּחַ בָּאָה וְעוֹקַרְתּוֹ וְהוֹפַכְתּוֹ עַל פָּנָיו, שֶׁנֶּאֱמַר וְהָיָה כְּעַרְעָר בָּעֲרָבָה וְלֹא יִרְאֶה כִּי־יָבוֹא טוֹב וְשָׁכַן חֲרֵרִים בַּמִּדְבָּר אֶרֶץ מְלֵחָה וְלֹא תֵשֵׁב. אֲבָל כָּל שֶׁמַּעֲשָׂיו מְרֻבִּים מֵחָכְמָתוֹ לְמָה הוּא דוֹמֶה, לְאִילָן שֶׁעֲנָפָיו מוּעָטִין וְשָׁרָשָׁיו מְרֻבִּין, שֶׁאֲפִילוּ כָּל־הָרוּחוֹת שֶׁבָּעוֹלָם בָּאוֹת וְנוֹשְׁבוֹת בּוֹ אֵין מְזִיזִין אוֹתוֹ מִמְּקוֹמוֹ, שֶׁנֶּאֱמַר וְהָיָה כְּעֵץ שָׁתוּל עַל־מַיִם וְעַל־יוּבַל יְשַׁלַּח שָׁרָשָׁיו, וְלֹא יִרְאֶה כִּי־יָבֹא חֹם, וְהָיָה עָלֵהוּ רַעֲנָן וּבִשְׁנַת בַּצֹּרֶת לֹא יִדְאָג, וְלֹא יָמִישׁ מֵעֲשׂוֹת פֶּרִי.

יח רַבִּי אֶלְעָזָר (בֶּן־) חִסְמָא אוֹמֵר, קִנִּין וּפִתְחֵי נִדָּה הֵן הֵן גּוּפֵי הֲלָכוֹת. תְּקוּפוֹת וְגִמַטְרִיָּאוֹת פַּרְפְּרָאוֹת לַחָכְמָה.

CHAPTER IV

1 Ben Zoma says: Who is wise? He who learns from every man, as it is said (PSALMS 119:99): "From all who have taught me I have gained wisdom." Who is strong? He who subdues his passions, for it is said (PROVERBS 16:32): "He who is slow to anger is better than the strong; and he who rules his spirit is better than he who conquers a city." Who is rich? He who rejoices in his portion, for it is said (PSALMS 128:2): "When you eat of the toil of your hands, happy shall you be, and it shall be well with you." (*Happy shall you be* — in this world; *and it shall be well with you* — in the World-to-Come.) Who is honored? He who honors his fellow man, for it is said, (SAMUEL I 2:30): "...for those who honor Me I will honor, and they who despise Me shall be regarded in contempt."

2 Ben Azzai says: Run to perform even a slight mitzvah as you would for an important one, and flee from sin, for one mitzvah will lead to another mitzvah, and one sin will lead to another sin, for the reward of a mitzvah is inherent in the mitzvah and the recompense of a sin is the sin itself.

פרק ד

א בֶּן־זוֹמָא אוֹמֵר, אֵיזֶהוּ חָכָם, הַלּוֹמֵד מִכָּל־אָדָם, שֶׁנֶּאֱמַר מִכָּל מְלַמְּדַי הִשְׂכַּלְתִּי כִּי עֵדְוֺתֶיךָ שִׂיחָה לִי. אֵיזֶהוּ גִבּוֹר, הַכּוֹבֵשׁ אֶת־יִצְרוֹ, שֶׁנֶּאֱמַר טוֹב אֶרֶךְ אַפַּיִם מִגִּבּוֹר וּמוֹשֵׁל בְּרוּחוֹ מִלֹּכֵד עִיר. אֵיזֶהוּ עָשִׁיר, הַשָּׂמֵחַ בְּחֶלְקוֹ, שֶׁנֶּאֱמַר יְגִיעַ כַּפֶּיךָ כִּי תֹאכֵל אַשְׁרֶיךָ וְטוֹב לָךְ. אַשְׁרֶיךָ בָּעוֹלָם הַזֶּה וְטוֹב לָךְ לָעוֹלָם הַבָּא. אֵיזֶהוּ מְכֻבָּד, הַמְכַבֵּד אֶת הַבְּרִיּוֹת, שֶׁנֶּאֱמַר כִּי מְכַבְּדַי אֲכַבֵּד וּבֹזַי יֵקָלּוּ.

ב בֶּן־עַזַּאי אוֹמֵר, הֱוֵי רָץ לְמִצְוָה קַלָּה וּבוֹרֵחַ מִן־הָעֲבֵרָה, שֶׁמִּצְוָה גּוֹרֶרֶת מִצְוָה וַעֲבֵרָה גוֹרֶרֶת עֲבֵרָה שֶׁשְּׂכַר מִצְוָה מִצְוָה וּשְׂכַר עֲבֵרָה עֲבֵרָה.

3 He used to say: Do not despise any man, and do not deem anything unworthy of consideration; for there is no man who does not have his hour and no thing that does not have its place.

4 Rabbi Levitas of Yavneh says: Be exceedingly humble in spirit for the hope of earthly man is but worms [decay]. Rabbi Yochanan ben Beroka says: He who desecrates the Name of God in secret, will be punished publicly, whether the desecration is perpetrated in error or intentionally.

5 Rabbi Ishmael his son says: He who learns in order to teach will be granted the opportunity to learn and to teach; but he who learns in order to practice will be granted the opportunity to learn and to teach, to observe and to practice. Rabbi Tzadok says: Do not make of them [the words of the Torah] a crown with which to aggrandize yourself, nor an axe with which to strike. Thus Hillel used to say: "He who makes improper use of the crown [of Torah] shall perish." From this you may learn that he who derives selfish gain from the words of Torah takes his life away from the world.

6 Rabbi Yosei says: He who honors the Torah, will himself be honored by mankind; but he who dishonors the Torah, will himself be dishonored by mankind.

ג׳ הוּא הָיָה אוֹמֵר, אַל־תְּהִי־בָז לְכָל־אָדָם וְאַל־תְּהִי מַפְלִיג לְכָל־דָּבָר, שֶׁאֵין לְךָ אָדָם שֶׁאֵין לוֹ שָׁעָה וְאֵין לְךָ דָּבָר שֶׁאֵין לוֹ מָקוֹם.

ד׳ רַבִּי לְוִיטַס אִישׁ יַבְנֶה אוֹמֵר, מְאֹד מְאֹד הֱוֵי שְׁפַל רוּחַ שֶׁתִּקְוַת אֱנוֹשׁ רִמָּה. רַבִּי יוֹחָנָן בֶּן בְּרוֹקָא אוֹמֵר, כָּל־הַמְחַלֵּל שֵׁם שָׁמַיִם בַּסֵּתֶר נִפְרָעִין מִמֶּנּוּ בַּגָּלוּי. אֶחָד שׁוֹגֵג וְאֶחָד מֵזִיד בְּחִלּוּל הַשֵּׁם.

ה׳ רַבִּי יִשְׁמָעֵאל בְּנוֹ אוֹמֵר, הַלּוֹמֵד עַל־מְנָת לְלַמֵּד מַסְפִּיקִים בְּיָדוֹ לִלְמוֹד וּלְלַמֵּד, וְהַלּוֹמֵד עַל־מְנָת לַעֲשׂוֹת מַסְפִּיקִים בְּיָדוֹ לִלְמוֹד וּלְלַמֵּד, לִשְׁמוֹר וְלַעֲשׂוֹת. רַבִּי צָדוֹק אוֹמֵר, אַל תַּעֲשֵׂם עֲטָרָה לְהִתְגַּדֵּל־בָּהֶם וְלֹא קַרְדֹּם לַחְפּוֹר־בָּהֶם, וְכַךְ הָיָה הִלֵּל אוֹמֵר, וּדְאִשְׁתַּמַּשׁ בְּתָגָא חֲלָף, הָא לָמַדְתָּ, כָּל־הַנֶּהֱנֶה מִדִּבְרֵי תוֹרָה נוֹטֵל חַיָּיו מִן־הָעוֹלָם.

ו׳ רַבִּי יוֹסֵי אוֹמֵר, כָּל־הַמְכַבֵּד אֶת־הַתּוֹרָה גּוּפוֹ מְכֻבָּד עַל־הַבְּרִיּוֹת וְכָל־הַמְחַלֵּל אֶת־הַתּוֹרָה גּוּפוֹ מְחֻלָּל עַל־הַבְּרִיּוֹת.

7 Rabbi Ishmael his son says: He who avoids a judicial position, rids himself of hatred, robbery, and perjury, but he who arrogantly renders legal decisions — is foolish, wicked, and brutish.

8 He used to say: Do not judge alone, for none may judge alone, except One. And do not say: "Accept my view," for it is they and not you who have the authority.

9 Rabbi Yonatan says: He who fulfills the Torah even out of poverty, will in the end fulfill it out of wealth; and he who neglects the Torah out of wealth, will in the end neglect it out of poverty.

10 Rabbi Meir says: Limit your business activities, and occupy yourself with the Torah instead; and be of humble spirit before all men; and if you neglected the Torah, you will have many others who did so, opposite you; but if you toil in the Torah, He has abundant reward to give you.

11 Rabbi Eliezer ben Ya'akov says: He who performs one mitzvah, gains for himself one advocate; and he who commits one sin, acquires for himself one accuser. Repentance and good deeds are as a shield against punishment. Rabbi Yochanan Ha-Sandlar says: Every assembly which is for the sake of Heaven [a

ז רַבִּי יִשְׁמָעֵאל בְּנוֹ אוֹמֵר, הַחוֹשֵׂךְ עַצְמוֹ מִן־הַדִּין פּוֹרֵק מִמֶּנּוּ אֵיבָה וְגָזֵל וּשְׁבוּעַת שָׁוְא, וְהַגַּס לִבּוֹ בְּהוֹרָאָה שׁוֹטֶה רָשָׁע וְגַס רוּחַ.

ח הוּא הָיָה אוֹמֵר, אַל־תְּהִי דָן יְחִידִי שֶׁאֵין דָּן יְחִידִי אֶלָּא אֶחָד, וְאַל־תֹּאמַר קַבְּלוּ דַעְתִּי שֶׁהֵם רַשָּׁאִים וְלֹא אָתָּה.

ט רַבִּי יוֹנָתָן אוֹמֵר, כָּל־הַמְקַיֵּם אֶת־הַתּוֹרָה מֵעֹנִי סוֹפוֹ לְקַיְּמָהּ מֵעשֶׁר. וְכָל־הַמְבַטֵּל אֶת־הַתּוֹרָה מֵעשֶׁר סוֹפוֹ לְבַטְּלָהּ מֵעֹנִי.

י רַבִּי מֵאִיר אוֹמֵר, הֱוֵי מְמַעֵט בְּעֵסֶק וַעֲסֹק בַּתּוֹרָה וֶהֱוֵה שְׁפַל־רוּחַ בִּפְנֵי כָל־אָדָם וְאִם־בָּטַלְתָּ מִן־הַתּוֹרָה יֶשׁ־לְךָ בְּטֵלִים הַרְבֵּה כְּנֶגְדֶּךָ וְאִם־עָמַלְתָּ בַתּוֹרָה יֶשׁ־לוֹ שָׂכָר הַרְבֵּה לִתֶּן לָךְ.

יא רַבִּי אֱלִיעֶזֶר בֶּן־יַעֲקֹב אוֹמֵר, הָעוֹשֶׂה מִצְוָה אַחַת קוֹנֶה לוֹ פְּרַקְלִיט אֶחָד, וְהָעוֹבֵר עֲבֵרָה אַחַת קוֹנֶה לוֹ קַטֵּיגוֹר אֶחָד. תְּשׁוּבָה וּמַעֲשִׂים טוֹבִים כִּתְרִיס בִּפְנֵי הַפֻּרְעָנוּת. רַבִּי יוֹחָנָן הַסַּנְדְּלָר אוֹמֵר, כָּל־

noble purpose], will in the end endure; but that which is not for the sake of Heaven, will in the end not endure.

12 Rabbi Elazar ben Shammua says: Let the honor of your student be as dear to you as your own; and the honor of your friend, as the reverence due to your teacher; and the reverence due to your teacher, as the reverence due to Heaven.

13 Rabbi Yehudah says: Be cautious in teaching, for an error in teaching constitutes a deliberate sin. Rabbi Shimon says: There are three crowns: the crown of Torah, the crown of priesthood, and the crown of kingship; but the crown of a good name excels them all.

14 Rabbi Nehorai says: Go into voluntary exile to a place where there is Torah, and do not say that it will follow you, for it is your associates who will preserve it in your hand; and do not rely on your own understanding.

15 Rabbi Yannai says: We are not qualified to explain either why the wicked enjoy peace or the sufferings of the righteous. Rabbi Matia ben Charash says: Be the first to greet every man; and rather a tail among lions than a head among foxes.

16 Rabbi Ya'akov says: This world is like the vestibule before the World-to-Come; prepare

כְּנֵסִיָּה שֶׁהִיא לְשֵׁם שָׁמַיִם סוֹפָהּ לְהִתְקַיֵּם, וְשֶׁאֵינָהּ לְשֵׁם שָׁמַיִם אֵין סוֹפָהּ לְהִתְקַיֵּם.

יב רַבִּי אֶלְעָזָר בֶּן שַׁמּוּעַ אוֹמֵר, יְהִי כְבוֹד תַּלְמִידְךָ חָבִיב עָלֶיךָ כְּשֶׁלָּךְ וּכְבוֹד חֲבֵרְךָ כְּמוֹרָא רַבָּךְ וּמוֹרָא רַבָּךְ כְּמוֹרָא שָׁמָיִם.

יג רַבִּי יְהוּדָה אוֹמֵר, הֱוֵה זָהִיר בְּתַלְמוּד שֶׁשִּׁגְגַת תַּלְמוּד עוֹלָה זָדוֹן. רַבִּי שִׁמְעוֹן אוֹמֵר, שְׁלשָׁה כְתָרִים הֵן, כֶּתֶר תּוֹרָה וְכֶתֶר כְּהֻנָּה וְכֶתֶר מַלְכוּת. וְכֶתֶר שֵׁם טוֹב עוֹלֶה עַל גַּבֵּיהֶן.

יד רַבִּי נְהוֹרַאי אוֹמֵר, הֱוֵה גוֹלֶה לִמְקוֹם תּוֹרָה וְאַל־תֹּאמַר שֶׁהִיא תָבוֹא אַחֲרֶיךָ שֶׁחֲבֵרֶיךָ יְקַיְּמוּהָ בְיָדֶיךָ וְאֶל־בִּינָתְךָ אַל־תִּשָּׁעֵן.

טו רַבִּי יַנַּאי אוֹמֵר, אֵין בְּיָדֵינוּ לֹא מִשַּׁלְוַת הָרְשָׁעִים וְאַף לֹא מִיִּסּוּרֵי הַצַּדִּיקִים. רַבִּי מַתְיָא בֶן חָרָשׁ אוֹמֵר, הֱוֵי מַקְדִּים בִּשְׁלוֹם כָּל־אָדָם, וֶהֱוֵי זָנָב לַאֲרָיוֹת, וְאַל־תְּהִי רֹאשׁ לַשּׁוּעָלִים.

טז רַבִּי יַעֲקֹב אוֹמֵר, הָעוֹלָם הַזֶּה דּוֹמֶה לִפְרוֹזְדוֹר בִּפְנֵי הָעוֹלָם הַבָּא. הַתְקֵן

yourself in the vestibule, so that you may enter the banquet hall.

17 He used to say: One hour of repentance and good deeds in this world is worth more than the whole life of the World-to-Come; and one hour of spiritual satisfaction in the World-to-Come is worth more than the whole life of this world.

18 Rabbi Shimon ben Elazar says: Do not attempt to pacify your fellowman in the time of his anger; nor to comfort him while his departed one lies before him; nor question him at the time of his taking a vow; nor attempt to see him in the hour of his humiliation.

19 Shmuel Ha-Katan says: "Rejoice not when your enemy falls, and let not your heart exult when he stumbles; lest the Lord see it, and be displeased, and He turn away His wrath from him" (PROVERBS 24:17-18).

20 Elisha ben Avuyah says: He who learns in his youth, what is he like? Like ink written on new paper. And he who learns in his old age, what is he like? Like ink written on blotted paper. Rabbi Yosei bar Yehudah of Kfar Ha-Bavli says: He who learns from the young, what is he like? Like one who eats unripe grapes and drinks old wine. *Rabi* [Yehudah *Ha-Nasi*] said: Do not look only at the jar, but rather at its contents; there is a new jar full of old wine, and an old jar which does not hold even new wine.

עַצְמְךָ בִּפְרוֹזְדוֹר כְּדֵי שֶׁתִּכָּנֵס לִטְרַקְלִין.

יג הוּא הָיָה אוֹמֵר, יָפָה שָׁעָה אַחַת בִּתְשׁוּבָה וּמַעֲשִׂים טוֹבִים בָּעוֹלָם הַזֶּה מִכֹּל חַיֵּי הָעוֹלָם הַבָּא וְיָפָה שָׁעָה אַחַת שֶׁל-קוֹרַת רוּחַ בָּעוֹלָם הַבָּא מִכֹּל-חַיֵּי הָעוֹלָם הַזֶּה.

יח רַבִּי שִׁמְעוֹן בֶּן-אֶלְעָזָר אוֹמֵר, אַל-תְּרַצֶּה אֶת-חֲבֵרְךָ בִּשְׁעַת כַּעֲסוֹ וְאַל-תְּנַחֲמֵהוּ בְּשָׁעָה שֶׁמֵּתוֹ מֻטָּל לְפָנָיו וְאַל-תִּשְׁאַל לוֹ בִּשְׁעַת נִדְרוֹ וְאַל-תִּשְׁתַּדֵּל לִרְאוֹתוֹ בִּשְׁעַת קַלְקָלָתוֹ:

יט שְׁמוּאֵל הַקָּטָן אוֹמֵר, בִּנְפֹל אוֹיִבְךָ אַל-תִּשְׂמָח וּבִכָּשְׁלוֹ אַל-יָגֵל לִבֶּךָ, פֶּן-יִרְאֶה יְיָ וְרַע בְּעֵינָיו וְהֵשִׁיב מֵעָלָיו אַפּוֹ.

כ אֱלִישָׁע בֶּן אֲבוּיָה אוֹמֵר, הַלּוֹמֵד יֶלֶד, לְמָה הוּא דוֹמֶה לִדְיוֹ כְתוּבָה עַל-נְיָר חָדָשׁ, וְהַלּוֹמֵד זָקֵן לְמָה הוּא דוֹמֶה לִדְיוֹ כְתוּבָה עַל נְיָר מָחוּק: רַבִּי יוֹסֵי בַּר יְהוּדָה אִישׁ כְּפַר הַבַּבְלִי אוֹמֵר, הַלּוֹמֵד מִן הַקְּטַנִּים לְמָה הוּא דוֹמֶה לְאוֹכֵל עֲנָבִים קֵהוֹת וְשׁוֹתֶה יַיִן מִגִּתּוֹ, וְהַלּוֹמֵד מִן-הַזְּקֵנִים לְמָה הוּא דוֹמֶה לְאוֹכֵל עֲנָבִים בְּשׁוּלוֹת וְשׁוֹתֶה יַיִן יָשָׁן. רַבִּי אוֹמֵר, אַל-תִּסְתַּכֵּל בַּקַּנְקַן אֶלָּא בְּמַה שֶׁיֵּשׁ-בּוֹ, יֵשׁ קַנְקַן חָדָשׁ מָלֵא יָשָׁן. וְיָשָׁן שֶׁאֲפִלּוּ חָדָשׁ אֵין בּוֹ.

21 Rabbi Eliezer Ha-Kappar says: Envy, lust, and thirst for honor take a man out of the world.

22 He used to say: Those who are born are destined to die; and those who die, to be resurrected; and the living, to be judged; to know and to proclaim so that it be known that He is God, He is the Maker, He is the Creator, He is the Discerner, He is the Judge, He is the Witness, He is the Complainant and it is He who is destined to judge. Blessed be He, before Whom there is no wrongdoing, nor forgetfulness, nor partiality, nor taking of bribes; for all is His. And know that everything comes to be according to the reckoning. And let not your fancy assure you that the grave will be your refuge, for perforce were you formed, and perforce were you born, and perforce you live, and perforce you die, and perforce you will have to give account and reckoning before the Supreme King of kings, the Holy One, blessed be He.

כא רַבִּי אֶלְעָזָר הַקַּפָּר אוֹמֵר, הַקִּנְאָה וְהַתַּאֲוָה וְהַכָּבוֹד מוֹצִיאִים אֶת הָאָדָם מִן הָעוֹלָם.

כב הוּא הָיָה אוֹמֵר, הַיִּלּוֹדִים לָמוּת וְהַמֵּתִים לְהֵחָיוֹת וְהַחַיִּים לִדּוֹן, לֵידַע וּלְהוֹדִיעַ וּלְהִוָּדַע, שֶׁהוּא אֵל הוּא הַיּוֹצֵר הוּא הַבּוֹרֵא הוּא הַמֵּבִין הוּא הַדַּיָּן הוּא הָעֵד הוּא בַּעַל דִּין הוּא עָתִיד לָדוּן. בָּרוּךְ הוּא, שֶׁאֵין לְפָנָיו לֹא עַוְלָה וְלֹא שִׁכְחָה וְלֹא מַשּׂוֹא פָנִים וְלֹא מִקַּח שֹׁחַד, שֶׁהַכֹּל שֶׁלּוֹ. וְדַע שֶׁהַכֹּל לְפִי הַחֶשְׁבּוֹן, וְאַל־יַבְטִיחֲךָ יִצְרְךָ שֶׁהַשְּׁאוֹל בֵּית מָנוֹס לָךְ, שֶׁעַל כָּרְחֲךָ אַתָּה נוֹצָר וְעַל כָּרְחֲךָ אַתָּה נוֹלָד וְעַל כָּרְחֲךָ אַתָּה חַי וְעַל כָּרְחֲךָ אַתָּה מֵת וְעַל כָּרְחֲךָ אַתָּה עָתִיד לִתֵּן דִּין וְחֶשְׁבּוֹן לִפְנֵי מֶלֶךְ מַלְכֵי הַמְּלָכִים הַקָּדוֹשׁ בָּרוּךְ הוּא.

CHAPTER V

1 By ten Divine utterances was the world created. What does this fact teach us? Surely could not the world have been created by one Divine utterance? But it is to emphasize the punishment of the wicked, who destroy the world which was created by ten utterances, and to give a proper reward to the righteous, who maintain the world which was created by ten utterances.

2 The ten generations from Adam to Noah are to indicate to us how great is God's patience, for all the generations continued provoking Him until He brought upon them the waters of the Flood. The ten generations from Noah until Abraham are to indicate to us how great is God's patience, for all the generations continued provoking Him until Abraham came and earned for himself the merit of them all.

3 With ten trials was our father Abraham tried, and he stood firm through them all, to show us how great was the love of our father Abraham (peace be upon him) towards God.

פרק ה

א בַּעֲשָׂרָה מַאֲמָרוֹת נִבְרָא הָעוֹלָם. וּמַה תַּלְמוּד לוֹמַר וַהֲלֹא בְּמַאֲמָר אֶחָד יָכוֹל לְהִבָּרְאוֹת, אֶלָּא לְהִפָּרַע מִן־הָרְשָׁעִים שֶׁמְּאַבְּדִים אֶת־הָעוֹלָם שֶׁנִּבְרָא בַּעֲשָׂרָה מַאֲמָרוֹת וְלִתֵּן שָׂכָר טוֹב לַצַּדִּיקִים שֶׁמְּקַיְּמִין אֶת־הָעוֹלָם שֶׁנִּבְרָא בַּעֲשָׂרָה מַאֲמָרוֹת.

ב עֲשָׂרָה דוֹרוֹת מֵאָדָם עַד נֹחַ, לְהוֹדִיעַ כַּמָּה אֶרֶךְ אַפַּיִם לְפָנָיו שֶׁכָּל הַדּוֹרוֹת הָיוּ מַכְעִיסִים וּבָאִין עַד שֶׁהֵבִיא עֲלֵיהֶם אֶת־מֵי הַמַּבּוּל. עֲשָׂרָה דוֹרוֹת מִנֹּחַ עַד אַבְרָהָם, לְהוֹדִיעַ כַּמָּה אֶרֶךְ אַפַּיִם לְפָנָיו, שֶׁכָּל־הַדּוֹרוֹת הָיוּ מַכְעִיסִים וּבָאִין עַד שֶׁבָּא אַבְרָהָם אָבִינוּ וְקִבֵּל שְׂכַר כֻּלָּם.

ג עֲשָׂרָה נִסְיוֹנוֹת נִתְנַסָּה אַבְרָהָם אָבִינוּ וְעָמַד בְּכֻלָּם לְהוֹדִיעַ כַּמָּה חִבָּתוֹ שֶׁל־אַבְרָהָם אָבִינוּ.

4 Ten miracles were wrought for our fathers in Egypt and ten at the Sea of Reeds. Ten plagues did the Holy One, blessed be He, bring upon the Egyptians in Egypt and ten at the Sea of Reeds. Ten times did our fathers try the Holy One, blessed be He, in the wilderness, as it is said (NUMBERS 14:22): "...They have tried Me ten times and have not hearkened to My voice."

5 Ten miracles were wrought for our fathers in the Temple Sanctuary: No woman ever miscarried from the scent of the sacrificial meat; the sacrificial meat never became putrid; no fly was ever seen in the slaughterhouse; no unclean accident ever befell the High Priest on Yom Kippur; the rains never extinguished the fire of the woodpile on the altar; the wind did not prevail over the column of smoke that rose from the altar; there was never found a disqualifying defect in the *Omer* or in the two loaves [for Shavuot], or in the showbread [for the Sabbath]; the people stood tightly pressed together, yet they found ample space to prostrate themselves; never did a snake or scorpion do injury to anyone in Jerusalem; and no man ever said to his fellow: "There is insufficient space for me to lodge overnight in Jerusalem."

6 Ten things were created on Sabbath eve at twilight, namely: the mouth of the earth; the mouth of the well; the mouth of the ass; the rainbow; the manna; the staff; the *shamir*; the written letters; the writing; and the tablets of stone. And some add: also the harmful spirits, and the grave of Moses, and the ram of our father Abraham; and others include: also the tongs made by means of tongs [the first metal instrument].

ד עֲשָׂרָה נִסִּים נַעֲשׂוּ לַאֲבוֹתֵינוּ בְּמִצְרַיִם וַעֲשָׂרָה עַל הַיָּם. עֶשֶׂר מַכּוֹת הֵבִיא הַקָּדוֹשׁ בָּרוּךְ הוּא עַל הַמִּצְרִיִּים בְּמִצְרַיִם וְעֶשֶׂר עַל הַיָּם. עֲשָׂרָה נִסְיוֹנוֹת נִסּוּ אֲבוֹתֵינוּ אֶת הַקָּדוֹשׁ בָּרוּךְ הוּא בַּמִּדְבָּר, שֶׁנֶּאֱמַר וַיְנַסּוּ אֹתִי זֶה עֶשֶׂר פְּעָמִים וְלֹא שָׁמְעוּ בְּקוֹלִי.

ה עֲשָׂרָה נִסִּים נַעֲשׂוּ לַאֲבוֹתֵינוּ בְּבֵית הַמִּקְדָּשׁ. לֹא הִפִּילָה אִשָּׁה מֵרֵיחַ בְּשַׂר הַקֹּדֶשׁ, וְלֹא הִסְרִיחַ בְּשַׂר הַקֹּדֶשׁ מֵעוֹלָם, וְלֹא נִרְאָה זְבוּב בְּבֵית הַמִּטְבָּחַיִם, וְלֹא אֵרַע קֶרִי לְכֹהֵן גָּדוֹל בְּיוֹם הַכִּפֻּרִים, וְלֹא כִבּוּ הַגְּשָׁמִים אֵשׁ שֶׁל־עֲצֵי הַמַּעֲרָכָה, וְלֹא נִצְּחָה הָרוּחַ אֶת־עַמּוּד הֶעָשָׁן, וְלֹא נִמְצָא פְסוּל בָּעֹמֶר וּבִשְׁתֵּי הַלֶּחֶם וּבְלֶחֶם הַפָּנִים, עוֹמְדִים צְפוּפִים וּמִשְׁתַּחֲוִים רְוָחִים וְלֹא הִזִּיק נָחָשׁ וְעַקְרָב בִּירוּשָׁלַיִם מֵעוֹלָם, וְלֹא אָמַר אָדָם לַחֲבֵרוֹ צַר לִי הַמָּקוֹם שֶׁאָלִין בִּירוּשָׁלָיִם.

ו עֲשָׂרָה דְבָרִים נִבְרְאוּ בְּעֶרֶב שַׁבָּת בֵּין הַשְּׁמָשׁוֹת וְאֵלּוּ הֵן. פִּי הָאָרֶץ, פִּי הַבְּאֵר, פִּי הָאָתוֹן, הַקֶּשֶׁת וְהַמָּן וְהַמַּטֶּה וְהַשָּׁמִיר, הַכְּתָב וְהַמִּכְתָּב וְהַלּוּחוֹת. וְיֵשׁ אוֹמְרִין אַף הַמַּזִּיקִין וּקְבוּרָתוֹ שֶׁל־מֹשֶׁה וְאֵילוֹ שֶׁל־אַבְרָהָם אָבִינוּ. וְיֵשׁ אוֹמְרִים אַף צְבָת בִּצְבַת עֲשׂוּיָה.

7 There are seven marks of a boor, and seven of a wise man. The wise man does not speak before one who is greater than he is in wisdom and experience; he does not interrupt the words of his companion; he is not hasty to answer; he asks what is relevant to the subject and answers to the point; he speaks on the first point first and on the last point last; regarding that which he has not learned, he says: "I have not learned this"; and he acknowledges the truth. And the opposite of these traits is the mark of the boor.

8 Seven kinds of punishment come into the world for seven kinds of sins: When some give tithes and others do not, there comes a famine caused by drought; some will suffer hunger, while others will have plenty. When all resolve to withhold the tithes, there will be a famine caused by panic of war and drought. When all decide not to set apart *challah* from the dough, then there comes a famine of extermination. Pestilence comes into the world to execute the death penalties enumerated in the Torah, which are not in the purview of a court of justice; and for the improper use of the produce of the seventh year. The sword comes into the world for the delay of justice, and for the perversion of justice, and upon those who misinterpret the Torah.

9 Wild beasts come into the world because of perjury, and for the profanation of the Name of God. Exile comes into the world because of idolators, for incest, for murder, and because of nonobservance of the Sabbatical year of the Land. At four periods pestilence increases: in the fourth year; in the seventh year; in the

ז שִׁבְעָה דְבָרִים בַּגֹּלֶם וְשִׁבְעָה בֶּחָכָם. הֶחָכָם אֵינוֹ מְדַבֵּר בִּפְנֵי מִי שֶׁהוּא גָדוֹל מִמֶּנּוּ בְּחָכְמָה, וְאֵינוֹ נִכְנָס לְתוֹךְ דִּבְרֵי חֲבֵרוֹ, וְאֵינוֹ נִבְהָל לְהָשִׁיב, שׁוֹאֵל כָּעִנְיָן וּמֵשִׁיב כַּהֲלָכָה, וְאוֹמֵר עַל־רִאשׁוֹן רִאשׁוֹן וְעַל־אַחֲרוֹן אַחֲרוֹן, וְעַל מַה־שֶּׁלֹּא שָׁמַע אוֹמֵר לֹא שָׁמַעְתִּי, וּמוֹדֶה עַל־הָאֱמֶת, וְחִלּוּפֵיהֶן בַּגֹּלֶם.

ח שִׁבְעָה מִינֵי פוּרְעָנִיּוֹת בָּאִין לָעוֹלָם עַל־שִׁבְעָה גוּפֵי עֲבֵרָה. מִקְצָתָן מְעַשְּׂרִין וּמִקְצָתָן אֵינָן מְעַשְּׂרִין רָעָב שֶׁל־בַּצֹּרֶת בָּא מִקְצָתָן רְעֵבִים וּמִקְצָתָן שְׂבֵעִים, גָּמְרוּ שֶׁלֹּא לְעַשֵּׂר רָעָב שֶׁל מְהוּמָה וְשֶׁל־בַּצֹּרֶת בָּא, וְשֶׁלֹּא לִטּוֹל אֶת־הַחַלָּה רָעָב שֶׁל־כְּלָיָה בָּא. דֶּבֶר בָּא לָעוֹלָם עַל מִיתוֹת הָאֲמוּרוֹת בַּתּוֹרָה שֶׁלֹּא נִמְסְרוּ לְבֵית דִּין וְעַל פֵּרוֹת שְׁבִיעִית. חֶרֶב בָּאָה לָעוֹלָם עַל עִנּוּי הַדִּין וְעַל עִוּוּת הַדִּין וְעַל־הַמּוֹרִים בַּתּוֹרָה שֶׁלֹּא כַהֲלָכָה.

ט חַיָּה רָעָה בָּאָה לָעוֹלָם עַל שְׁבוּעַת שָׁוְא וְעַל חִלּוּל הַשֵּׁם. גָּלוּת בָּא לָעוֹלָם עַל עוֹבְדֵי עֲבוֹדָה זָרָה וְעַל גִּלּוּי עֲרָיוֹת וְעַל־שְׁפִיכוּת דָּמִים, וְעַל־הַשְׁמָטַת הָאָרֶץ: בְּאַרְבָּעָה פְרָקִים הַדֶּבֶר מִתְרַבֶּה, בָּרְבִיעִית וּבַשְּׁבִיעִית וּבְמוֹצָאֵי שְׁבִיעִית וּבְמוֹצָאֵי הֶחָג

year after the seventh year; and at the conclusion of the Festival of Sukkot each year. In the fourth year, because of the failure to give tithes to the poor in the third year; in the seventh year, because of failure to give tithes to the poor in the sixth year; in the year after the seventh year, because of improper use of the seventh-year produce; and at the conclusion of the Festival of Sukkot each year, for depriving the poor of the gifts due them.

10 There are four character types among men: He who says: "What is mine is mine and what is yours is yours" — is the average type; although some say, this is the character of Sodom. He who says: "What is mine is yours and what is yours is mine" is an ignoramus. He who says: "What is mine is yours and what is yours is yours" is a pious man. And he who says: "What is mine is mine and what is yours is mine" is a wicked man.

11 There are four kinds of dispositions: He who is easily provoked and easily pacified — his gain is canceled by his loss. He who is difficult to provoke and difficult to pacify — his loss is canceled by his gain. He who is difficult to provoke and easily pacified — is a pious man. He who is easily provoked and difficult to pacify — is a wicked man.

12 There are four types of students: Quick to learn and quick to forget — his gain is offset by his loss. Slow to learn and slow to forget — his loss is compensated by his gain. Quick to learn and slow to forget — is the best portion. Slow to learn and quick to forget — is the worst portion.

שֶׁבְּכָל־שָׁנָה וְשָׁנָה. בָּרְבִיעִית מִפְּנֵי מַעֲשַׂר עָנִי שֶׁבַּשְּׁלִישִׁית, בַּשְּׁבִיעִית מִפְּנֵי מַעֲשַׂר עָנִי שֶׁבַּשִּׁשִּׁית, וּבְמוֹצָאֵי שְׁבִיעִית מִפְּנֵי פֵּרוֹת שְׁבִיעִית, וּבְמוֹצָאֵי הֶחָג שֶׁבְּכָל־שָׁנָה וְשָׁנָה מִפְּנֵי גֶּזֶל מַתְּנוֹת עֲנִיִּים.

י אַרְבַּע מִדּוֹת בָּאָדָם. הָאוֹמֵר שֶׁלִּי שֶׁלִּי וְשֶׁלְּךָ שֶׁלָּךְ זוֹ מִדָּה בֵּינוֹנִית וְיֵשׁ אוֹמְרִים זוֹ מִדַּת סְדוֹם, שֶׁלִּי שֶׁלָּךְ וְשֶׁלְּךָ שֶׁלִּי עַם הָאָרֶץ, שֶׁלִּי שֶׁלָּךְ וְשֶׁלְּךָ שֶׁלָּךְ חָסִיד, שֶׁלִּי שֶׁלִּי וְשֶׁלְּךָ שֶׁלִּי רָשָׁע.

יא אַרְבַּע מִדּוֹת בַּדֵּעוֹת. נוֹחַ לִכְעוֹס וְנוֹחַ לִרְצוֹת יָצָא הֶפְסֵדוֹ בִּשְׂכָרוֹ, קָשֶׁה לִכְעוֹס וְקָשֶׁה לִרְצוֹת יָצָא שְׂכָרוֹ בְּהֶפְסֵדוֹ, קָשֶׁה לִכְעוֹס וְנוֹחַ לִרְצוֹת חָסִיד, נוֹחַ לִכְעוֹס וְקָשֶׁה לִרְצוֹת רָשָׁע.

יב אַרְבַּע מִדּוֹת בַּתַּלְמִידִים. מָהִיר לִשְׁמוֹעַ וּמָהִיר לְאַבֵּד יָצָא שְׂכָרוֹ בְּהֶפְסֵדוֹ, קָשֶׁה לִשְׁמוֹעַ וְקָשֶׁה לְאַבֵּד יָצָא הֶפְסֵדוֹ בִּשְׂכָרוֹ, מָהִיר לִשְׁמוֹעַ וְקָשֶׁה לְאַבֵּד זוֹ חֵלֶק טוֹב, קָשֶׁה לִשְׁמוֹעַ וּמָהִיר לְאַבֵּד זוֹ חֵלֶק רַע.

13 There are four types of donors to *tzedakah*: He who desires to give but that others should not give — begrudges the privilege of others. He who desires that others should give, but will not give himself — begrudges himself. He who gives and also wants others to give — is pious. He who will not give and does not want others to give — is wicked.

14 There are four types of people who attend the house of study: He who attends the house of study but does not practice its teachings still earns the reward for attending. He who practices but does not attend the house of study, earns the reward for practicing. He who attends and practices is a pious man. He who does not attend and does not practice is a wicked man.

15 There are four types among those who sit before the Sages: a sponge, a funnel, a strainer and a sieve. A sponge, which absorbs everything; a funnel, which receives at one end and spills out at the other; a strainer, which lets the wine pass through and retains the dregs; and a sieve, which lets out the flour dust and retains the fine flour.

16 All love which depends on some sensual object will soon pass away when the object passes away; but if it does not depend on a sensual object, it will never pass away. Which love was dependent upon a sensual object? The love of Amnon and Tamar. And which did not depend on any such object? The love of David and Jonathan.

יג אַרְבַּע מִדּוֹת בְּנוֹתְנֵי צְדָקָה. הָרוֹצֶה שֶׁיִּתֵּן וְלֹא יִתְּנוּ אֲחֵרִים עֵינוֹ רָעָה בְּשֶׁל־אֲחֵרִים, יִתְּנוּ אֲחֵרִים וְהוּא לֹא יִתֵּן עֵינוֹ רָעָה בְּשֶׁלּוֹ, יִתֵּן וְיִתְּנוּ אֲחֵרִים חָסִיד, לֹא יִתֵּן וְלֹא יִתְּנוּ אֲחֵרִים רָשָׁע.

יד אַרְבַּע מִדּוֹת בְּהוֹלְכֵי בֵית הַמִּדְרָשׁ. הוֹלֵךְ וְאֵינוֹ עוֹשֶׂה שְׂכַר הֲלִיכָה בְּיָדוֹ, עוֹשֶׂה וְאֵינוֹ הוֹלֵךְ שְׂכַר מַעֲשֶׂה בְּיָדוֹ, הוֹלֵךְ וְעוֹשֶׂה חָסִיד, לֹא הוֹלֵךְ וְלֹא עוֹשֶׂה רָשָׁע.

טו אַרְבַּע מִדּוֹת בְּיוֹשְׁבִים לִפְנֵי חֲכָמִים, סְפוֹג וּמַשְׁפֵּךְ מְשַׁמֶּרֶת וְנָפָה. סְפוֹג שֶׁהוּא סוֹפֵג אֶת־הַכֹּל, וּמַשְׁפֵּךְ שֶׁמַּכְנִיס בְּזוֹ וּמוֹצִיא בְזוֹ, מְשַׁמֶּרֶת שֶׁמּוֹצִיאָה אֶת־הַיַּיִן וְקוֹלֶטֶת אֶת הַשְּׁמָרִים, וְנָפָה שֶׁמּוֹצִיאָה אֶת־הַקֶּמַח וְקוֹלֶטֶת אֶת־הַסֹּלֶת.

טז כָּל־אַהֲבָה שֶׁהִיא־תְלוּיָה בְדָבָר בָּטֵל דָּבָר בָּטְלָה אַהֲבָה, וְשֶׁאֵינָהּ תְּלוּיָה בְדָבָר אֵינָהּ בְּטֵלָה לְעוֹלָם. אֵיזוֹ הִיא אַהֲבָה שֶׁהִיא־תְלוּיָה בְדָבָר זוֹ אַהֲבַת אַמְנוֹן וְתָמָר, וְשֶׁאֵינָהּ תְּלוּיָה בְדָבָר זוֹ אַהֲבַת דָּוִד וִיהוֹנָתָן.

17 Any controversy which is for the sake of Heaven [a noble purpose], will result in abiding value; but that which is not for the sake of Heaven, shall not in the end be of permanence. Which controversy was for the sake of Heaven? The controversy between Hillel and Shammai. And which was not for the sake of Heaven? The controversy of Korach and all his company.

18 He who leads the people to righteousness, no sin shall occur through him; but he who leads the people to sin, shall not be granted the opportunity to repent. Moses was righteous and he led the people to righteousness; the righteousness of the people is ascribed to him, as it is said (DEUTERONOMY 33:21): "...He executed the justice of the Lord and His judgments with Israel." Jeroboam sinned and caused the people to sin; hence the sin of the people is ascribed to him, as it is said (KINGS I 15:30): "For the sins of Jeroboam [ben Nevat] which he sinned, and caused Israel to sin."

19 He who has the following three qualities is among the disciples of our father, Abraham; but he who has three other attributes is of the disciples of Bil'am the wicked. A good eye, and a humble spirit, and a modest soul, are the characteristics of the disciples of our father, Abraham. An evil eye, a haughty spirit, and an arrogant soul, are the characteristics of Bil'am the wicked. How does the lot of the disciples of our father Abraham differ from the lot of the disciples of Bil'am, the wicked? The disciples of our father Abraham enjoy this world and inherit the World-to-Come, as it is said

יז כָּל מַחֲלֹקֶת שֶׁהִיא לְשֵׁם שָׁמַיִם סוֹפָהּ לְהִתְקַיֵּם וְשֶׁאֵינָהּ לְשֵׁם שָׁמַיִם אֵין סוֹפָהּ לְהִתְקַיֵּם. אֵיזוֹ הִיא מַחֲלֹקֶת שֶׁהִיא לְשֵׁם שָׁמַיִם זוֹ מַחְלֹקֶת הִלֵּל וְשַׁמַּאי, וְשֶׁאֵינָהּ לְשֵׁם שָׁמַיִם זוֹ מַחֲלֹקֶת קֹרַח וְכָל-עֲדָתוֹ.

יח כָּל-הַמְזַכֶּה אֶת-הָרַבִּים אֵין חֵטְא בָּא עַל-יָדוֹ וְכָל-הַמַּחֲטִיא אֶת-הָרַבִּים אֵין מַסְפִּיקִין בְּיָדוֹ לַעֲשׂוֹת תְּשׁוּבָה. מֹשֶׁה זָכָה וְזִכָּה אֶת-הָרַבִּים זְכוּת הָרַבִּים תָּלוּי בּוֹ שֶׁנֶּאֱמַר צִדְקַת יְיָ עָשָׂה וּמִשְׁפָּטָיו עִם-יִשְׂרָאֵל. יָרָבְעָם בֶּן-נְבָט חָטָא וְהֶחֱטִיא אֶת-הָרַבִּים, חֵטְא הָרַבִּים תָּלוּי בּוֹ, שֶׁנֶּאֱמַר עַל-חַטֹּאות יָרָבְעָם אֲשֶׁר חָטָא וַאֲשֶׁר הֶחֱטִיא אֶת-יִשְׂרָאֵל.

יט כָּל-מִי שֶׁיֵּשׁ-בּוֹ שְׁלֹשָׁה דְבָרִים הַלָּלוּ הוּא מִתַּלְמִידָיו שֶׁל-אַבְרָהָם אָבִינוּ, וּשְׁלֹשָׁה דְבָרִים אֲחֵרִים הוּא מִתַּלְמִידָיו שֶׁל-בִּלְעָם הָרָשָׁע. עַיִן טוֹבָה וְרוּחַ נְמוּכָה וְנֶפֶשׁ שְׁפָלָה מִתַּלְמִידָיו שֶׁל-אַבְרָהָם אָבִינוּ, עַיִן רָעָה וְרוּחַ גְּבוֹהָה וְנֶפֶשׁ רְחָבָה מִתַּלְמִידָיו שֶׁל-בִּלְעָם הָרָשָׁע. מַה בֵּין תַּלְמִידָיו שֶׁל-אַבְרָהָם אָבִינוּ לְתַלְמִידָיו שֶׁל-בִּלְעָם הָרָשָׁע. תַּלְמִידָיו שֶׁל-אַבְרָהָם אָבִינוּ

(PROVERBS 8:21): "That I may cause those that love Me to inherit substance, and I will fill their treasures"; but the disciples of Bil'am the wicked inherit Gehinnom and descend into the pit of destruction, as it is written (PSALMS 55:24): "But You, O God, will bring them down into the pit of destruction; bloody and deceitful men shall not live out half their days, but as for me, I will trust in You."

20 Yehudah ben Teima says: Be strong as a leopard, light as an eagle, swift as a deer, and mighty as a lion, to do the will of your Father Who is in Heaven. He used to say: The impudent is destined for Gehinnom and the shamefaced is destined for *Gan Eden.* May it be Your will, O Lord our God, that You rebuild Your city speedily in our days, and grant us our portion in Your Torah.

21 He used to say: At five years of age [one is ready] for the study of Torah; at ten for the study of Mishnah; at thirteen, for the fulfillment of mitzvot; at fifteen, for the study of Talmud; at eighteen, for marriage; at twenty, for a career; at thirty, for strength; at forty, for understanding; at fifty, for giving counsel; at sixty, to reach old age; at seventy, the hoary head; at eighty, for strength in old age; at ninety, in decline; at one hundred, it is as if he had died and passed away and departed from this world.

22 Ben Bag Bag says: Study Torah again and again, for everything is contained in it; constantly examine it; and grow old and gray with it, and

אוֹכְלִין בָּעוֹלָם הַזֶּה וְנוֹחֲלִין הָעוֹלָם הַבָּא, שֶׁנֶּאֱמַר לְהַנְחִיל אֹהֲבַי יֵשׁ וְאֹצְרֹתֵיהֶם אֲמַלֵּא. תַּלְמִידָיו שֶׁל־בִּלְעָם הָרָשָׁע יוֹרְשִׁין גֵּיהִנֹּם וְיוֹרְדִין לִבְאֵר שַׁחַת, שֶׁנֶּאֱמַר וְאַתָּה אֱלֹהִים תּוֹרִדֵם לִבְאֵר שַׁחַת, אַנְשֵׁי דָמִים וּמִרְמָה לֹא־יֶחֱצוּ יְמֵיהֶם וַאֲנִי אֶבְטַח־בָּךְ.

כ יְהוּדָה בֶּן תֵּימָא אוֹמֵר, הֱוֵי עַז כַּנָּמֵר, וְקַל כַּנֶּשֶׁר, וְרָץ כַּצְּבִי וְגִבּוֹר כָּאֲרִי, לַעֲשׂוֹת רְצוֹן אָבִיךְ שֶׁבַּשָּׁמַיִם. הוּא הָיָה אוֹמֵר, עַז פָּנִים לְגֵיהִנָּם, וּבֹשֶׁת פָּנִים לְגַן עֵדֶן. יְהִי רָצוֹן מִלְּפָנֶיךָ יְיָ אֱלֹהֵינוּ וֵאלֹהֵי אֲבוֹתֵינוּ שֶׁיִּבָּנֶה בֵּית הַמִּקְדָּשׁ בִּמְהֵרָה בְיָמֵינוּ וְתֵן חֶלְקֵנוּ בְּתוֹרָתֶךָ:

כא הוּא הָיָה אוֹמֵר, בֶּן־חָמֵשׁ שָׁנִים לַמִּקְרָא, בֶּן־עֶשֶׂר שָׁנִים לַמִּשְׁנָה, בֶּן־שְׁלֹשׁ עֶשְׂרֵה לַמִּצְוֹת, בֶּן־חֲמֵשׁ עֶשְׂרֵה לַתַּלְמוּד, בֶּן־שְׁמֹנֶה עֶשְׂרֵה לַחֻפָּה, בֶּן־עֶשְׂרִים לִרְדּוֹף, בֶּן־שְׁלֹשִׁים לַכֹּחַ, בֶּן־אַרְבָּעִים לַבִּינָה, בֶּן־חֲמִשִּׁים לָעֵצָה, בֶּן־שִׁשִּׁים לַזִּקְנָה, בֶּן־שִׁבְעִים לַשֵּׂיבָה, בֶּן־שְׁמוֹנִים לַגְּבוּרָה, בֶּן־תִּשְׁעִים לָשׁוּחַ, בֶּן־מֵאָה כְּאִלּוּ מֵת וְעָבַר וּבָטֵל מִן הָעוֹלָם.

כב בֶּן בַּג בַּג אוֹמֵר, הֲפָךְ־בָּהּ וַהֲפָךְ־בָּהּ דְּכֹלָּא־בָהּ, וּבָהּ תֶּחֱזֵה וְסִיב וּבְלֵה בָהּ

depart not from it, for there is no better pursuit for you than the Torah.

23 Ben Hei Hei says: According to the effort [aggravation] is the reward.

CHAPTER VI

The Sages taught the following in the style of the Mishnah. Blessed be He, Who chose them and their teaching.

1 Rabbi Meir says: He who occupies himself with Torah with a sincere purpose merits many things; moreover, he is deserving that in his merit the whole world exists. He is called: friend, beloved; he loves God, he loves mankind, he pleases God, he pleases mankind; and it invests him with humility and reverence,

וּמִמֶּנָּה לֹא תָזוּעַ, שֶׁאֵין לְךָ מִדָּה טוֹבָה הֵימֶנָּה.

כג בֶּן־הֵא הֵא אוֹמֵר,
לְפֻם צַעֲרָא אַגְרָא.

פרק ו

שָׁנוּ חֲכָמִים בִּלְשׁוֹן הַמִּשְׁנָה בָּרוּךְ שֶׁבָּחַר בָּהֶם וּבְמִשְׁנָתָם.

א רַבִּי מֵאִיר אוֹמֵר, כָּל הָעוֹסֵק בַּתּוֹרָה לִשְׁמָהּ זוֹכֶה לִדְבָרִים הַרְבֵּה. וְלֹא עוֹד אֶלָּא שֶׁכָּל־הָעוֹלָם כֻּלּוֹ כְּדַי הוּא לוֹ, נִקְרָא רֵעַ, אָהוּב, אוֹהֵב אֶת־הַמָּקוֹם, אוֹהֵב אֶת־הַבְּרִיּוֹת, מְשַׂמֵּחַ אֶת הַמָּקוֹם, מְשַׂמֵּחַ אֶת הַבְּרִיּוֹת. וּמַלְבַּשְׁתּוֹ עֲנָוָה וְיִרְאָה,

and qualifies him to be righteous and pious, upright and faithful. It distances him from sin, and draws him closer to virtue. Through him men benefit from counsel and sound wisdom, understanding and strength, as it is said (PROVERBS 8:14): "Counsel is mine and sound wisdom: I am insight. Mine is strength." It gives him kingship and dominion and sound wisdom and discerning judgment. To him are revealed secrets of the Torah and he becomes like a fountain that ever gathers strength and like a river which is never ceasing; yet he remains modest, patient, ever forgiving of insults; and it [the Torah] makes him great and exalted over all creatures.

2 Rabbi Yehoshua ben Levi says: Every day a Heavenly voice goes forth from Mount Horev proclaiming these words: "Woe to the people for their disregard of the Torah!" For he who does not occupy himself with the Torah is considered rebuked, as it is said (PROVERBS 11:22): "As a golden ring in the snout of a swine, so is a fair woman who is without discretion." And it says further (EXODUS 32:16): "And the tablets were the work of God, and the writing was the writing of God, graven upon the tablets." Read not "graven" [*charut*], but rather "freedom" [*cherut*]; for none may be considered free except he who occupies himself with the study of Torah, and he who occupies himself with the study of Torah will be exalted, as it is said (NUMBERS 21:19): "And from Mattanah to Nachaliel and from Nachaliel to Bamot" (the place-names being symbolic of great spiritual attainment).

3 He who learns from his fellow even one chapter, or one law, or one verse, or one expression, or

וּמַכְשַׁרְתּוֹ לִהְיוֹת צַדִּיק וְחָסִיד וְיָשָׁר וְנֶאֱמָן, וּמְרַחַקְתּוֹ מִן־הַחֵטְא וּמְקָרַבְתּוֹ לִידֵי זְכוּת, וְנֶהֱנִין מִמֶּנּוּ עֵצָה וְתוּשִׁיָּה, בִּינָה וּגְבוּרָה, שֶׁנֶּאֱמַר לִי עֵצָה וְתוּשִׁיָּה אֲנִי בִינָה לִי גְבוּרָה, וְנוֹתֶנֶת לוֹ מַלְכוּת וּמֶמְשָׁלָה וְחִקּוּר דִּין, וּמְגַלִּין לוֹ רָזֵי תוֹרָה, וְנַעֲשֶׂה כְּמַעְיָן הַמִּתְגַּבֵּר וּכְנָהָר שֶׁאֵינוֹ פוֹסֵק וֶהֱוֵי צָנוּעַ וְאֶרֶךְ רוּחַ וּמוֹחֵל עַל עֶלְבּוֹנוֹ, וּמְגַדַּלְתּוֹ וּמְרוֹמַמְתּוֹ עַל־כָּל הַמַּעֲשִׂים.

ב אָמַר רַבִּי יְהוֹשֻׁעַ בֶּן־לֵוִי, בְּכָל־יוֹם וָיוֹם בַּת־קוֹל יוֹצֵאת מֵהַר חוֹרֵב וּמַכְרֶזֶת וְאוֹמֶרֶת אוֹי לָהֶם לַבְּרִיּוֹת מֵעֶלְבּוֹנָהּ שֶׁל תּוֹרָה, שֶׁכָּל־מִי שֶׁאֵינוֹ עוֹסֵק בַּתּוֹרָה נִקְרָא נָזוּף, שֶׁנֶּאֱמַר נֶזֶם זָהָב בְּאַף חֲזִיר אִשָּׁה יָפָה וְסָרַת טָעַם. וְאוֹמֵר, וְהַלֻּחֹת מַעֲשֵׂה אֱלֹהִים הֵמָּה וְהַמִּכְתָּב מִכְתַּב אֱלֹהִים הוּא חָרוּת עַל־הַלֻּחֹת, אַל תִּקְרָא חָרוּת אֶלָּא חֵרוּת, שֶׁאֵין לָךְ בֶּן־חֹרִין אֶלָּא מִי שֶׁעוֹסֵק בְּתַלְמוּד תּוֹרָה, וְכָל־מִי שֶׁעוֹסֵק בַּתּוֹרָה תָּדִיר, הֲרֵי זֶה מִתְעַלֶּה שֶׁנֶּאֱמַר וּמִמַּתָּנָה נַחֲלִיאֵל וּמִנַּחֲלִיאֵל בָּמוֹת.

ג הַלּוֹמֵד מֵחֲבֵרוֹ פֶּרֶק אֶחָד אוֹ הֲלָכָה אַחַת אוֹ פָּסוּק אֶחָד אוֹ דִבּוּר אֶחָד אוֹ

even a single letter, must pay him honor; for so we find with David, King of Israel, who learned only two things from Achitofel, and yet he called him his teacher, his guide, and his close friend, as it is said (PSALMS 55:14): "But it was you, a man my equal, my guide and my confidant." Surely this contains an inference from minor to major; if David, the King of Israel, who learned from Achitofel only two things, called him his teacher, his guide, and his close friend — how much more ought one who learns from his fellowman one chapter or one law, one verse, one expression, or even one letter, to pay him honor! And honor is inherent only in Torah, for it is said (PROVERBS 3:35): "The wise shall inherit honor"; "And the upright shall inherit the good" (PROVERBS 28:10); and "good" implies Torah, as it is said (PROVERBS 4:2): "For I give you good doctrine; forsake not my Torah."

4 This is the way of the Torah: To eat bread and salt; to drink water by measure; to sleep upon the ground; and to live a life of hardship while you study the Torah diligently. If you do so, "...happy shall you be, and it shall be well with you" (PSALMS 128:2): *happy shall you be* — in this world, *and it shall be well with you* — in the World-to-Come. Do not seek greatness for yourself, and strive not after honor. Let your good deeds exceed your learning. And crave not for the table of kings, for your table is greater than their table, and your crown is greater than their crown; and your Employer is faithful to pay you the reward for your work.

5 Greater is the Torah than the priesthood and the kingship: for the kingship is acquired by thirty

אֲפִילוּ אוֹת אַחַת צָרִיךְ לִנְהַג בּוֹ כָּבוֹד, שֶׁכֵּן מָצִינוּ בְּדָוִד מֶלֶךְ יִשְׂרָאֵל שֶׁלֹּא לָמַד מֵאֲחִיתֹפֶל אֶלָּא שְׁנֵי דְבָרִים בִּלְבָד קְרָאוֹ רַבּוֹ אַלּוּפוֹ וּמְיֻדָּעוֹ, שֶׁנֶּאֱמַר וְאַתָּה אֱנוֹשׁ כְּעֶרְכִּי אַלּוּפִי וּמְיֻדָּעִי. וַהֲלֹא דְבָרִים קַל וָחֹמֶר, וּמַה דָּוִד מֶלֶךְ יִשְׂרָאֵל שֶׁלֹּא לָמַד מֵאֲחִיתֹפֶל אֶלָּא שְׁנֵי דְבָרִים בִּלְבָד קְרָאוֹ רַבּוֹ אַלּוּפוֹ וּמְיֻדָּעוֹ, הַלּוֹמֵד מֵחֲבֵרוֹ פֶּרֶק אֶחָד אוֹ הֲלָכָה אַחַת אוֹ פָּסוּק אֶחָד אוֹ דִבּוּר אֶחָד אוֹ אֲפִילוּ אוֹת אַחַת, עַל־אַחַת כַּמָּה וְכַמָּה שֶׁצָּרִיךְ לִנְהַג בּוֹ כָּבוֹד. וְאֵין כָּבוֹד אֶלָּא תוֹרָה, שֶׁנֶּאֱמַר כָּבוֹד חֲכָמִים יִנְחָלוּ וּתְמִימִים יִנְחֲלוּ טוֹב. וְאֵין טוֹב אֶלָּא תוֹרָה, שֶׁנֶּאֱמַר כִּי לֶקַח טוֹב נָתַתִּי לָכֶם תּוֹרָתִי אַל־תַּעֲזֹבוּ.

ד כָּךְ הִיא דַּרְכָּהּ שֶׁל תּוֹרָה, פַּת בַּמֶּלַח תֹּאכֵל וּמַיִם בַּמְּשׂוּרָה תִּשְׁתֶּה וְעַל הָאָרֶץ תִּישָׁן וְחַיֵּי צַעַר תִּחְיֶה וּבַתּוֹרָה אַתָּה עָמֵל. אִם אַתָּה עוֹשֶׂה כֵן אַשְׁרֶיךָ וְטוֹב לָךְ, אַשְׁרֶיךָ בָּעוֹלָם הַזֶּה וְטוֹב לָךְ לָעוֹלָם הַבָּא. אַל־תְּבַקֵּשׁ גְּדֻלָּה לְעַצְמְךָ וְאַל־תַּחְמֹד כָּבוֹד. יוֹתֵר מִלִּמּוּדְךָ עֲשֵׂה, וְאַל־תִּתְאַוֶּה לְשֻׁלְחָנָם שֶׁל־מְלָכִים, שֶׁשֻּׁלְחָנְךָ גָּדוֹל מִשֻּׁלְחָנָם, וְכִתְרְךָ גָּדוֹל מִכִּתְרָם וְנֶאֱמָן הוּא בַּעַל מְלַאכְתְּךָ, שֶׁיְּשַׁלֵּם לָךְ שְׂכַר פְּעֻלָּתְךָ.

ה גְּדוֹלָה תּוֹרָה יוֹתֵר מִן הַכְּהֻנָּה וּמִן הַמַּלְכוּת, שֶׁהַמַּלְכוּת נִקְנֵית בִּשְׁלֹשִׁים מַעֲלוֹת,

qualifications, and the priesthood by twenty-four; while the Torah is acquired by forty-eight qualifications, namely: by study, by attentive listening, by ordered speech, by the consideration of the heart, by perfect understanding, by meditation, by awe, by reverence, by modesty, by cheerfulness, by close association with the Sages, by communion with colleagues, by earnest discussions with the students, by prudence, by knowledge of the Scriptures and the Mishnah, by moderation in sleep, moderation in conversation, moderation in pleasure, moderation in jest, and moderation in business; by patience, by a good heart, by trust in the Sages, and by acceptance of suffering.

6 [The Torah is acquired by one] who knows his place; who is content with his lot; who puts a fence about his words; who claims no credit for himself; who is beloved; who loves God; who loves mankind; who loves kindness; who loves reproof; who loves rectitude; who distances himself from honor; who is not arrogant about his learning; who is not happy in rendering decisions; who shares the burden with his fellowman, who judges his friend favorably; who guides him in the truth, and in peace; whose mind is fully directed to his study; who asks and answers; listens and adds to his knowledge; who learns in order to teach, and studies in order to do good deeds; who makes his teacher wiser; who notes with care his learning, and reports a saying in the name of its author. For so you have learned: Whoever conveys a saying in the name of its author, brings deliverance to the world, as it is said (ESTHER 2:22): "and Esther told the king thereof in Mordecai's name."

וְהַכְּהֻנָּה — בְּעֶשְׂרִים וְאַרְבַּע, וְהַתּוֹרָה נִקְנֵית בְּאַרְבָּעִים וּשְׁמוֹנָה דְבָרִים: בְּתַלְמוּד, בִּשְׁמִיעַת הָאֹזֶן, בַּעֲרִיכַת שְׂפָתַיִם, בְּבִינַת הַלֵּב, בְּשִׂכְלוּת הַלֵּב, בְּאֵימָה, בְּיִרְאָה, בַּעֲנָוָה, בְּשִׂמְחָה, בְּשִׁמּוּשׁ חֲכָמִים, בְּדִקְדּוּק חֲבֵרִים, וּבְפִלְפּוּל הַתַּלְמִידִים, בְּיִשּׁוּב, בְּמִקְרָא, בְּמִשְׁנָה, בְּמִעוּט שֵׁנָה, בְּמִעוּט שִׂיחָה, בְּמִעוּט תַּעֲנוּג, בְּמִעוּט שְׂחוֹק, בְּמִעוּט דֶּרֶךְ אֶרֶץ, בְּאֶרֶךְ אַפַּיִם, בְּלֵב טוֹב, בֶּאֱמוּנַת חֲכָמִים, וּבְקַבָּלַת הַיִּסּוּרִין.

ו הַמַּכִּיר אֶת מְקוֹמוֹ, וְהַשָּׂמֵחַ בְּחֶלְקוֹ, וְהָעוֹשֶׂה סְיָג לִדְבָרָיו, וְאֵינוֹ מַחֲזִיק טוֹבָה לְעַצְמוֹ, אָהוּב, אוֹהֵב אֶת הַמָּקוֹם, אוֹהֵב אֶת הַבְּרִיּוֹת, אוֹהֵב אֶת הַצְּדָקוֹת, אוֹהֵב אֶת הַתּוֹכָחוֹת, אוֹהֵב אֶת הַמֵּישָׁרִים, מִתְרַחֵק מִן הַכָּבוֹד, וְלֹא מֵגִיס לִבּוֹ בְּתַלְמוּדוֹ, וְאֵינוֹ שָׂמֵחַ בְּהוֹרָאָה, נוֹשֵׂא בְּעֹל עִם חֲבֵרוֹ, מַכְרִיעוֹ לְכַף זְכוּת, מַעֲמִידוֹ עַל הָאֱמֶת, מַעֲמִידוֹ עַל הַשָּׁלוֹם, מִתְיַשֵּׁב לִבּוֹ בְּתַלְמוּדוֹ, שׁוֹאֵל וּמֵשִׁיב, שׁוֹמֵעַ וּמוֹסִיף, הַלּוֹמֵד עַל מְנָת לְלַמֵּד, וְהַלּוֹמֵד עַל מְנָת לַעֲשׂוֹת, הַמַּחְכִּים אֶת רַבּוֹ, וְהַמְכַוֵּן אֶת שְׁמוּעָתוֹ, וְהָאוֹמֵר דָּבָר בְּשֵׁם אוֹמְרוֹ. הָא לָמַדְתָּ, שֶׁכָּל הָאוֹמֵר דָּבָר בְּשֵׁם אוֹמְרוֹ מֵבִיא גְאֻלָּה לָעוֹלָם, שֶׁנֶּאֱמַר "וַתֹּאמֶר אֶסְתֵּר לַמֶּלֶךְ בְּשֵׁם מָרְדֳּכָי".

7 Great is the Torah, for it gives life to those who practice it in this world and in the World-to-Come, as it is said (PROVERBS 4:22): "For they are life to those who find them, and healing to all their flesh." And it says (PROVERBS 3:8): "It shall be health to your body and marrow to your bones." And it says (PROVERBS 3:18): "She is a tree of life to those who lay hold upon her, and happy is everyone who retains her." And it says (PROVERBS 1:9): "For they shall be an ornament of grace unto your head, and chains [of honor] about your neck." And it says (PROVERBS 4:9): "She shall give to your head an ornament of grace; a crown of glory shall she deliver to you." And it says (PROVERBS 3:16): "Length of days is in her right hand; and in her left hand, riches and honor." And it says (PROVERBS 3:2): "For length of days, and long life, and peace, shall they add to you."

8 Rabbi Shimon ben Menasia says in the name of Rabbi Shimon ben Yochai: Beauty, strength, riches, honor, wisdom, old age, a hoary head, and children are comely to the righteous and comely to the world, as it is written (PROVERBS 16:31): "The hoary head is a crown of glory; it is found in the way of righteousness." And it says (PROVERBS 14:24): "The crown of the wise is their riches." And it says (PROVERBS 17:6): "Children's children are the crown of old men; and the glory of children are their fathers." And it says (PROVERBS 20:29): "The glory of young men is their strength; and the beauty of old men is the hoary head." And it says (ISAIAH 24:23): "Then the moon shall be confounded, and the sun ashamed, when the Lord of hosts shall reign on Mount Zion and in Jerusalem,

ז גְדוֹלָה תּוֹרָה שֶׁהִיא נוֹתֶנֶת חַיִּים לְעוֹשֶׂיהָ בָּעוֹלָם הַזֶּה וּבָעוֹלָם הַבָּא, שֶׁנֶּאֱמַר כִּי־חַיִּים הֵם לְמֹצְאֵיהֶם וּלְכָל־בְּשָׂרוֹ מַרְפֵּא, וְאוֹמֵר רִפְאוּת תְּהִי לְשָׁרֶּךָ וְשִׁקּוּי לְעַצְמוֹתֶיךָ, וְאוֹמֵר עֵץ־חַיִּים הִיא לַמַּחֲזִיקִים בָּהּ וְתֹמְכֶיהָ מְאֻשָּׁר, וְאוֹמֵר כִּי לִוְיַת־חֵן הֵם לְרֹאשֶׁךָ וַעֲנָקִים לְגַרְגְּרֹתֶיךָ, וְאוֹמֵר תִּתֵּן לְרֹאשְׁךָ לִוְיַת־חֵן עֲטֶרֶת תִּפְאֶרֶת תְּמַגְּנֶךָּ, וְאוֹמֵר כִּי בִי יִרְבּוּ יָמֶיךָ וְיוֹסִיפוּ לְּךָ שְׁנוֹת חַיִּים, וְאוֹמֵר אֹרֶךְ יָמִים בִּימִינָהּ בִּשְׂמֹאולָהּ עֹשֶׁר וְכָבוֹד, וְאוֹמֵר כִּי אֹרֶךְ יָמִים וּשְׁנוֹת חַיִּים וְשָׁלוֹם יוֹסִיפוּ לָךְ.

ח רַבִּי שִׁמְעוֹן בֶּן מְנַסְיָא אוֹמֵר מִשּׁוּם רַבִּי שִׁמְעוֹן בֶּן יוֹחַאי: הַנּוֹי, וְהַכֹּחַ, וְהָעֹשֶׁר, וְהַכָּבוֹד, וְהַחָכְמָה, וְהַזִּקְנָה, וְהַשֵּׂיבָה, וְהַבָּנִים — נָאֶה לַצַּדִּיקִים וְנָאֶה לָעוֹלָם, שֶׁנֶּאֱמַר (שם טז, לא): "עֲטֶרֶת תִּפְאֶרֶת שֵׂיבָה, בְּדֶרֶךְ צְדָקָה תִּמָּצֵא", וְאוֹמֵר (שם יד, כד): "עֲטֶרֶת חֲכָמִים עָשְׁרָם"; וְאוֹמֵר (שם יז, ו): "עֲטֶרֶת זְקֵנִים בְּנֵי בָנִים, וְתִפְאֶרֶת בָּנִים אֲבוֹתָם", וְאוֹמֵר (שם כ, כט): "תִּפְאֶרֶת בַּחוּרִים כֹּחָם, וַהֲדַר זְקֵנִים שֵׂיבָה"; וְאוֹמֵר (ישעיה כד, כג): "וְחָפְרָה הַלְּבָנָה וּבוֹשָׁה הַחַמָּה, כִּי־מָלַךְ יְיָ צְבָאוֹת בְּהַר צִיּוֹן וּבִירוּשָׁלַיִם וְנֶגֶד זְקֵנָיו

and before His elders gloriously." Rabbi Shimon ben Menasia says: These seven qualifications, which the Sages enumerated as pertaining to the righteous, were all realized in *Rabi* [*Yehudah Ha-Nasi*] and in his sons.

9 Rabbi Yosei ben Kisma said: Once I was traveling on the road, when a man met me, and greeted me with "*Shalom.*" I returned the greeting with "*Shalom.*" He said to me: "Rabbi, from what place are you?" I replied: "I come from a great city of sages and scholars." He said to me: "Rabbi, if you were willing to live with us in our place, I would give you a million golden dinars and precious stones and pearls." I said to him: "My son, if you were to give me all the silver and gold and precious stones and pearls in the world, I would not live anywhere except in a place of Torah"; for in the hour of man's departure, neither silver nor gold nor precious stones and pearls accompany him, but Torah and good deeds alone, as it is said (PROVERBS 6:22): "When you go, it shall lead you; when you sleep, it shall keep you; and when you awaken, it shall talk with you." *When you go, it shall lead you* — in this world; *when you sleep, it shall keep you* — in the grave; *and when you awaken, it shall talk with you* — in the World-to-Come. And likewise it is written in the Book of Psalms by David, King of Israel (PSALMS 119:72): "The Torah of Your mouth is better unto me than thousands of gold and silver." And it says (HAGGAI 2:8): "The silver is Mine, and the gold is Mine, says the Lord of hosts."

10 Five possessions has the Holy One, blessed be He, declared in this world, namely: The Torah is His own special possession; Heaven and earth are a

כָּבוֹד". רַבִּי שִׁמְעוֹן בֶּן מְנַסְיָא אוֹמֵר: אֵלּוּ שֶׁבַע מִדּוֹת, שֶׁמָּנוּ חֲכָמִים לַצַּדִּיקִים, כֻּלָּם נִתְקַיְּמוּ בְּרַבִּי וּבְבָנָיו.

ט אָמַר רַבִּי יוֹסֵי בֶּן קִסְמָא: פַּעַם אַחַת הָיִיתִי מְהַלֵּךְ בַּדֶּרֶךְ, וּפָגַע בִּי אָדָם אֶחָד, וְנָתַן לִי שָׁלוֹם וְהֶחֱזַרְתִּי לוֹ שָׁלוֹם. אָמַר לִי: רַבִּי, מֵאֵיזֶה מָקוֹם אַתָּה? אָמַרְתִּי לוֹ: מֵעִיר גְּדוֹלָה שֶׁל חֲכָמִים וְשֶׁל סוֹפְרִים אֲנִי. אָמַר לִי: רַבִּי, רְצוֹנְךָ שֶׁתָּדוּר עִמָּנוּ בִּמְקוֹמֵנוּ? וַאֲנִי אֶתֵּן לְךָ אֶלֶף אֲלָפִים דִּינְרֵי זָהָב וַאֲבָנִים טוֹבוֹת וּמַרְגָּלִיּוֹת. אָמַרְתִּי לוֹ: בְּנִי, אִם אַתָּה נוֹתֵן לִי כָּל כֶּסֶף וְזָהָב וַאֲבָנִים טוֹבוֹת וּמַרְגָּלִיּוֹת שֶׁבָּעוֹלָם, אֵינִי דָר אֶלָּא בִּמְקוֹם תּוֹרָה, לְפִי שֶׁבִּשְׁעַת פְּטִירָתוֹ שֶׁל אָדָם אֵין מְלַוִּין לוֹ לָאָדָם לֹא כֶסֶף וְלֹא זָהָב וְלֹא אֲבָנִים טוֹבוֹת וּמַרְגָּלִיּוֹת, אֶלָּא תּוֹרָה וּמַעֲשִׂים טוֹבִים בִּלְבַד, שֶׁנֶּאֱמַר (משלי ו, כב): "בְּהִתְהַלֶּכְךָ תַּנְחֶה אֹתָךְ, בְּשָׁכְבְּךָ תִּשְׁמֹר עָלֶיךָ, וַהֲקִיצוֹתָ הִיא תְשִׂיחֶךָ". "בְּהִתְהַלֶּכְךָ תַּנְחֶה אֹתָךְ" — בָּעוֹלָם הַזֶּה; "בְּשָׁכְבְּךָ תִּשְׁמֹר עָלֶיךָ" — בַּקֶּבֶר; "וַהֲקִיצוֹתָ הִיא תְשִׂיחֶךָ" — לָעוֹלָם הַבָּא. וְכֵן כָּתוּב בְּסֵפֶר תְּהִלִּים עַל יְדֵי דָוִד מֶלֶךְ יִשְׂרָאֵל (תהלים קיט, עב): "טוֹב-לִי תוֹרַת-פִּיךָ מֵאַלְפֵי זָהָב וָכָסֶף", וְאוֹמֵר (חגי ב, ח): "לִי הַכֶּסֶף וְלִי הַזָּהָב, אָמַר יְיָ צְבָאוֹת".

י חֲמִשָּׁה קִנְיָנִים קָנָה (לוֹ) הַקָּדוֹשׁ בָּרוּךְ הוּא בְּעוֹלָמוֹ וְאֵלּוּ הֵן. תּוֹרָה קִנְיָן אֶחָד, שָׁמַיִם וָאָרֶץ קִנְיָן אֶחָד, אַבְרָהָם קִנְיָן אֶחָד, יִשְׂרָאֵל

special possession; Abraham is a special possession; Israel is a special possession; the Temple is a special possession. How do we know that the Torah is a special possession? As it is written (PROVERBS 8:22): "The Lord possessed me in the beginning of His way, before His works of old." How do we know that Heaven and earth are a special possession? As it is written (ISAIAH 66:1): "Thus says the Lord: The Heaven is My throne, and the earth is My footstool; where is the house that you build unto Me? And where is the place of My rest?" And it says (PSALMS 104:24): "O Lord, how manifold are Your works! In wisdom have You made them all; the earth is full of Your riches." How do we know that Abraham is a special possession? As it is written (GENESIS 14:19): "And he blessed him and said: Blessed be Abram of the Most High God, Possessor of Heaven and earth." How do we know that Israel is a special possession? As it is written (EXODUS 15:16): "...till Your people pass over, O Lord, till the people pass over, which you have purchased." And it says (PSALMS 16:3): "As for the holy people who are upon earth, they are the excellent ones in whom is all My delight." How do we know that the Temple is a special possession? As it is said (EXODUS 15:17): "...the Sanctuary, O Lord, which Your hands have established." And it says (PSALMS 78:54): "And He brought them to the realm of His Sanctuary; even to this mountain, which His right hand had purchased."

11 Everything that the Holy One, blessed be He, created in His world, He created solely for His glory, as it is said (ISAIAH 43:7): "Even everything that is called by My Name, and which I have created for My glory, I have formed it, yea, I have made it." And it says (EXODUS 15:18): "The Lord shall reign for ever and ever."

קִנְיָן אֶחָד, בֵּית הַמִּקְדָּשׁ קִנְיָן אֶחָד. תּוֹרָה מִנַּיִן, דִּכְתִיב יְיָ קָנָנִי רֵאשִׁית דַּרְכּוֹ קֶדֶם מִפְעָלָיו מֵאָז. שָׁמַיִם וָאָרֶץ מִנַּיִן, דִּכְתִיב כֹּה אָמַר יְיָ הַשָּׁמַיִם כִּסְאִי וְהָאָרֶץ הֲדֹם רַגְלָי אֵי־זֶה בַיִת אֲשֶׁר תִּבְנוּ־לִי וְאֵי־זֶה מָקוֹם מְנוּחָתִי. וְאוֹמֵר מָה רַבּוּ מַעֲשֶׂיךָ יְיָ כֻּלָּם בְּחָכְמָה עָשִׂיתָ מָלְאָה הָאָרֶץ קִנְיָנֶךָ. אַבְרָהָם מִנַּיִן, דִּכְתִיב וַיְבָרְכֵהוּ וַיֹּאמַר בָּרוּךְ אַבְרָם לְאֵל עֶלְיוֹן קֹנֵה שָׁמַיִם וָאָרֶץ. יִשְׂרָאֵל מִנַּיִן, דִּכְתִיב עַד־יַעֲבֹר עַמְּךָ יְיָ עַד יַעֲבֹר עַם־זוּ קָנִיתָ. וְאוֹמֵר לִקְדוֹשִׁים אֲשֶׁר בָּאָרֶץ הֵמָּה וְאַדִּירֵי כָּל־חֶפְצִי־בָם. בֵּית הַמִּקְדָּשׁ מִנַּיִן, דִּכְתִיב מָכוֹן לְשִׁבְתְּךָ פָּעַלְתָּ יְיָ מִקְּדָשׁ אֲדֹנָי כּוֹנְנוּ יָדֶיךָ. וְאוֹמֵר וַיְבִיאֵם אֶל־גְּבוּל קָדְשׁוֹ הַר זֶה קָנְתָה יְמִינוֹ:

יב כָּל מַה־שֶּׁבָּרָא הַקָּדוֹשׁ בָּרוּךְ הוּא בְּעוֹלָמוֹ לֹא בְרָאוֹ אֶלָּא לִכְבוֹדוֹ, שֶׁנֶּאֱמַר כֹּל הַנִּקְרָא בִשְׁמִי וְלִכְבוֹדִי בְּרָאתִיו יְצַרְתִּיו אַף עֲשִׂיתִיו. וְאוֹמֵר, יְיָ יִמְלֹךְ לְעֹלָם וָעֶד.

Glossary

The following glossary provides a partial explanation of some of the foreign words and phrases used in this book. The spelling and explanations reflect the way the specific word is used herein. Often, there are alternate spellings and meanings for the words.

AHAVAT YISRAEL: love of one's fellow Jews.
AMORA'IM: (A.) the Sages whose opinions comprise the Gemara.
ANSHEI KNESSET HA-GEDOLAH: the Men of the Great Assembly.
AVODAH: labor; worship; the Temple Service.
BAR MITZVAH: a Jewish boy of 13, the age at which he assumes religious obligations; the celebration marking that occasion.
BARAITA(-OT): (A.) a Tannaic compilation which is not included in the MISHNAH.
BEIT DIN: a Jewish court of law.
BEIT HA-MIDRASH: a house of study; a synagogue.
BEIT HA-MIKDASH: the Holy Temple.
BRIT MILAH: the ritual of circumcision.
CHACHAM: a wise man.
CHASSID: one who behaves with lovingkindness and compassion; followers of the ethical teachings of the Ba'al Shem Tov.
CHESSED: lovingkindness.
DIN TORAH: lit., Torah law; a dispute judged by a Rabbinical court in accordance with the HALACHAH.
ERETZ YISRAEL: the Land of Israel.
GEMILUT CHASADIM: the practice of lovingkindness.
HALACHAH: Jewish law.
KADDISH: the mourner's prayer.
KEHILLAH(-OT): Jewish community(-ies) or congregation(s).
LAG BA-OMER: the 33rd day in the Counting of the OMER, the seven-week period of semi-mourning between Pesach and Shavuot.
MISHNAH: the compiled, codified of the Oral Law; a paragraph or chapter of the Oral Law.
MITZVAH(-OT): commandment(s) of the Torah.

MUSAR: the study of Torah ethics and values.
NEBACH: (Y.) "Poor thing!"
OMER: the barley offering sacrificed on Pesach in the BEIT HA-MIKDASH.
RIBBONO SHEL OLAM: Master of the Universe.
SHECHINAH: the Divine Presence.
SHEMONEH ESREH: the Eighteen Benedictions, or *Amidah* prayer.
SIDDUR: the prayer book.
SIMCHAH: happiness; a joyous occasion.
TZADDIK: a righteous, pious man; a holy man.
TZEDAKAH: charity; righteousness.
TALLIT: a prayer shawl.
TALMID CHACHAM: a Torah scholar.
TEFILLIN: phylacteries.
YESHIVAH(-OT): academy(-ies) of Torah study.

Index

Abraham 37, 48, 64, 130
Akavia ben Mahalalel 155
Akiva, Rabbi 18, 40, 46, 50, 53, 68, 80, 87, 90, 91, 170
Alexander the Great 134
Anshei Knesset Ha-Gedolah 133
Antignos of Socho 33, 81, 136
Antoninus, Emperor 8, 9, 147
Aristoblus 139
Avtalyon 25, 139

Baal Shem Tov 41, 42
Bar Kochba 146, 158, 164, 174
Ben Azzai 177
Ben Bag Bag 193
Ben Hei Hei 193
Ben Zoma 5, 20, 21, 45, 101, 177
Berdichev, Rabbi Levi Yitzchak of 27, 130
Bruriah 158, 165

Cain 97
Chafetz Chayim 10, 16, 41, 111-12
Chaggai, Zechariah, and Malachi 133, 141
Chalafta ben Dosa of Kfar Chananiah, Rabbi 162
Chanina (Chananiah) ben Chachinai 160
Chanina (Chananiah) ben Teradyon, Rabbi 157, 165
Chanina, Rabbi 156
Chanina ben Dosa, Rabbi 21, 70, 166

Dosa ben Harkinas, Rabbi 167

Dostai, Rabbi, ben Rabbi Yannai 163
Dubner Maggid 109, 110, 131

Elazar ben Arach 30, 40, 60, 153
Elazar ben Azariah 66, 87, 175
Elazar ben Chisma, Rabbi 176
Elazar ben Shammua, Rabbi 184
Elazar ben Yehudah of Bartota 162
Elazar Ha-Moda'i, Rabbi 168
Eliezer (Elazar) Ha-Kappar, Rabbi 45, 192
Eliezer ben Hurkanos, Rabbi 151
Eliezer ben Ya'akov, Rabbi 182
Elijah 7, 129
Elisha ben Avuyah 165, 173, 191
Ezra 133, 171

Gamliel ben Rabbi Yehuda *Ha-Nasi*, Rabban 148
Gamliel the Elder, *Rabban* 28, 144
Gan Eden 6, 196
Gehinnom 6, 9, 107

Hadrian, Emperor 26, 146, 147
Herod 71, 72
Hillel 17, 39, 40, 61, 118, 119, 140, 171
Hurkanos 139

Levitas, Rabbi 178

Maimonides 6, 31, 45, 48, 54, 62, 64
Matia ben Charash, Rabbi 188
Meir, Rabbi 71, 84, 163

Index 275

Mendel of Kotsk, Rebbe   37
Mishnah   147, 155, 160, 164, 175, 182, 184
Moses   18, 41, 48, 98, 121, 170, 171

Nechunia ben Ha-Kanah, Rabbi   161
Nehorai (Nechemiah), Rabbi   186
Nero, Emperor   163
Nittai of Arbel   12, 137

Rashi   31, 39, 76

Sabbatical year   142
Sadigurer Rebbe   19
Salanter, Yisrael, Rabbi   19
Shammai   81, 140, 143
Shlomo of Karlin, Rabbi   42
Shlomtzion, Queen   139
Shemayah   71, 139
Shimon ben Elazar   90, 106, 108, 189
Shimon ben Gamliel the Elder, *Rabban*   25, 145
Shimon ben Natanel, Rabbi   153
Shimon ben Shatach   49, 138
Shimon ben Yochai   5, 158
Shimon *Ha-Tzaddik*   65, 87, 93, 134
Shmuel Ha-Katan   190
Solomon, King   17, 21, 23, 26, 27, 86

Tarfon, Rabbi   18, 41, 154
Tzadok, Rabbi   179

Vespasian, General (Emperor)   149, 150
Vilna Gaon   133

Ya'akov ben Kurshai, Rabbi   5, 188
Yannai, Rabbi   187
Yehoshua ben Chananiah, Rabbi   151
Yehoshua ben Levi, Rabbi   7, 30, 194
Yehoshua ben Perachiah   137
Yehudah bar Illai, Rabbi   185
Yehudah ben Tabbai   49, 138
Yehudah ben Teima   192
Yehudah *Ha-Nasi*, Rabbi (*Rabi*)   8, 44, 50, 146
Yishmael ben Elisha, Rabbi   169
Yishmael ben Rabbi Yosei, Rabbi   182
Yishmael ben Yochanan (ben Beroka), Rabbi   179
Yochanan ben Beroka, Rabbi   178
Yochanan ben Zakkai, *Rabban*   30, 43, 55, 83, 149, 171
Yochanan Ha-Sandlar, Rabbi   183
Yonatan, Rabbi   182
Yosei bar Yehudah, Rabbi   192
Yosei ben Kisma, Rabbi   197
Yosei ben Yoezer of Tzeredah   11, 30, 136
Yosei *Ha-Kohen*, Rabbi   152

Zusya of Hanipol, Reb   40

Sponsors

ALIZA SAVETSKY

In loving memory of her mother
Miriam Abromowitz
מרים בת צבי אלימלך פריידא ז״ל
נפטרה כו׳ אב תשמ״ז

My mother Miriam, a true בת תורה, touched the lives of all who knew her, giving unselfishly of herself to family and friends alike. Her children were her true pride and joy, and she denied herself many material comforts in order to provide them with a good Torah education.

Surviving Auschwitz, she was determined to tell the world the truth about the Holocaust, and she was never reluctant to speak her mind. Her worldly knowledge and goodness of heart benefited many who knew her.

Words cannot begin to express how much I miss her. With her death it seemed as if a part of my being was taken from me. At the tender age of twenty-six, I felt bitterness, anger, and confusion. Although time heals, the scars remain.

My mother was a true אשת חיל in every sense of the word. She passed on to me her strong belief in Hashem and Torah, and that is something I will cherish forever.

Sponsors

CANTOR LEIB RASKIN
THE GOLDKORN FAMILY

In loving memory of
Dina Raskin
דינה בת ר׳ זאב ז״ל
our dear wife, mother, mother-in-law,
grandmother and great-grandmother.
נפטרה ביום ט״ז תמוז תש״ן
July 8, 1990
ירושלים

Sponsors

REBECCA AND SHABTAI KEVELSON

In loving memory of their parents

איש התורה והחסד
ר׳ שמואל בנימין בן ר׳ יהודה לייב הלוי קבלסון זצ״ל
נפטר ו׳ תשרי תשכ״ג
והצדקת
מרת לאה פריידא בת ר׳ חיים שלום ע״ה
נפטרה ט׳ מרחשון תשכ״ז
ומרבה הצדקה
ר׳ שמואל בן ר׳ יצחק פלאט ז״ל
נפטר כ׳ אלול תשל״ב
והנדיבה
מרת שרה שיינדל בת ר׳ אברהם ע״ה
נפטרה כ״ח תשרי תש״מ

יהא זכרם ברוך ות.נ.צ.ב.ה.

Sponsors

SOL SCHWARTZ

In loving memory
לזכר נשמות הקדושים
אבי
ר׳ אליעזר בן ר׳ חננאל הכהן שווארץ
אמי
מרת הינדא בה"ר צבי אריה פרידמן
אחיותי
חיה שייndיל, שרה, לאה,
ופריידא עם בעליה וילדיה
שנהרגו עקה"ש בשואה הי"ד

אשתי החשובה והיקרה, רודפת צדקה וחסד
מרת בתיה בת ר׳ אריה ע"ה
נפטרה בשם טוב
ח׳ מרחשון תשמ"ה

אחותי בת שבע בת ר׳ אליעזר הכהן
אחותי פריל בת ר׳ אליעזר הכהן
ובעלה ר׳ אשר ישעיה בן ר׳ שאול ביטרמן
גיסי ר׳ שמואל זאב בן ר׳ ישראל אהרן הכהן גרינפלד
אחי חננאל

חמי וחמותי
ר׳ אריה בן ר׳ יצחק סמואלס
ומרת חוה בת ר׳ אלכסנדר זיסקינד

Sponsors

CHARLOTTE AND MORRIS GREEN
משה אליעזר ורעיתו שיינדל פערל גרין

In loving memory of their fathers
לעילוי נשמות אבותיהם
Joseph J. Green
יעקב יוסף בן הרב צבי הירש גרין ז"ל
and
Simon Apfel
שמעון בן שמואל חיים אפפעל ז"ל
(Jerusalem — New York)